MULTICULTUR/

James A. E

MW01087700

(continued)

Immigrant-Origin Students in Community College

Navigating Risk and Reward in Higher Education

EDITED BY

Carola Suárez-Orozco
Olivia Osei-Twumasi

TEACHERS COLLEGE PRESS

TEACHERS COLLEGE | COLUMBIA UNIVERSITY
NEW YORK AND LONDON

Published by Teachers College Press, 1234 Amsterdam Avenue, New York, NY 10027

Copyright © 2019 by Teachers College, Columbia University

Cover design by adam b. bohannon. Cover illustration by Qvasimodo art / iStock by Getty Images.

All rights reserved. No part of this publication may be reproduced or transmitted in any form or by any means, electronic or mechanical, including photocopy, or any information storage and retrieval system, without permission from the publisher. For reprint permission and other subsidiary rights requests, please contact Teachers College Press, Rights Dept.: tcpressrights@tc.columbia.edu

Library of Congress Cataloging-in-Publication Data

Names: Suárez-Orozco, Carola, 1957– editor. | Osei-Twumasi, Olivia, editor.
Title: Immigrant-origin students in community college : navigating risk and reward in
   higher education / Edited by Carola Suarez-Orozco, Olivia Osei-Twumasi.
Description: New York : Teachers College Press, [2019] | Series: Multicultural education
   series | Includes bibliographical references and index.
Identifiers: LCCN 2019014866 (print) | ISBN 9780807761946 (pbk.) |
   ISBN 9780807761953 (case) | ISBN 9780807778036 (ebook)
Subjects: LCSH: Children of immigrants—Education (Higher)—United States. |
   Community colleges—United States. | Children of immigrants—Services for—
   United States. | Multicultural education—United States.
Classification: LCC LC3746 .I56 2019 (print) | LCC LC3746 (ebook) |
   DDC 378.198290973—dc23
LC record available at https://lccn.loc.gov/2019014866
LC ebook record available at https://lccn.loc.gov/2019980978

ISBN 978-0-8077-6194-6 (paper)
ISBN 978-0-8077-6195-3 (hardcover)
ISBN 978-0-8077-7803-6 (ebook)

Printed on acid-free paper
Manufactured in the United States of America

Contents

Series Foreword

This engaging and informative volume, coedited by Carola Suárez-Orozco and Olivia Osei-Twumasi, details the major findings of a carefully designed and implemented mixed-methods study of 600 diverse immigrant-origin community college students in New York City. Although this book describes immigrant-origin students, many of its findings have important implications for other groups of diverse students whose first entry to higher education is in community colleges, namely most African Americans, American Indians, and many low-income and working-class students who are the first generation of their families to attend a college or university. Because half of all undergraduates in the United States attend community colleges (see Chapter 1 of this volume), the findings in this book have salient, significant, and wide applicability for reforming higher education to make it more accessible and equitable.

This book describes effective educational interventions as well as the barriers that community colleges experience in educating immigrant-origin students. It also details innovative and creative ways in which the barriers and problems can be examined and reduced. A significant democratic promise of community colleges is that they provide an entry to higher education for students from a range of ethnic, racial, cultural, language, income-level, and immigrant-status groups; usually have open admissions; and are located close to homes and families. Community colleges also have much lower tuition costs than most 4-year colleges.

Despite their promises and possibilities, community colleges face a number of intractable problems that merit serious attention, discourse, analysis, and reform. Fewer than 40% of the students who enter community colleges obtain an undergraduate degree or certificate within 6 years. The problems that community colleges experience result from both the personal and cultural challenges that immigrant-origin and low-income students experience, as well as from the organizational structures within community colleges that are not culturally responsive to the needs of their students. The multiple and complex problems that immigrant-origin students experience in community colleges result from a number of factors in their lives. These issues include often serving as cultural mediators and translators for their immigrant families; working long hours to help supplement the income of their families; and simultaneously learning academic English while mastering key concepts in disciplines such as mathematics, biology, and chemistry.

Structural reforms are essential within community colleges to enable them to increase the percentage of students who transition from community colleges to 4-year colleges and university and who earn certificates. Some reforms should be targeted to immigrant-origin students because nearly a third (30%) of community college students are foreign-born or the children of immigrants (see Chapter 1 of this volume). This incisive and well-researched book describes the institutional structures within community colleges that need to be reformed in order to make them more culturally responsive to their students.

The attitudes, perceptions, and behaviors of community college instructors and administrators must become more positive toward immigrant-origin students in order to bring about institutional reform. One of the illuminating interview studies described in this book indicates that many community college administrators and faculty have a deficit conception of immigrant-origin students, while at the same time admiring them for their resiliency, work ethic, and perseverance. This book also describes ways in which the implementation of reform strategies such as culturally responsive teaching (Gay, 2018) and fund-of-knowledge approaches (Moll & Gonzalez, 2004) can be effectively used to transform the institutional structure of community colleges.

American classrooms are experiencing the largest influx of immigrant students since the beginning of the 20th century. Approximately 12.6 million new immigrants—documented and undocumented—settled in the United States in the years from 2000 to 2016 (Zong, Batalova, & Hallock, 2018). Less than 10% came from nations in Europe, and most came from Mexico, nations in South Asia, East Asia, Latin America, the Caribbean, and Central America. Today, an increasing number come from Africa, India, and China. The influence of this increasingly diverse population on U.S. schools, colleges, and universities is and will continue to be enormous.

Schools in the United States are more diverse today than they have been since the early 1900s, when a multitude of immigrants entered the United States from Southern, Central, and Eastern Europe (Banks, 2005). In 2017, the National Center for Education Statistics estimated that the percentage of students from ethnic minority groups made up more than 52% of the students in prekindergarten through 12th grade in U. S. public schools, an increase from 39.2% in 2001 (National Center for Education Statistics, 2017). Language and religious diversity is also increasing in the U.S. student population. A Center for Migration Studies publication estimated that 21.6% of Americans aged 5 and above (65.5 million) spoke a language other than English at home in 2016 (Camarota & Ziegler, 2017). This percentage has doubled since 1990, and almost tripled since 1980. The significant number of immigrants from nations such as India and China has also greatly increased religious diversity in the United States. Harvard professor Diana L. Eck (2001) calls the United States the "most religiously diverse nation on earth" (p. 4). Islam is now the fastest-growing religion in the United States, as well as in several European nations such as France, the United Kingdom, and the Netherlands (Banks, 2009; O'Brien, 2016).

The major purpose of the Multicultural Education Series is to provide preservice educators, practicing educators, graduate students, scholars, and policymakers with an interrelated and comprehensive set of books that summarizes and analyzes important research, theory, and practice related to the education of ethnic, racial, cultural, and linguistic groups in the United States and the education of mainstream students about diversity. The dimensions of multicultural education, developed by Banks (2004) and described in the *Handbook of Research on Multicultural Education* and in the *Encyclopedia of Diversity in Education* (Banks, 2012), provide the conceptual framework for the development of the publications in the Series. The dimensions are content integration, the knowledge construction process, prejudice reduction, equity pedagogy, and an empowering institutional culture and social structure. The books in the Multicultural Education Series also provide research, theoretical, and practical knowledge about the behaviors and learning characteristics of students of color (Conchas & Vigil, 2012; Lee, 2007), language minority students (Gándara & Hopkins, 2010; Valdés, 2001; Valdés, Capitelli, & Alvarez, 2011), low-income students (Cookson, 2013; Gorski, 2018), and other minoritized population groups, such as students who speak different varieties of English (Charity Hudley & Mallinson, 2011), and LGBTQ youth (Mayo, 2014).

A number of other books in the Multicultural Education Series describe problems related to diversity in higher education and ways in which it can be reformed. These books include *Engaging the "Race Question": Accountability and Equity in U. S. Higher Education* by Alicia C. Dowd and Estela Mara Bensimon (2015); *Race, Empire, and English Language Teaching: Creating Responsible and Ethical Anti-Racist Practice* by Suhanthie Motha (2014); *Achieving Equity for Latino Students: Expanding the Pathway to Higher Education Through Public Policy* by Frances Contreras (2011); *Americans by Heart: Undocumented Latino Students and the Promise of Higher Education* by William Perez (2011); and *Asians in the Ivory Tower: Dilemmas of Racial Inequality in American Higher Education* by Robert T. Teranishi (2010).

Despite the challenges that it faces, the community college in the United States remains a beacon of hope for many immigrant-origin students, as well as for students from other marginalized and low-income groups. It provides an opportunity for immigrant-origin students and students from low-income communities who did not receive excellent high school educations a second chance and an opportunity to actualize their intellectual gifts and to attain academic success beyond their expectations. The community college in the United States is a precious national treasure that deserves wide public support because of its potential to become a great equalizer of higher education. A quote often attributed to Mahatma Gandhi states, "A nation's greatness is measured by how it treats its weakest members." The quality of higher education that the United States constructs and implements for its immigrant-origin population and other marginalized groups will be a significant marker of its quest for global leadership, influence, and distinction.

—*James A. Banks*

REFERENCES

Banks, C. A. M. (2005). *Improving multicultural education: Lessons from the intergroup education movement.* New York, NY: Teachers College Press.

Banks, J. A. (2004). Multicultural education: Historical development, dimensions, and practice. In J. A. Banks & C. A. M. Banks (Eds.), *Handbook of research on multicultural education* (2nd ed., pp. 3–29). San Francisco, CA: Jossey-Bass.

Banks, J. A. (Ed.). (2009). *The Routledge international companion to multicultural education.* New York, NY and London, UK: Routledge.

Banks, J. A. (2012). Multicultural education: Dimensions of. In J. A. Banks (Ed.). *Encyclopedia of diversity in education* (Vol. 3, pp. 1538–1547). Thousand Oaks, CA: Sage.

Camarota, S. A., & Ziegler, K. (2017, October). 65.5 million U.S. residents spoke a foreign language at home in 2016. *The Center for Immigration Studies.* Retrieved from cis.org /Report/655-Million-US-Residents-Spoke-Foreign-Language-Home-2016

Charity Hudley, A. H., & Mallinson, C. (2011). *Understanding language variation in U.S. schools.* New York, NY: Teachers College Press.

Conchas, G. Q., & Vigil, J. D. (2012). *Streetsmart schoolsmart: Urban poverty and the education of adolescent boys.* New York, NY: Teachers College Press.

Contreras, F. (2011). *Achieving equity for Latino students: Expanding the pathway to higher education through public policy.* New York, NY: Teachers College Press

Cookson, P. W. Jr. (2013). *Class rules: Exposing inequality in American high schools.* New York, NY: Teachers College Press.

Dowd, A. C., & Bensimon, E. M. (2015). *Engaging the "race question": Accountability and equity in U. S. higher education.* New York, NY: Teachers College Press.

Eck, D. L. (2001). *A new religious America: How a "Christian country" has become the world's most religiously diverse nation.* New York, NY: HarperSanFrancisco.

Gándara, P., & Hopkins, M. (Eds.). (2010). *Forbidden language: English language learners and restrictive language policies.* New York, NY: Teachers College Press.

Gay, G. (2018). *Culturally responsive teaching: Theory, research, and practice* (3rd ed.). New York, NY: Teachers College Press.

Gorski, P. C. (2018). *Reaching and teaching students in poverty: Strategies for erasing the opportunity gap* (2nd ed.). New York, NY: Teachers College Press.

Lee, C. D. (2007). *Culture, literacy, and learning: Taking bloom in the midst of the whirlwind.* New York, NY: Teachers College Press.

Mayo, C. (2014). *LGBTQ youth and education: Policies and practices.* New York, NY: Teachers College Press.

Moll, L. C. & Gonzalez, N. (2004). Engaging life: A funds-of-knowledge approach to multicultural education. In J. A. Banks & C. A. M. Banks (Eds.), *Handbook of research on multicultural education* (pp. 699–715). San Francisco, CA: Jossey-Bass.

Motha, S. (2014). *Race, empire and English language teaching: Creating responsible and ethical anti-racist practice.* New York, NY: Teachers College Press.

National Center for Education Statistics. (2017). *Enrollment and percentage distribution of enrollment in public elementary and secondary schools, by race/ethnicity and region: Selected years, fall 1995 through fall 2025.* Retrieved from nces.ed.gov/programs/digest /d15/tables/dt15_203.50.asp

O'Brien, P. (2016). *The Muslim question in Europe: Political controversies and public philosophies.* Philadelphia, PA: Temple University Press.

Pérez, W. (2011). *Americans by heart: Undocumented Latino students and the promise of higher education*. New York, NY: Teachers College Press.

Teranishi, R. T. (2010). *Asians in the ivory tower: Dilemmas of racial inequality in American higher education*. New York, NY: Teachers College Press.

Valdés, G. (2001). *Learning and not learning English: Latino Students in American schools*. New York, NY: Teachers College Press.

Valdés, G., Capitelli, S., & Alvarez, L. (2011). *Latino children learning English: Steps in the journey*. New York, NY: Teachers College Press.

Zong, J., Batalova, J., & Hallock, J. (2018, February). *Frequently requested statistics on immigrants and immigration in the United States*. The Migration Policy Institute. Retrieved from www.migrationpolicy.org/article/frequently-requested-statistics-immigrants-and-immigration-united-states#Demographic

CHAPTER 1

Introduction

What Are the Opportunities, Challenges, and Experiences of Immigrant-Origin Students in Community Colleges?

Carola Suárez-Orozco, Olivia Osei-Twumasi,
Robert T. Teranishi, & Marcelo Suárez-Orozco

The transition, it just really knocks you down and you feel lost. There is no one that is going to walk you through anything.

—21-year-old, Black, female, second-generation immigrant community college student

I am really shy . . . when I speak publicly, I feel scrambled . . . when it comes out, it doesn't come out the way I wanted to say it, so I just usually don't speak.

—21-year-old, Latina, second-generation immigrant community college student

I find the immigrant . . . students work much harder because they feel the sacrifices their parents are doing to get them through school. . . . They know what the family is doing to get them there—that pressure is what makes them go.

—Community College Human Anatomy and Physiology instructor

Immigrant students are more serious; they want to learn more.

—Community College CAMS instructor

I notice that the immigrants tend to be more respectful than American-born students.

—Community College Anatomy and Physiology instructor

Over the last two generations, large-scale migration has shaped and reshaped nearly all aspects of American life: our economy and society, our culture and politics, and our identities. Higher education—like all other settings—is experiencing ever more diverse students in its classrooms particularly in community colleges. Over 40% of all undergraduates attend community colleges, and these rates are significantly higher for first generation to college and immigrant-origin students (Ma & Baum, 2016). As such administrators, faculty, and staff must endeavor to better understand and serve the rapidly growing number of highly diverse immigrant-origin students in these settings.

The first (foreign-born) and second generation (born in the United States to immigrant parents) share in common immigrant parents (Suárez-Orozco, Abo-Zena, & Kerivan-Marks, 2015) and together make up a quarter of children under the age of 18 and nearly a third of 18- to 32-year-olds (Rumbaut & Komaie, 2010). This population is certainly highly diverse (Suárez-Orozco, Frosso-Stefanidi, Marks, & Katsiaficas, 2018). First-generation immigrants, for example, are a complex group that includes naturalized citizens, lawful permanent residents (LPRs), certain legal nonimmigrants (e.g., persons in the United States on student or work visas), those admitted under refugee or asylum status, and persons residing without authorization in the United States. Broadly speaking, immigrant-origin students typically face acculturative challenges including learning a new academic language and the characteristics of the new culture, while at the same time learning and maintaining their family's culture of origin (Marks, Godoy, & Garcia Coll, 2013; Oppedal & Toppelberg, 2016). Although many immigrant-origin students do well and even thrive educationally, others encounter difficulties (Masten, Liebkind, & Hernández, 2012; Suárez-Orozco, Abo-Zena, & Kerivan-Marks, 2015).

Immigrant-origin students are entering higher education in ever increasing numbers; in the period 2007–2008, *nearly a quarter* (23%) of the approximately 22.3 million undergraduates in U.S. postsecondary education were first- or second-generation immigrant-origin students (Knapp, Kelly-Reid, & Ginder, 2009). Indeed, nearly a third of the college-age population is of immigrant origin—nearly 30% of all young adults between the ages of 18 and 34 were born abroad (the immigrant first generation) or had parents who were foreign-born (the second generation) (Rumbáut & Komaie, 2010).

Importantly, for more *than half of all immigrant-origin students*, the first step toward higher education is most likely to be by way of a quintessentially American institution—the community college system (Teranishi, C. Suárez-Orozco, & M. Suárez-Orozco, 2011). But what do we know about immigrant-origin students' experiences in community colleges? Who are they? What are their hopes, ambitions, and dreams? How do they negotiate their way into and through these institutions? What obstacles and frustrations do they encounter along their journeys? How well are they understood (or misunderstood) by community college faculty, administrators, and staff? What is the role of relationships—with other students, with faculty and staff—in their journeys? Above all, what can community colleges do to better help this growing population of new Americans succeed? These are some of the questions to which we set out to find answers in a mixed-methods study of more than 600 diverse immigrant-origin students attending three community colleges in New York City.

Community colleges are a significant point of reference for growing numbers of immigrant-origin students. The most recently available data (from 2011–2012) suggest that almost a third of community college students (30%) are foreign-born or the children of immigrants (AACC, 2015). The nation's more than 1,200 community colleges offer an accessible and affordable postsecondary education well suited to accommodate many of the needs of immigrant students. By and large, community colleges offer open access for general education classes, more affordable tuition, classes designed to improve English-language skills (especially in urban areas), and specialized training for the labor force. Community colleges may also serve to foster civil and cultural engagement in the local community, catering to working adults with evening courses and often offering postsecondary education in proximity to homes and jobs. For some, community colleges offer the possibility to transfer to 4-year institutions. Nonetheless, despite the promise and potential of community colleges for serving immigrant-origin and other underprivileged students, there are concerns about their effectiveness. For example, fewer than 40% of entrants to community colleges complete any type of undergraduate degree or certificate within 6 years (Bailey, Jaggars, & Jenkins, 2015).

Since community colleges now have the largest concentration of immigrants in higher education (Teranishi et al., 2011), it is important to gain a deep and multidimensional understanding of the experiences of new Americans in this educational context. As the nation increasingly focuses on a college completion agenda, not simply promoting *access* to higher education but also taking into account the proportion of Americans who *finish* college with a degree or certificate, the unique perspectives and needs of immigrant-origin students have largely been ignored. The low completion and transfer rates at community colleges, however, have brought into question these institutions' role in meeting the completion agenda as well as the extent to which community colleges are, in fact, a source of social mobility for underserved students (Schudde & Goldrick-Rab, 2015). Although immigrant students enter community colleges seeking social mobility, are some instead experiencing stasis? What serves to foster fruitful journeys, and what, in turn, frustrates them?

THE DEMOGRAPHIC IMPERATIVE

The growth of immigrant students in community colleges is tied to larger demographic trends and the sharp growth of the first- and second-generation immigrant population in the United States since 1965. Since then, the number of immigrants has increased more than fourfold, and their share as a percentage of the U.S. population has been rising steadily (Passel & D'Vera, 2008). As of 2014, immigrants in the United States and their U.S.–born children numbered approximately

81 million people, or 26% of the overall U.S. population (Zong & Batalova, 2017). Furthermore, between 2005 and 2050, while the U.S. population is projected to expand by 48%, immigrants are expected to make up 82% of the total growth. Thus, by 2050, it is estimated that about one in three people in the United States will be foreign-born or the child of immigrant parents (Passel & D'Vera, 2008). The majority of immigrants in the United States arrive from Latin America (53.0%) and Asia (30.6%), though the fastest-growing group is from Africa (from 1.4% to 4.8% in 35 years)[1] (Zong & Batalova, 2017).

Immigrants tend to be younger than the population as a whole—indeed, they are in their prime childbearing years, thus contributing to the growth of the U.S.–born second generation. The share of children (under age 18) in immigrant families rose from 13.4% of all children in 1990 to 25.5% in 2015 (Zong & Batalova, 2017). These trends will continue to drive an increase in the numbers of college-age immigrant-origin youth in the coming years (Rumbáut & Komaie, 2010). In immigrant hubs such as New York City and Los Angeles, these trends are even more dramatic. In New York City in 2011, immigrants and their U.S.–born children accounted for approximately 60% of the city's population. More than a third (37%) of New York City residents were foreign-born, and almost half of all children under 18 had at least one immigrant parent (New York City, Department of City Planning [NYC], 2013). A similar dynamic is unfolding in the greater Los Angeles and San Francisco Bay areas, where 75% of all children have at least one immigrant parent (Data Points, 2017).

Thus, immigrants and their children are a significant demographic force in American society and nationwide represent the fastest-growing sector of the student population. Inevitably, the children of immigrants will become essential players in the U.S. labor force in the decades to come (Passell, 2011). Arguably, then, it is a societal imperative to understand who they are and how to best serve them across academic settings—including community colleges, the higher education setting that they are most likely to enter first—both for their own future well-being and for the economic growth of the nation moving forward.

As noted earlier, the population of immigrant-origin students, however, is far from monolithic and needs to be understood in terms of the contours of its heterogeneity (Erisman & Looney, 2007; Teranishi et al., 2011). Although some students are exceptionally well prepared to compete in higher education, others are not. On one end of the spectrum are groups who enter with parents who have higher rates of bachelor's and advanced degrees than those of the U.S. native-born population; at the other end are immigrants who arrive with parents who have very low levels of educational attainment (Teranishi et al., 2011; Zong & Batalova, 2017). Furthermore, many who immigrate to the United States as adolescents enter low-quality, highly segregated schools and are often ill-prepared to apply to competitive colleges or universities (C. Suárez-Orozco, M. M. Suárez-Orozco, & Todorova, 2008). Therefore, community colleges offer a promising and affordable pathway into higher education.

A SNAPSHOT OF IMMIGRANT-ORIGIN STUDENTS
IN COMMUNITY COLLEGES

In the United States today, half of all undergraduates attend community colleges. Yet community colleges remain both ambiguous and neglected in the higher education literature (Deil-Amen, 2015. In the period 2011–2012, 7.4 million students were enrolled at one of more than 1,200 community colleges nationwide. The most recently available data (from 2011–2012) suggest that *almost a third* of community college students (30%) were foreign-born or the children of immigrants (American Association of Community Colleges [AACC], 2015), roughly the same as the percentage of immigrant-origin individuals who fell into this age range (Rumbáut & Komaie, 2010). Breaking this statistic down further, 6.5% were foreign-born U.S. citizens, 5.6% were resident aliens or other eligible noncitizens,[2] and 16.0% were U.S.–born citizens with at least one foreign-born parent. Finally, 1.5% were international students, that is, foreign students with visas.[3]

First- and second-generation immigrant students are more likely to start their postsecondary education at community colleges than their nonimmigrant-origin undergraduate peers are. A study focusing on the City University of New York (CUNY) system found, for example, that 48% of entering freshmen in 1997 were foreign-born, up from 33% in 1990 (Bailey & Weininger, 2002). It also found that 60% of the foreign-born students had begun their studies in an associate's degree program. Among the foreign-born, a greater proportion of first-time students who had attended high school outside the United States began their CUNY studies in an associate's program (67%) than those who had attended high school in the United States did (59%).

Nationwide, during the period 2011–2012, 41% of nonimmigrant students[4] began their college careers at community colleges; by contrast, 62% of foreign-born noncitizens, 46% of foreign-born citizens, and 46% of second-generation immigrant students first attended community colleges (U.S. Department of Education, 2012). Asian, Hispanic, and White first- and second-generation immigrants are more likely to enroll in community colleges than their third-generation peers are.[5] Notably, Latinx students of all immigrant generations are more likely to start out in community colleges than in 4-year schools (Staklis & Horn, 2012).

THE PARTICULAR CHALLENGES FACING
IMMIGRANT-ORIGIN STUDENTS

Immigrant-origin students share many characteristics with other nontraditional students; in addition, they have specific characteristics and needs beyond those of typical community college students. Immigrant students are more likely to be the first in their families to attend college and thus often lack familiarity with higher education in general and the U.S. educational system in particular

(C. Suárez-Orozco et al., 2008; Teranishi et al., 2011). They share with other nontraditional students concerns about affordability since costs typically figure importantly in their decision to attend a community college. Although immigrant adults have a lower unemployment rate than native-born adults do, their wages are consistently lower than those of their peers.[6] The lower wages prevalent among immigrant adults (particularly Latinx immigrants) make it difficult for them or their children to afford to attend college. Research shows that although immigrant students tend to have financial needs, they often lack information about how to finance their college costs. Immigrant-origin students are less likely than other students to apply for student loans. Further, data show that they tend to be debt adverse and to cover most of their college costs themselves (Teranishi et al., 2011). Financially independent immigrant adults and the children of immigrants underuse financial aid, and many are confused about access to aid because of their own U.S. resident status or that of their parents (Teranishi et al., 2011). Furthermore, although naturalized citizens and legal permanent residents are eligible for in-state tuition, the same is not true for nonpermanent residents and undocumented students, depending on their state of residency. Undocumented students specifically are entirely ineligible for federal aid as well as for state aid in many states, a situation that greatly limits their opportunities for postsecondary education (Suárez-Orozco, Abo-Zena, & Kerivan-Marks, 2015; Teranishi et al., 2011).

With ever-present financial concerns, many immigrant-origin students work at least part-time while studying (Teranishi et al., 2011). They also have multiple home obligations either with new families they have formed or with their families of origin as they often act as cultural and linguistic brokers for relatives (Dorner, Orellana, & Jiménez, 2008). Mexican and Central American immigrant students often have responsibilities and obligations to their family, including running errands, caring for siblings, translating for their parents, and contributing to the household income; similar obligations are not as prevalent among native-born students (Fuligni, Tseng, & Lam, 1999). Another study of college students in New York City found that immigrant college students spent significantly more time each week on family responsibilities than their native-born peers did (Katsiaficas et al., 2015).

"Under-matching" is another particular challenge that many immigrant-origin students face as they enter higher education. An immigrant pattern of debt adversity, less access to financial aid, lack of understanding of the college pathway system (and the relative advantages of attending Tier 1 colleges as opposed to less competitive colleges), and a sense of responsibility and obligation to the family lead many immigrant students who would qualify for admission to higher tiered institutions to "under-match"—that is, choose the cheaper, more local option of attending a community college. Although a practical choice for many, community colleges' notoriously low transfer rates have the potential to sideline students who might have received higher levels of support at a 4-year institution that typically provides more resources (Holland, 2013).

Some immigrant-origin students entering community colleges have already completed much of their education outside the United States; for students who have a strong educational foundation, the primary educational challenge will be acquiring academic English-language skills. Other immigrant-origin students have received all or a significant portion of their education in U.S. schools that are segregated and inadequately resourced; these students may be underprepared academically and will need to undergo a period of remediation. In a study of an urban community college, 85% of immigrants required remediation as first-time freshmen, often because of deficient English-language skills. By comparison, 55% of native-born students required such remediation (Teranishi et al., 2011). It is important to consider the saliency of issues of remediation on persistence for degree attainment by immigrant-origin students, yet the needs of each of the groups described above are quite different.

This point brings us to a key issue related to immigration, especially for the first generation. Most, though of course not all, immigrants speak a language other than English at home and thus must learn a new language as part of the educational process. Although there is growing evidence of bilingual cognitive advantages (Bialystok, 1999), attaining high levels of academic English proficiency is a long and arduous process that typically takes at least 5 to 7 years of high-quality exposure (Collier, 1989). However, many immigrant-origin students do not receive this kind of instruction and, consequently, enter community colleges with an inadequate command of academic English that affects both their ability to understand content in the classroom and their ability to participate fully or earn high grades. Academic language proficiency is a sine qua non for academic success. Indeed, many immigrants attend community colleges specifically to improve their English-language skills. Bailey and Weininger (2002) highlight the "classic adjustment role" that community colleges can play for students who are well prepared academically but lack English-language skills. They argue that community colleges are well positioned to help newcomers with their English-language skills so that their strong underlying academic preparation can come to the fore. Furthermore, English as a Second Language (ESL) courses provide immigrants with a range of benefits in addition to the development of their language skills, including opportunities to receive peer support and informal counseling from their ESL instructors. These programs are not without their challenges, however. In addition to a shortage of ESL faculty, low levels of funding, and few ESL courses that offer college-level credit, attrition rates in ESL courses are often high. Since ESL courses are usually prerequisites for college-level courses, these high attrition rates are a serious problem.

There is no doubt that too many immigrant youths encounter a myriad of challenges—economic obstacles, xenophobia, language acquisition difficulties, acculturative needs, underresourced neighborhoods and schools, and the like. As a result, they struggle to gain their bearings in an educational system that may put them on a downward trajectory (C. Suárez-Orozco et al., 2008; García Coll & Marks, 2011; Portes & Zhou, 1993; Suárez-Orozco et al., 2015). However, many previous studies have established that immigrant students bring with them clusters of strength and resilience. They arrive in their new lands with distinct social and cultural resources (Perreira, Harris, & Lee, 2006). Their high aspirations (Fuligni, 2001; Portés & Rumbáut, 2006), dual frames of reference (C. Suárez-Orozco & M. Suárez-Orozco, 1995), optimism (Kao & Tienda, 1995), dedicated hard work, positive attitudes toward school (C. Suárez-Orozco & M. Suárez-Orozco, 1995), and ethic of family support for advanced learning (Li, 2004) contribute to the situation in which some immigrant youth educationally outperform expectations or their native-born peers who have had similar constellations of impediments (Perreira et al., 2006).

In this volume, we move beyond immigrant-origin students as merely English learners or remedial students and consider the notion of the "whole" student promoted by John Dewey. We take both ecological (Brofenbrenner & Morris, 2006) and risk and resilience (Kia-Keating et al., 2011) perspectives. Thus, we recognize that students are embedded within larger social systems that include proximal systems such as their families (e.g., generation to college, socioeconomic status, documentation status), campus they attend state (e.g., tuition policies), and national policies (e.g., immigration policies). We also recognize that while many students face a host of hurdles, many also demonstrate remarkable resiliency. To understand patterns, we need to consider the interaction of the resources of and the risks facing the individual within the contexts she navigates (Suárez-Orozco, Frosso-Stefanidi, Marks, & Katsiaficas, 2018).

COMMUNITY COLLEGES AS SITES OF OPPORTUNITY?

Evidence shows that immigrant-origin students attain rates of graduation similar to those of other students (U.S. Bureau of Labor Statistics, 2017). Second-generation immigrant-origin students are almost indistinguishable from students from the third generation and beyond in terms of rates of graduation from certificate programs and receipt of associate's and bachelor's degrees. Foreign-born immigrants with citizenship also perform similarly, although foreign-born immigrants without citizenship (mostly green card holders) are less likely to attain a bachelor's degree and more likely to attain a certificate or an associate's degree (U.S. Bureau of Labor Statistics, 2017).

Nevertheless, students who begin their higher educational trajectory in community colleges are substantially *less likely* to attain a bachelor's degree than students who start at a 4-year institution are (U.S. Department of Education, 2012). Something happens along the way to transferring despite students' stated intentions to earn at least a bachelor's degree (Bailey & Weininger, 2002). Cabrera, Burkum, and La Nasa (2005) demonstrated that even among highly academically prepared students, only 30% who first attended 2-year colleges completed a bachelor's degree, as compared with 78% who went straight to 4-year colleges. Directly entering a 4-year college—rather than using a community college as a stepping-stone—has become a key predictor of eventual bachelor's degree attainment. As a result, the role of community colleges as drivers of mobility has become a source of controversy, with several analysts arguing that beginning tertiary education in a community college may actually impede a student's mobility (Goldrick-Rab et al., 2007; Grubb, 1991). This situation is particularly true for minorities (Latinx in particular), who have even steeper rates of noncompletion than their White peers do (Alexander, Garcia, González, Grimes, & O'Brien, 2007; Fry, 2002).

Nevertheless, community colleges continue to offer the promise of helping nontraditional students overcome barriers and serving as a stepping stone to further opportunities in higher education. Community colleges have lower rates of tuition than 4-year institutions do, open access admissions, and convenient locations and class times. They provide classes designed for English language learners and offer remedial education for second-chance students. For these reasons, community colleges are potentially well suited to meet the educational needs of immigrant students seeking to obtain an affordable postsecondary education, learn English-language skills, and gain skills to prepare for the labor market. Community colleges provide immigrants with opportunities to move up the economic ladder and have a genuine shot at advancement in the knowledge economy. As the "Ellis Island and workhorses of higher education" (Connell, 2008, p. 1), community colleges are accessible to millions of immigrant students. For those struggling to overcome the barriers of poverty, limited English skills, and inadequate academic preparation, community colleges offer opportunities and a pathway to a brighter future.

And yet to date, there has been little systematic inquiry into the experiences of immigrant-origin community college students from diverse backgrounds in these settings. We sought to undertake an in-depth inquiry using a variety of strategies and perspectives in order to learn from immigrant students as well as from those who endeavor to serve them about their experiences.

THE RESEARCH ON IMMIGRANTS IN COMMUNITY COLLEGE (RICC) STUDY

The Research on Immigrants in Community College (RICC) Study funded by the W. T. Grant Foundation and the Ford Foundation was designed to shed light on two questions: In what ways do community colleges serve as sites of possibilities (Fine & Jaffe-Walter, 2007)? In what ways do they fail to meet their potential for these students?

We chose as the site for research New York City, a place with one of the most diverse and dynamic populations of any city in the world. Immigrants and children of immigrants comprise nearly 6 in 10 residents, and half of the population speak a language other than English at home. Our participants included first- and second-generation immigrant students as well as nonimmigrant students, who served as a comparison group. They originated in many countries whose populations are generally grouped in the U.S. ethnic or racial categories of Asian, Latinx, Black, and White.

The RICC Study employed a variety of methodological strategies to answer our research questions and shed light on the day-to-day experiences of immigrant-origin students in community college settings. This was a multiphase, embedded, mixed-methods study, with each phase informing the next (Creswell & Plano Clark, 2011) (see online appendix for details on the RICC methodology and information on all instruments). The first year's long intensive qualitative Phase 1 informed the development of student surveys, which were then collected during Phase 2. A subsample of matched student qualitative interviews, along with faculty, and administrator interviews as well as administrative records (including grades) were conducted during Phase 3 (see Figure 1.1).

The overarching goal of the study was to deeply understand the experience of immigrant-origin students in community college campuses. We were also interested in systematically examining community college classrooms as spaces of learning as well as examining other campus settings outside of classrooms that could have implications for (1) fostering relational engagement (Bensimon, 2007, p. 2), (2) accessing social capital (Deil-Amen, 2015), and (3) stimulating academic engagement (C. Suárez-Orozco et al., 2008; Kuh, Cruce, Shoup, Kinzie, & Gonyea, 2008) and success.

The principal investigators of this study consisted of an interdisciplinary team. Carola Suárez-Orozco is a cultural developmental psychologist with a longstanding research interest in the experiences of immigrant students. Robert Teranishi is a sociologist focusing on higher education and educational policy. Marcelo Suárez-Orozco is an educational anthropologist with expertise in the immigration experience and higher education. In the last phase of our study, Olivia Osei-Twumasi, an educational economist, joined our analytical team, bringing a fresh new lens. Our mutual expertise worked synthetically in the development of research strategies and theoretical approaches with which we approached our inquiry and interpreted the emerging findings.

All of this book's chapters were authored or coauthored by scholars who were intimately involved in the development of protocols designed for this research project, in the fieldwork, in the data collection, or in the data analysis—and in many cases in multiple dimensions of the research. Five of the authors (or coauthors) developed their dissertations from this project (Stacey Alicea, Tasha Darbes, Sandra Dias, Heather Herrera, and Dalal Katsiaficas). Margary Martin was the

Figure 1.1. Multiphase Embedded Mixed-Methods Design

project director for 2 years of the project. Many of the other authors worked as analysts in different phases of the project. Taken together, the various forms of data collected during this study yield a rich picture of the experiences of immigrant-origin students in community colleges as well as information about their specific needs and the factors that can aid their success.

PLAN OF THE BOOK

This book's chapters draw on various types of data and focus on different contexts and experiences as well as on different points of view. In Part I, "The Challenges Immigrant-Origin Students Face in Community College," we set the stage by having the authors provide some nuanced, in-depth insights into the *specific* challenges that immigrant-origin community college students encounter as they enter these settings. In what ways are their experiences somewhat different from those of their nonimmigrant-origin peers? What are the specific challenges that they face?

In Chapter 2, "Emerging into Adulthood for Immigrant-Origin Community College Students," Dalal Katsiaficas addresses the specific developmental challenges of immigrant-origin young adults. Sociologists have argued that young adults today are no longer taking on the roles of adulthood in the ways in which previous generations did. Likewise, developmental psychologists have claimed that those between the ages of 18 and 25 today tend to delay taking on the roles typically associated with adulthood, with many experiencing a phase of prolonged emerging adulthood. But how do immigrant-origin students experience this developmental phase? The data suggest important differences in the ways in which immigrant young adults move through emerging adulthood and the ways in which their non-immigrant peers do. In Chapter 3, Tasha Darbes examines "The Pathways of English Learners in Community Colleges: Persistence and Push-Out." She explores how language learners experience their classes, the impact of gatekeeping policies such as testing and remediation on them, and the particular obstacles that these students face as they traverse their academic pathways. In Chapter 4, "Resilience in the Face of Adversity: Undocumented Students in Community Colleges," Olivia Osei-Twumasi and Guadalupe López Hernández examine the effects that undocumented status has on the lives of students in community colleges, drawing in part on data from the RICC study as well as from other data sources.

In Part II, "The Role of Community College Settings," the authors examine contexts that include the classroom environment, out-of-class time spent on campus, and counseling services. In Chapter 5, "Classroom Engagement in Community Colleges: Moving Beyond Student and Instructor Dimensions to a Dynamic Settings Approach," Stacey Alicea and Carola Suárez-Orozco present evidence from structured classroom observations developed for this study to systematically examine the dimensions of academic, relational, and cognitive engagement. The data from these 60 observations show promise for future interventions to improve the classroom experiences of diverse community college students.

Chapter 6, "The Prevalence and Relevance of Microaggressions in Community College Classrooms," by Carola Suárez-Orozco, Saskias Casanova, Margary Martin, Dalal Katsiaficas, and Sukhmani Singh, also draws on standardized observations of 60 classrooms across three campuses. The authors reliably assess microaggressions and determine the types used, the contexts in which they were delivered, and who the targets and instigators were. This chapter provides insights into how these undermining interactions are enacted and the kinds of classrooms in which they occur. The subsequent chapter, Chapter 7, "The Use of Out-of-Class Time on Campus of Immigrant-Origin Students," by Olivia Osei-Twumasi, Carola-Suárez Orozco, Edwin Hernandez, Monique Corral, and Janet Cerda, challenges the notion that immigrant-origin community college students do not spend much time on their campuses. The authors show the various ways in which students use college spaces and discuss what uses of time on campus are most conducive for academic success. Another key aspect of college settings is the services they provide and the extent to which these are accessed by students. In Chapter 8, Sandra I. Dias considers "Immigrant-Origin Community College Students' Help-Seeking Orientation and Use of Counseling Services." Young adults of college age face greater mental health challenges than those faced by previous generations, but are immigrant-origin young adult students availing themselves of counseling services on campus? If not, why not?

The next grouping, Part III, "The Importance of Relationships in Community Colleges," highlights the important role of interpersonal relationships on community college campuses, especially for immigrant-origin students. In Chapter 9, "Immigrant-Origin Community College Students' Experiences with Faculty: Relational Agency or Relational Helplessness?" Carola Suárez-Orozco, Natacha M. Cesar-Davis, and Alfredo Novoa analyze and reflect on such students' experiences—positive, negative, and ideal—with faculty on community college campuses, providing important insights. By comparing the responses of students who reported high levels of relational engagement on their surveys with those who reported low levels, they also present intriguing emerging themes, revealing the contrasting experiences of these groups of students. Chapter 10, "Through a Lens of Deficit: Faculty and Administrator Perceptions of Immigrant-Origin Students," by Heather Herrera, Margary Martin, and Natacha M. Cesar-Davis, provides a distinct point of view that was voiced in interviews with faculty and administrators. Lamentably, the authors found that many faculty and administrators viewed their students through such a lens. In the following chapter, Chapter 11, "The Significance of Networks of Relationships for Immigrant-Origin Students," Stacey Alicea draws on social network data to depict the significance of networks of relationships in the lives of immigrant-origin community college students. She finds that immigrant-origin students in the RICC study had relatively small, disconnected networks consisting largely of other students and argues that cultivating and leveraging social networks on community college campuses may be an effective way of connecting students with the resources they need to achieve their educational goals. Part III ends with Chapter 12, "The Role of Instructor Relationships in Predicting Academic

Outcomes Among Immigrant-Origin Community College Students," by McKenna Parnes, Sarah Schwartz, Carola Suárez-Orozco, and Olivia Osei-Twumasi. The authors present a model that predicts academic engagement. Drawing on the RICC survey data, their quantitative analysis aligns with the qualitative data presented earlier in this section, all pointing to the significance of relationships in academic engagement.

Part IV, "And Now What?," addresses a persistent dilemma. In Chapter 13, "Dreams Versus Realities: Graduation Rates of Immigrant-Origin Community College Students," Olivia Osei-Twumasi and Juliana Karras-Jean Gilles draw attention to the disconcerting divide between students' high expectations of achieving academic success and the reality of the low transfer and graduation rates of community college students. Furthermore, they explore how this divide specifically plays out in the lives of immigrant-origin students. Finally, in Chapter 14, "(Re) Designing Institutional Practices and Policies to Serve Immigrant Students in Community Colleges," Robert T. Teranishi, Cecilia Rios-Aguilar, and Cynthia M. Alcantar make astute recommendations for effective strategies of practice that build on the many strengths of immigrant-origin students. Lastly, they turn to federal, state, and local administrative policy recommendations to best foster the educational flourishing of community colleges' most rapidly growing student population.

Taken together, the components of this rich study provide various perspectives, placing students at the center but also including administrators and faculty. The study draws on multiple innovative sources of data analyzed with a variety of strategies by a multiethnic, multilingual, multidisciplinary research team to piece together an in-depth quilt of the lives of immigrant-origin students in community colleges.

NOTES

1. In these figures, the term *immigrants* (also known as *the foreign-born*) refers to people residing in the United States who were not U.S. citizens at birth. This population includes naturalized citizens, lawful permanent residents (LPRs), certain legal nonimmigrants (e.g., persons on student or work visas), those admitted with refugee or asylum status, and persons residing in the United States without authorization.

2. Specifically, "other eligible noncitizens" are those admitted into the United States as legal immigrants for the purpose of obtaining permanent resident alien status.

3. International students are those intending to return to their countries of origin upon completion of their studies and are not considered immigrant students. They are more likely to enroll in public or 4-year colleges than in community colleges. International students are not the focus of this study.

4. Other U.S. citizens may be the grandchildren of immigrants, or their families may have been in the United States for many generations; the data do not generally make it possible to distinguish more closely among this group (nonimmigrant students).

5. However, Black second-generation immigrants were more likely to start their education at 4-year schools than Black third-generation or higher students were; they also appear

to be overrepresented at elite schools (e.g., see Douglass, Roebken, & Thomson [2007] for enrollment figures for UC Berkeley).

6. The median weekly wage for immigrants who worked full-time, for example, was 20% less than it was for native-born workers in 2015 ($681 versus $837) (U.S. Bureau of Labor Statistics, 2017).

REFERENCES

Alexander, B. C., Garcia, V., González, L., Grimes, G., & O'Brien, D. (2007). Barriers in the transfer process for Hispanic and Hispanic immigrant students. *Journal of Hispanic Higher Education, 6*(2), 174–184.

American Association of Community Colleges (AACC). (2015). *Data points: Coming to America.* Washington, DC: Author. Retrieved from www.aacc.nche.edu/Publications /datapoints/Documents/DataPoints_Coming2America_final.pdf

Bailey, T. R., Jaggars, S. S., & Jenkins, D. (2015). *Redesigning America's community colleges.* Cambridge, MA: Harvard University Press.

Bailey, T. R., & Weininger, E. B. (2002). Performance, graduation, and transfer of immigrants and natives in City University of New York Community Colleges. *Educational Evaluation and Policy Analysis, 24*(4), 359–377.

Bensimon, E. M. (2007). The underestimated significance of practitioner knowledge in the scholarship of student success. *The Review of Higher Education, 30*(4), 441–469.

Bialystok, E. (1999). Cognitive complexity and attentional control in the bilingual mind. *Child Development, 70*(3), 636–644.

Bronfenbrenner, U., & Morris, P. A. (2006). The bioecological model of human development. In W. Danon (Ed.), *Handbook of child psychology* (pp. 793–828). Hoboken, NJ: Wiley.

Cabrera, A. F., Burkum, K. R., & La Nasa, S. M. (2005). Pathways to a four-year degree. In A. Seidman (Ed.), *College student retention: Formula for student success* (pp. 155–214). Westport, CT: Praeger Publishers.

Collier, V. P. (1989). How long? A synthesis of research on academic achievement in a second language. *TESOL Quarterly, 23*(3), 509–531.

Connell, C. (2008). The vital role of community colleges in the education and integration of immigrants. Sabastopol, CA: Grantmakers Concerned with Immigrants and Refugees.

Creswell, J. W., & Clark, V. L. P. (2017). *Designing and conducting mixed methods research.* Thousand Oaks, CA: Sage.

Data Points. (2017). *Half of California children have immigrant parent.* Palo Alto, CA: Lucile Packard Foundation. Retrieved from www.kidsdata.org/blog/?p=7804

Deil-Amen, R. (2011). Socio-academic integrative moments: Rethinking academic and social integration among two-year college students in career-related programs. *The Journal of Higher Education, 82*(1), 54–91.

Deil-Amen, R. (2015). The "traditional" college student: A smaller and smaller minority and its implications for access institutions. In M. Stevens & M. Kirst (Eds.), *Remaking college: The changing ecology of higher education* (pp. 134–165). Palo Alto, CA: Stanford University Press.

Dorner, L. M., Orellana, M. F., & Jiménez, R. (2008). "It's one of those things that you do to help the family": Language brokering and the development of immigrant adolescents. *Journal of Adolescent Research, 23*(5), 515–543.

Douglass, J. A., Roebken, H., & Thomson, G. (2007). *The immigrant university: Assessing the dynamics of race, major and socioeconomic characteristics at the University of California.* A Student Experience in the Research University (SERU) Project Research Paper. Research & Occasional Paper Series: CSHE. 19.07. Berkeley, CA: Center for Studies in Higher Education.

Erisman, W., & Looney, S. (2007). *Opening the door to the American Dream: Increasing higher education access and success for immigrants.* Washington, DC: Institute for Higher Education Policy.

Fine, M., & Jaffe-Walter, R. (2007). Swimming: On oxygen, resistance, and possibility for immigrant youth under siege. *Anthropology & Education Quarterly, 38*(1), 76–96.

Fry, R. (2002). *Latinos in higher education: Many enroll, too few graduate.* Pew Hispanic Center. Washington, DC: Pew Research Center.

Fuligni, A. J. (2001). A comparative longitudinal approach among children of immigrant families. *Harvard Educational Review, 71*(3), 566–578.

Fuligni, A. J., Tseng, V., & Lam, M. (1999). Attitudes toward family obligations among American adolescents with Asian, Latin American, and European backgrounds. *Child Development, 70*(4), 1030–1044.

García Coll, C., & Marks, A. (Eds.). (2011). *The immigrant paradox in children and adolescents: Is becoming American a developmental risk?* Washington, DC: American Psychological Association Press.

Goldrick-Rab, S., Faye Carter, D., & Winkle Wagner, R. (2007). What higher education has to say about the transition to college. *Teachers College Record, 109*(10), 2444–2481.

Grubb, W. N. (1991). The decline of the community college transfer rates: Evidence from national longitudinal surveys. *Journal of Higher Education, 62*(2), 194–222.

Holland, M. M. (2013). *Unequal playing fields, same game: The college application process for students at diverse high schools.* Cambridge, MA: Harvard University Press.

Kao, G., & Tienda, M. (1995). Optimism and achievement: The educational performance of immigrant youth. *Social Science Quarterly, 76*(1), 1–19.

Katsiaficas, D., Suárez-Orozco, C., & Dias, S. I. (2015). "When do I feel like an adult?" Latino and Afro-Caribbean immigrant-origin community college students' conceptualizations and experiences of (emerging) adulthood. *Emerging Adulthood, 3*(2), 98–112.

Kia-Keating, M., Dowdy, E., Morgan, M. L., & Noam, G. G. (2011). Protecting and promoting: An integrative conceptual model for healthy development of adolescents. *Journal of Adolescent Health, 48*(3), 220–228.

Knapp, L. G., Kelly-Reid, J. E., & Ginder, S. A. (2009). Postsecondary institutions and price of attendance in the United States: Fall 2008 and degrees and other awards conferred: 2007–08, and 12-month enrollment 2007–08. *First look. NCES 2009–165.* Washington, DC: National Center for Education Statistics.

Kuh, G. D., Cruce, T. M., Shoup, R., Kinzie, J., & Gonyea, R. M. (2008). Unmasking the effects of student engagement on first-year college grades and persistence. *The Journal of Higher Education, 79*(5), 540–563.

Li, G. (2004). Family literacy: Learning from an Asian immigrant family. In F. B. Boyd, C. H. Brock, & M. S. Rozendal (Eds.), *Multicultural and multilingual literacy and language: Contexts and practices* (pp. 304–321). New York, NY: The Guilford Press.

Ma, J., & Baum, S. (2016). Trends in community colleges: Enrollment, prices, student debt, and completion. *College Board Research Brief.* Retrieved from trends.collegeboard .org/content/trends-community-colleges-enrollment-prices-student-debt-and -completion-april-2016

Marks, A. K., Godoy, C. M., & Garcia Coll, C. (2013). An ecological approach to understanding immigrant child and adolescent developmental competencies. In L. Gershoff, R. Mistry, & D. Crosby (Eds.), *The contexts of child development* (pp. 75–89). New York, NY: Oxford University Press.

Masten, A. S., Liebkind, K., & Hernández, D. J. (2012). *Realizing the potential of immigrant youth.* Cambridge, UK: Cambridge University Press.

New York City, Department of City Planning. (2013). *The newest New Yorkers.* New York, NY: New York City, Department of City Planning. Retrieved from cmsny.org/the-newest-new-yorkers-2013

Oppedal, B., & Toppelberg, C. (2016). Culture competence: A developmental task of acculturation. In J. W. Berry & D. L. Sam (Eds.), *The Cambridge handbook of acculturation psychology revised* (pp. 71–92). Cambridge, UK: Cambridge University Press.

Passel, J. S. (2011). Demography of immigrant youth: Past, present, and future. *The Future of Children, 21*(1), 19–41.

Passel, J. S., & D'Vera, C. (2008). *US Population Projections: 2005–2050.* Washington, DC: Pew Research Center Social & Demographic Trends.

Perreira, K. M., Harris, K. M., & Lee, D. (2006). Making it in America: High school completion by immigrant and native youth. *Demography, 43,* 511–536.

Portés, A., & Rumbáut, R. G. (2006). *Immigrant America: A portrait.* Berkeley: University of California Press.

Portes, A., & Zhou, M. (1993). The new second generation: Segmented assimilation and its variants. *The Annals of the American Academy of Political and Social Science, 530*(1), 74–96.

Rumbáut, R. G., & Komaie, G. (2010). Immigration and adult transitions. *The Future of Children, 20*(1), 43–66.

Schudde, L., & Goldrick-Rab, S. (2015). On second chances and stratification: How sociologists think about community colleges. *Community College Review, 43*(1), 27–45.

Staklis, S., & Horn, L. (2012). *New Americans in postsecondary education: A profile of immigrant and second-generation American undergraduates. Stats in Brief. NCES 2012–13.* Washington, DC: National Center for Education Statistics.

Suárez-Orozco, C., Abo-Zena, M., & Kerivan-Marks, A. (Eds.). (2015). *Transitions: The development of the children of immigrants.* New York, NY: New York University Press.

Suárez-Orozco, C., Frosso-Stefanidi, M., Marks, A., & Katsiaficas, D. (2018). An integrative risk and resilience model for understanding the adaptation of immigrant-origin children and youth. *American Psychologist, 73*(6), 781–796.

Suárez-Orozco, C., Katsiaficas, D., Birchall, O., Alcantar, A. M., Hernandez, E., Garcia, Y., . . . Teranishi, R. (2015). Undocumented undergraduates on college campuses: Understanding their challenges, assets, and what it takes to make an UndocuFriendly campus. *Harvard Education Review, 85*(3), 427–463.

Suárez-Orozco, C., & Suárez-Orozco, M. (1995). *Transformations: Immigration, family life & achievement motivation among Latino adolescents.* Cambridge, MA: Harvard University Press.

Suárez-Orozco, C., Suarez-Orozco, M. M., & Todorova, I. (2008). *Learning a new land: Immigrant students in American society.* Cambridge, MA: Harvard University Press.

Teranishi, R. T., Suárez-Orozco, C., & Suárez-Orozco, M. (2011). Immigrants in community colleges: Effective practices for large and growing population in U.S. higher education. *The Future of Children, 21*(1), 153–169.

U.S. Bureau of Labor Statistics. (2017). *Table 5. Median usual weekly earnings of full-time wage and salary workers for the foreign born and native born by selected characteristics, 2015–2016 annual averages.* Washington, DC: U.S. Bureau of Labor Statistics. Retrieved from www.bls.gov/news.release/forbrn.t05.htm

U.S. Department of Education. (2012). National Center for Education Statistics, 2011–12 Beginning Postsecondary Students Longitudinal Study, First Follow-Up (BPS:12/14).

Zong, Z., & Batalova, J. (2017). *Frequently requested statistics on immigration and immigrants in the United States.* Washington, DC: Migration Policy Institute. Retrieved from www.migrationpolicy.org/article/frequently-requested-statistics-immigrants-and-immigration-united-states

Part I

THE CHALLENGES IMMIGRANT-ORIGIN STUDENTS FACE IN COMMUNITY COLLEGES

CHAPTER 2

Emerging into Adulthood for Immigrant-Origin Community College Students

Dalal Katsiaficas

In the United States young adults are increasingly from immigrant backgrounds—either having immigrated to the United States themselves or being the children of immigrant parents. Currently, the number of immigrant-origin young adults (ages 18 to 34) has grown to nearly 20 million (Rumbaut & Komaie, 2010), with one in four of those between the ages of 16 and 24 in the United States being either first- or second-generation immigrants (Batalova & Fix, 2011). Despite their growing numbers, little attention has been paid to the experiences of immigrant-origin young adults during this developmental phase or to their engagement in a variety of social institutions. Immigrant-origin students are more likely than non-immigrant students to begin their postsecondary careers at community colleges (Chapa & De La Rosa, 2004; Teranishi, C. Suárez-Orozco, & M. M. Suárez-Orozco, 2011) though we know little about their emergence into adulthood in this setting (Teranishi et al., 2011).

EMERGING INTO ADULTHOOD

There is great debate in the fields of sociology and psychology regarding this phase of life. Sociologists have mainly viewed this period as an extended part of the transition to adult roles that includes getting married, having children, finishing school, moving away from home, and entering the workforce (Settersten & Ray, 2010). Trends in reaching these discrete markers have shifted dramatically over the past 50 years, with the average age of marriage, birth of the first child, and entrance into the full-time workforce steadily occurring later in life for young people in postindustrialized nations (Arnett, 2003, 2006; Arnett & Taber, 1994). Furthermore, cultural psychologists have noted that the point at which an individual has left adolescence and become an adult is a culturally defined moment that varies significantly from person to person (Arnett & Taber, 1994). The criteria for adulthood that emerging adults cite as central to their identities have also shifted beyond these sociological transitions to adult roles. Extensive survey and interview data on ethnically diverse emerging adults in the United States demonstrate that the top criteria for adulthood include accepting responsibility for oneself, becoming capable of making independent decisions, and becoming financially independent from one's parents, regardless of ethnic background (Arnett, 1998, 2003, 2004). These delays in the onset of feeling like an adult and the shifting markers of adulthood have led developmental psychologists, most notably Jeffery Jensen Arnett (2000), to argue that this transitional period is more than a staging ground for adulthood and that it should be recognized as a unique and important life-course developmental stage in its own right, referred to as *emerging adulthood* (Arnett, 2000).

The hallmark of emerging adulthood is feeling neither fully adult nor still an adolescent but feeling like one is somewhere "in between" (Arnett, 2006). This period of life is characterized as a time when one has high hopes about the future (Arnett, 2006) and a time ripe with opportunities for one to make transformational life changes such as entering college (Arnett, 2004, 2006). It is also a period of great instability for many, particularly in the domains of romantic relationships, work, and place of residence (Arnett, 2004). In addition, this stage of life is marked by further exploration of identities in the domains of sexuality, religion and spirituality, personal values, and political identities (Ghavami, Katsiaficas, & Rogers, 2016; Schwartz et al., 2013). Ethnic identity exploration takes on new importance during emerging adulthood (Syed & Azmitia, 2009) as this is often a time when young people find themselves in shifting contexts that promote further examination and negotiation of their identities (Phinney, 2006). Some scholars assert that this period of life is marked by "self-focus" with few social obligations, particularly for White middle-class college students (Arnett, 2006, p. 10). Others contend that this phase is one ripe for developing a sense of contribution to family and community that is critical to positive youth development (Katsiaficas, 2017; Katsiaficas et al., 2018; Lerner, Brentano, Dowling, & Anderson, 2002).

These characterizations of this stage of life, however, have been drawn from very narrowly focused populations. Nearly all studies regarding emerging adulthood in the United States thus far have been with predominantly White middle-class samples in 4-year college settings (Arnett, 2003; Syed & Mitchell, 2013). Given the increasing demographic diversity of the emerging adult population in the United States and the variety of settings in which these individuals find themselves, there is a growing need for research with non-White samples outside of 4-year college settings (Syed & Mitchell, 2013).

DEVELOPMENTAL CHALLENGES AND RESILIENCE FOR IMMIGRANT-ORIGIN EMERGING ADULTS

On top of the normative developmental tasks of young adults during this phase of life, immigrant-origin emerging adults also have to contend with the dual forces of acculturation and enculturation. Immigrant-origin emerging adults are *acculturating* to their host contexts. Broadly defined, *psychological acculturation* refers to the naturally occurring, dynamic process of negotiating and developing between two cultures (such as majority and minority, or immigrant and host) (Berry, Poortinga, Segall, & Dasen, 1992). As immigrant-origin emerging adults come of age, they often have to deal with different domains of acculturation, depending on the various settings within which they find themselves embedded. Research on 4-year institutions has demonstrated the importance of institutional environments as the staging grounds for the developmental tasks of emerging adulthood (Arnett, 2004), yet work with students in community colleges is still a nascent field.

At the same time, immigrant-origin youth experience *enculturation* to their native culture from their family members and coethnic peers. Though not a universal situation, many immigrant-origin families bring with them from their home countries the collectivistic values of familism and family interdependence that stand in stark contrast to the more typical mainstream U.S. individualistic schemas (Tseng, 2004). Research on immigrant populations documents the importance of *family interdependence,* particularly among Asian-Pacific and Latinx families. In addition, anthropological studies have shown that many cultures elevate and prize collectivistic values such as interdependence and duties and obligations to others more highly than they do individualistic markers as the key transition to adulthood (Markus & Kitayama, 1991; Shweder et al., 2007).

The cultural demands of family interdependence on emerging adults highlight lifelong financial and emotional support among family members, living close to or with parents, and consulting parents on important decisions (Tseng, 2004). Also referred to as *social responsibility,* these obligations are rooted in relationships with others and are defined as a sense of responsibility and duty that extends beyond the self (Wray-Lake & Syvertsen, 2011). This sense of social responsibility can be for family members, peers, or one's immediate community or can go beyond them to a sense of civic obligation (Wray-Lake & Syvertsen, 2011). As youth in immigrant families transition to adulthood, there are significant increases in their levels of family responsibilities (Fuligni & Pedersen, 2002) and civic engagement (Flanagan & Levine, 2010; Suárez-Orozco, Hernández, & Casanova, 2015) during this developmental period.

A manifestation of such cultural beliefs is a sense of family obligations (Fuligni, 2007; Fuligni, Tseng, & Lam, 1999) that have been examined extensively with adolescent populations. Family obligations comprise three domains: (1) attitudes toward providing family assistance, (2) respect for the family, and (3) the importance of providing support in the future after they (adolescents) have become adults (Fuligni et al., 1999). As immigrant-origin adolescents emerge into adulthood, there is an increase in all domains of family obligation. These increases were observed regardless of ethnic group membership; however, Latinx and Asians had a stronger sense of family obligations in all three domains than their European American peers did (Fuligni & Pedersen, 2002; Fuligni et al., 1999). These ethnic differences held true regardless of immigrant generation (Fuligni et al., 1999).

These findings also varied by socioeconomic status, with lower income emerging adults feeling a stronger sense of family financial obligations than more affluent emerging adults did.

Contribution for immigrant youth also occurs beyond the family context and can take the form of civic engagement, which often occurs as a means of giving back to the community by translating for community members and by tutoring and mentoring youth (Flanagan & Levine, 2010; Katsiaficas, 2017; Suárez-Orozco et al., 2015). Although unable to participate in voting, many immigrant and undocumented college students are often highly engaged in their communities by participating in rallies and/or community organizing (Flanagan & Levine, 2010; Nicholls, 2013). In addition, many undocumented and immigrant youth develop support groups in college, establish advocacy organizations in their communities, and also organize through online networks (e.g., Facebook, Twitter, blogs) to disseminate messages and information about resources (Nicholls, 2013).

These findings perhaps suggest not only that this time of life is driven by "self-focus" but also that values of family interdependence come to the forefront during this period (Katsiaficas, Suárez-Orozco, & Dias, 2014). Despite the centrality of family responsibilities and obligations (Fuligni, 2007) and of values of family interdependence (Tseng, 2004) in the lives of immigrant-origin community college students, we still know very little about how they operate for these students.

CHAPTER AIMS

The aim of this chapter is to explore how immigrant-origin community college students characterize the developmental period as they emerge into adulthood. Given the saliency of competing social responsibilities during this time of life, it is important to examine the ways in which these responsibilities play a role in the transition to adulthood. Much of the literature on emerging adulthood based on studies with White middle-class college student samples has suggested that many in this age group do not feel that they have reached adulthood (Arnett, 2000). I began by considering the demographic sociological markers of adulthood in regard to our immigrant-origin community college participants. Next, I asked participants to share what they perceived as important criteria for adulthood through a sentence-completion task. I then considered how the participants' responses aligned with the sociological markers. My findings demonstrate how the participants' criteria for adulthood should be incorporated as these more accurately reflect both the realities and the maturity of these participants.

Data were specifically drawn from the survey data of the Research on Immigrants in Community College (RICC) Study (see online appendix for details of the methodology). These data were coded by two researchers to determine overarching themes, with inter-rater reliability established at a minimum

Figure 2.1. Word Cloud of Completion Responses to the Statement "You know you're an adult when . . ."

threshold of .85 kappa coefficient. Frequency analyses were conducted, and responses were entered into a word-cloud generator that visually depicts the frequency of occurrence of word usage by word size (Wordle, 2014) (see Figure 2.1).

FORMAL ROLES: DEMOGRAPHIC MARKERS OF ADULTHOOD

The ways in which participants reached the five sociological major life role transition criteria for being an adult—finishing school, getting married, living alone, being financially independent, and having children—were examined. Roughly half of the RICC sample reported that they were financially independent when it came to college expenses, with 51.7% reporting that their parents did not contribute financially to their education. Notably, however, the majority of participants had not achieved *any of the other criteria,* including moving out of their parents' home, getting married, or having children. Since the participants were all attending community college, none had completed their schooling.

DO IMMIGRANT-ORIGIN COMMUNITY COLLEGE STUDENTS FEEL LIKE ADULTS?

Participants were asked to respond to the statement "I consider myself to be an adult." The majority of the participants (71.0%) responded that they either "agreed" (44.6%) or "strongly agreed" (26.4%) that they consider themselves to be adults. Nearly a fifth (19.0%) of emerging adults responded that they "neither agreed nor disagreed," suggesting the classic ambivalence toward adult status characteristic of this time of life. Only a tenth (9.9%) of participants "disagreed" (8.3%) or "strongly disagreed" (1.6%) with the statement, suggesting that they felt that they had not yet reached adult status. There were no differences in feeling like an adult along lines of gender, race/ethnicity, or generational status. Feeling like an adult did vary by age, however, peaking among 23-year-olds, and it was at its lowest levels with 19-year-olds.

You Know You Are an Adult When . . .

The survey participants ($N = 644$) were asked to complete the following sentence: "You know you're an adult when . . . ." Their responses provided insight into the ways in which they conceptualized the criteria of adulthood. Analysis of the sentence completion data revealed three main themes emerging as criteria for adulthood: responsibilities (66.3%), independence (26.3%), and adult role transitions (10.7%).

Responsibilities. Responsibility or competing responsibilities were the primary marker of adulthood, with two-thirds of participants listing "responsibilities," "being responsible," and "responsibility" in their responses.

The coding revealed that immigrant-origin community college students wrote about these multiple responsibilities in many ways. Exemplary responsibility responses to the sentence prompt "You know you're an adult when . . ." included the following:

> You fulfill ALL of your responsibilities and DO NOT take the easy way out. [Second-generation Latina, age 19]

> You have responsibilities in life, like work, school, [and] bills. [Second-generation Latino, age 22]

> [You] have juggled so many things on your plate, and not once did you think of quitting anything. [Second-generation mixed/other ethnicity woman, age 18]

> You assume your responsibilities and start planning for the future. [First-generation Latino, age 18]

Assuming *financial* responsibility was directly stated or implied in 24.8% of the responsibility responses. Sample responses about assuming *financial* responsibility included the following:

> You can handle your financial responsibilities. [Second-generation Latino, age 24]

> I pay for school. [First-generation Latina, age 20]

> You pay rent and utilities. [First-generation Black woman, age 19]

> You can support yourself. [Second-generation Latina, age 20]

> [You're] able to take full responsibilities for yourself. [Second-generation Black man, age 18].

Taking on responsibilities for others included responses that denoted taking care of others (and made up 5.9% of the responsibility responses). Participants completed the statement "You know you're an adult when . . ." with the following:

I started to think not only for myself but also for others in every aspect. [First-generation Asian woman, age 21]

I started to have responsibilities at home. [First-generation Latino, age 21]

You can fully take care of yourself and others. [Second-generation Black woman, age 19]

Having responsibilities as a marker of adulthood significantly varied by gender, with 74.1% of female participants and 56.9% of male participants noting this theme. In addition, responsibilities as a marker of adulthood significantly varied by ethnic group (Latinx, 73.9%; Black, 62.8%; multiracial, 62.7%; White, 62.3%; Asian; 54.9%). No generational or age differences were detected.

Independence. The second most common criterion for adulthood was independence, with 26.3% of participants listing it as a marker of adulthood. These were responses that described being independent or self-reliant, becoming capable of making independent decisions, and/or becoming financially independent (Arnett, 1998, 2003). Sample responses completing the statement "You know you are an adult when . . ." included the following.

You can be independent in every aspect of life. [First-generation mixed/other ethnicity man, age 23]

You are self-sufficient. [Second-generation Latina, age 23]

You start making your own decisions without help from anybody. [Second-generation Asian man, age 19]

No statistically significant gender, ethnic, generational, or age differences were detected for this theme.

Adult role transitions. The third most common theme was adult role transitions, with 10.7% of participants listing them as a marker of adulthood. Their responses addressed taking on a new role in life and included one of the five "traditional" sociological markers of adulthood: getting married, leaving home, completing school, entering the workforce, and having children (Settersten, 2005). Examples of these responses included the following:

You're married. [Second-generation White woman, age 18]

[You] have to raise a child. [Second-generation Latina, age 18]

There were statistically significant gender differences across this theme. Men were more likely to list adult role transitions than women were; 14.6% of men provided role transition responses, proportionally nearly twice as many as women did (7.5%). Latinx were the most likely to provide role transition responses (30.8%) while White participants were the least likely to do so (16.9%); Black and Asian participants fell in between (24.6% and 23.5%, respectively). There were no generational or age differences detected for this theme.

Juggling Responsibilities Beyond Formal Roles

Beyond examining formal social roles, the RICC survey considered the competing responsibilities in immigrant-origin students' lives that existed in addition to the demands of school (i.e., their work, family, and community responsibilities).

Working. Nearly half (46.0%) of participants worked outside of school. The majority of participants worked between 20 and 29 hours per week (25.4%). There were statistically significant ethnic differences regarding whether or not participants worked outside of school. White participants had the highest percentage (66.2%) of students working outside of school, with Asian participants having the lowest percentage (36.4%); the percentages of all other ethnic/racial groups fell between these two figures.

Family responsibilities. The majority of participants (60.9%) reported having had responsibilities for helping their parents or relatives during the past month. Those who reported having such responsibilities on average participated in slightly more than two family-related activities during that period ($M = 2.30, SD = 1.04$). For the nearly two-thirds of participants who had family responsibilities, activities ranged from providing advice or advocating for family members (81.0%) to helping with child or elder care (72.6%), helping their family members with translation (54.7%), and engaging in some other specific activity (which they listed on the form) (31.9%). Those "other" activities included performing household tasks such as cooking and cleaning and providing financial help such as paying bills or giving money to family members. Although there were no significant group differences with regard to whether or not participants engaged in these activities, there were significant ethnic differences in how often they participated in them. Latinx participants reported having participated in family responsibility activities more often than White and Black participants did ($F [4,363] = 6.23, p < .001$).

Community responsibilities. Three quarters (74.6%) of participants reported having participated in at least one community responsibility activity in the past month. On average, participants reported participating in nearly three community activities during that time period ($M = 2.88, SD = 2.51$). These activities ranged from mentoring young people (46.9%) to volunteering at a place of worship, school, or community center (45.1%); providing a community member with advocacy or advice (42.7%); engaging in a cause about which they cared (40.5%); helping someone with translation (39.9%); assisting with child or elder care (37.5%); and coaching young people (36.8%). There were no significant group differences by gender, generational status, or ethnicity regarding whether or not or how often participants engaged in community responsibilities.

IN SUM

These analyses provide a descriptive portrait of low-income, ethnically diverse immigrant-origin students aged 18 to 25 in community colleges. Most notably, these results show that the majority of participants did not meet the traditionally used sociological criteria of adulthood—getting married, having children, leaving the parental home, entering the workforce, and finishing school. In addition, the majority of participants did not cite these adult role transitions as their criteria for adulthood. The findings indicate that the participants were postponing many of the adult role transitions until they were at least in their late 20s. The findings also show that the majority continued to live at home with their families, were financially interdependent with their parents, and were unmarried and childless, suggesting that the conditions under which emerging adulthood occurs were present for this sample.

A number of demographic trends can help to place this finding in perspective. During the past 50 years, there have been significant increases in the age at which youth achieve these markers (Arnett & Taber, 1994). However, these overall trends become more nuanced as we examine a snapshot of the current national data for immigrant-origin individuals aged 18 to 34 from the 2008 Current Population Survey (Rumbaut & Komaie, 2010). Furthermore, and perhaps most important, income inequality has been steadily increasing since 1970 (Rosenbaum, Ahearn, & Becker, 2015).

Although first-generation individuals aged 18 to 34 tend to reach the sociological markers of adulthood at higher frequencies than second-generation individuals do, this sample showed the lowest levels of them reaching adult roles. More participants in this sample lived at home with parents than national trends reveal for others in this age group. However, this finding is characteristic of young people living in cities with high-cost housing (Rumbaut & Komaie, 2010). This result perhaps reflects the difficult economic realities of attending school full-time while living in a large urban center in the wake of the Great Recession of 2008. Despite the fact that most community college students report having plans to attain a bachelor's degree, only one in five (20%) attain one after 8 years, and almost half (46%) do not receive any credential at all after 8 years (Rosenbaum et al., 2015). The length of time that it takes to complete a degree within a community college setting precludes many young people's emergence into adult roles.

Immigrant-origin community college students often find themselves caught in an economic undertow that disrupts their pathways to adulthood. These survey results further highlight how increasingly elusive reaching these adult milestones can be in the wake of national and global economic hardships and under these circumstances.

Yet in spite of these preclusions to their attaining adult status, the results reveal that the majority of these participants felt as though they had reached adulthood. These findings stand in stark contrast to the work of Arnett (2006) and others who assert that ambivalence toward achieving adult status is characteristic of this time of life. The hallmark of emerging adulthood, feeling "in-between," may therefore uniquely be a trait for those who have the luxury of exploration, something that might not be possible for low-income, ethnically diverse immigrant-origin community college students. Instead, these students are neither postponing adulthood nor feeling like adults; rather, they are managing to find a path to adulthood despite the constrictions of their economic and social realities. Therefore, it is important to understand the ways in which immigrant-origin community college students make sense of their own adult identities and what they consider to be markers of adulthood.

The sense of adulthood that these participants feel is reflected in their own criteria of adulthood and their high level of engagement in the competing responsibilities of work, family, and community. There are many contributing factors that can impede academic persistence. Immigrant-origin students often find themselves in urban institutions that serve "nontraditional" students (Kuh, Vesper, & Krehbiel, 1994, p. 2) of diverse racial and ethnic backgrounds who attend college part-time, live off-campus and commute to class, work more than 20 hours a week, and often have spent some time out of school before returning to college (Horn, Berger, & Carroll, 2004; Kuh et al., 1994). Managing these multiple impediments in addition to dealing with competing social responsibilities sets immigrant-origin students apart from their native-born middle-class peers who may have the luxury of immersing themselves exclusively in the college campus experience without these constraints. It is not surprising that students who manage such multiple work, family, and school demands are at higher risk of not persisting in their studies (Bailey, Jenkins, & Leinbach, 2005; Valentine et al., 2009). These results further suggest that competing responsibilities are key to understanding this developmental period for this population. In many ways this result corroborates the work of Arnett (2003) and Nelson, Badger, and Wu (2004), who found that responsibility and independence are critical to the ways in which college students conceptualize adulthood.

These results also differ from the existing literature, however, by pointing to the ways in which this population is "other focused" and how social responsibilities go beyond taking responsibility for oneself as discussed in the extant literature. Park, Twenge, and Greenfield (2013), examining nationally representative data on adolescents, found that concern for others increased during the 2008 recession. Although only a small percentage of the participants explicitly listed engaging in social responsibilities as their main criterion for adulthood, the majority reported having engaged in these responsibilities for their families and communities. Emerging adulthood, therefore, is a time when social responsibility comes to the forefront for this population.

There were significant gender differences in the criteria for adulthood. Proportionally, more females listed responsibilities as markers of adulthood than their male peers did. Yet an examination of the behaviors participants reported did not reflect any gender differences in whether or how often they engaged in family or community responsibilities. In addition, although cited less often than responsibilities as a key marker of adulthood, adult role transitions were more often cited by male participants than by their female peers on the sentence completion task. This finding suggests that there are key gender differences in conceptualizations of adulthood but not necessarily in the ways in which immigrant-origin emerging adults engage with these social responsibilities.

In addition, there were significant ethnic differences. Latinx listed having responsibilities as a criterion for adulthood more often than other ethnic groups did. Latinx also participated in family responsibilities more often than their peers from other ethnic groups did. These findings suggest that ethnic differences are not only reflected in the criteria for adulthood but also in the behaviors of immigrant-origin emerging adults. This chapter further corroborates the extant literature regarding the role of familism and the high value that Latinx place on family obligations, a finding that is well documented in the literature (Fuligni et al., 1999).

Taken together, the values and expectations passed down through the dual forces of enculturation and acculturation each play a role in shaping how immigrant-origin students emerge into adulthood. Community college contexts serve as the nexus where home and school and enculturative and acculturative influences converge and where managing multiple cultural values comes to the forefront. It is critical to examine the ways in which immigrant-origin students engage with their families and communities as these activities have important implications for the kinds of people they will become (Lerner, Dowling, & Anderson, 2003; Suárez-Orozco et al., 2015) as well as for the kinds of societies we will become (Suárez-Orozco et al., 2015) in the long term. In the shorter term, it is crucial that the institutions serving them recognize their students as the complex, whole, emerging young adults that they are.

REFERENCES

Arnett, J. J. (1998). Learning to stand alone: The contemporary American transition to adulthood in cultural and historical context. *Human Development, 41*, 295–315.

Arnett, J. J. (2000). Emerging adulthood: A theory of development from the late teens through the twenties. *American Psychologist, 55*, 469–480.

Arnett, J. J. (2003). Conceptions of the transition to adulthood among emerging adults in American ethnic groups. *New Directions for Child and Adolescent Development, 2003*(100), 63–76. Retrieved from doi.org/10.1002/cd.75

Arnett, J. J. (2004). *Emerging adulthood: The winding road from the late teens through the twenties.* London, UK: Oxford University Press.

Arnett, J. J. (2006). Emerging adulthood: Understanding the new way of coming of age. In J. J. Arnett & J. L. Tanner (Eds.), *Emerging adults in America: Coming of age in the 21st century* (pp. 3–19). Washington, DC: American Psychological Association.

Arnett, J. J., & Taber, S. (1994). Adolescence terminable and interminable: When does adolescence end? *Journal of Youth & Adolescence, 23*, 517–537.

Bailey, T., Jenkins, D., & Leinbach, D. T. (2005). *Low-income and minority student completion study: Descriptive statistics from the 1992 high school cohort.* New York, NY: Columbia University, Teachers College, Community College Research Center. Retrieved from ccrc.tc.columbia.edu/Publication.asp?uid=206

Batalova, J., & Fix, M. (2011). *Up for grabs: The gains and prospects of first- and second-generation young adults.* Washington, DC: Migration Policy Institute.

Berry, J. W., Poortinga, Y. H., Segall, M. H., & Dasen, P. R. (1992). *Cross-cultural psychology: Research and implications.* New York, NY: Cambridge University Press.

Chapa, J., & De La Rosa, B. (2004). Latino population growth, socioeconomic and demographic characteristics, and implications for educational attainment. *Education and Urban Society, 36*(2), 130–149.

Flanagan, C., & Levine, P. (2010). Civic engagement and the transition to adulthood. *The Future of Children, 20*(1), 159–179.

Fuligni, A. J. (2007). Family obligation, college enrollment, and emerging adulthood in Asian and Latin American families. *Child Development Perspectives, 1*(2), 96–100. Retrieved from doi.org/10.1111/j.1750-8606.2007.00022.x

Fuligni, A. J., & Pedersen, S. (2002). Family obligation and the transition to young adulthood. *Developmental Psychology, 38*(5), 856–868.

Fuligni, A. J., Tseng, V., & Lam, M. (1999). Attitudes toward family obligations among American adolescents with Asian, Latin American, and European backgrounds. *Child Development, 70*(4), 1030–1044.

Ghavami, N., Katsiaficas, D., & Rogers, L. O. (2016). Toward an intersectional approach in developmental science: The role of race, gender, sexual orientation, and immigrant status. In S. S. Horn, M. Ruck, & L. Liben (Eds.), *Equity and justice in developmental sciences: Theoretical and methodological issues (advances in child development and behavior)* (Vol. 50, pp. 31–73). Retrieved from doi.org/http://dx.doi.org/10.1016/bs.acdb.2015.12.001

Katsiaficas, D. (2017). "I know I'm an adult when . . . I can care for myself and others": Social responsibilities and emerging into adulthood for community college students. *Emerging Adulthood.* doi:10.1177/2167696817698301

Katsiaficas, D., Hernandez, E., Alcantar, C. M., Gutierrez, M. N., Samayoa, E., & Williams, Z. (2018). "We'll get through this together": Collective contribution in the lives of Latino undocumented undergraduates. *Teachers College Record, 120*(12), 1–48.

Katsiaficas, D., Suárez-Orozco, C., & Dias, S. I. (2014). "When do I feel like an adult?": Latino and Afro-Caribbean immigrant-origin community college students' conceptualizations and experiences of (emerging) adulthood. *Emerging Adulthood.* Retrieved from doi.org/10.1177/2167696814548059

Kuh, G. D., Vesper, N., & Krehbiel, L. (1994). Student learning at metropolitan universities. In J. Smart (Ed.), *Higher education: Handbook of theory and research* (Vol. IX, pp. 1–44). New York, NY: Agathon.

Lerner, R. M., Brentano, C., Dowling, E. M., & Anderson, P. M. (2002). Positive youth development: Thriving as a basis of personhood and civil society. In C. S. Taylor, R. M. Lerner, & A. von Eye (Eds.), & G. Noam (Series Ed.), *New directions for youth development: Theory, practice and research: Pathways to positive youth development among gang and non-gang youth* (Vol. 95, pp. 11–33). San Francisco, CA: Jossey-Bass.

Lerner, R. M., Dowling, E. M., & Anderson, P. M. (2003). Positive youth development: Thriving as the basis of personhood and civil society. *Applied Developmental Science, 7*(3), 172–180.

Markus, H. R., & Kitayama, S. (1991). Culture and the self: Implications for cognition, emotion, and motivation. *Psychological Review, 98*(2), 224–253. Retrieved from doi.org/10.1037/0033-295X.98.2.224

Nelson, L. J., Badger, S., & Wu, B. (2004). The influence of culture in emerging adulthood: Perspectives of Chinese college students. *International Journal of Behavioral Development, 28*(1), 26–36. Retrieved from doi.org/10.1080/01650250344000244

Nicholls, W. (2013). *The DREAMers: How the undocumented youth movement transformed the immigrant rights debate.* Stanford, CA: Stanford University Press.

Park, H., Twenge, J. M., & Greenfield, P. M. (2013). The Great Recession: Implications for adolescent values and behavior. *Social Psychological and Personality Science, 5*(3), 310–318. doi:10.1177/1948550613495419

Phinney, J. S. (2006). Ethnic identity exploration in emerging adulthood. In J. J. Arnett & J. L. Tanner (Eds.), *Emerging adulthood: Coming of age in the 21st century* (pp. 117–134). Washington, DC: American Psychological Association.

Rosenbaum, J., Ahearn, C., & Becker, K. (2015). *The new forgotten half and research directions to support them.* New York, NY: William T. Grant Foundation.

Rumbaut, R. G., & Komaie, G. (2010). Immigration and adult transitions. *The Future of Children, 20*(1), 43–66.

Schwartz, S. J., Kim, S. Y., Whitbourne, S. K., Zamboanga, B. L., Weisskirch, R. S., Forthun, L. F., . . . Luyckx, K. (2013). Converging identities: Dimensions of acculturation and personal identity status among immigrant college students. *Cultural Diversity and Ethnic Minority Psychology, 19*(2), 155–165. Retrieved from doi.org/10.1037/a0030753

Settersten, R.A. (2005). Social policy and the transition to adulthood: Towards stronger institutions and individual capacities. In R. A. Settersten, F. F. Furstenberg, & R. G. Rumbaut (Eds.), *On the frontier of adulthood: Theory, research, & public policy* (pp. 534–560). Chicago, IL: University of Chicago Press.

Settersten, R. A., & Ray, B. (2011). *Not quite adults.* New York, NY: Bantam Books.

Shweder, R. A., Goodnow, J. J., Hatano, G., LeVine, R. A., Markus, H. R., & Miller, P. J. (2007). The cultural psychology of development: One mind, many mentalities. In W. Damon (Ed.), *Handbook of child psychology* (5th ed., Vol. 1, pp. 865–937). New York, NY: Wiley. Retrieved from doi.org/10.1002/9780470147658.chpsy0113

Suárez-Orozco, C., Hernández, M. G., & Casanova, S. (2015). "It's sort of my calling": The civic engagement and social responsibility of Latino immigrant-origin young adults. *Research in Human Development, 12*(1–2), 84–99. Retrieved from doi.org/10.1080/15427609.2015.1010350

Syed, M., & Azmitia, M. (2009). Longitudinal trajectories of ethnic identity during the college years. *Journal of Research on Adolescence, 19*(4), 601–624.

Syed, M., Azmitia, M., & Cooper, C. R. (2011). Identity and academic success among under-represented ethnic minorities: An interdisciplinary review and integration. *Journal of Social Issues, 67*(3), 442–468.

Syed, M., & Mitchell, L. L. (2013). Race, ethnicity, and emerging adulthood: Retrospect and prospects. *Emerging Adulthood, 1*(2), 83–95. Retrieved from doi.org/10.1177/2167696813480503

Teranishi, R. T., Suárez-Orozco, C., & Suárez-Orozco, M. M. (2011). Immigrants in community colleges. *The Future of Children, 21*(1), 153–169. Retrieved from doi.org/10.1353/foc.2011.0009

Tseng, V. (2004). Family interdependence and academic adjustment in college: Youth from immigrant and U.S.-born families. *Child Development, 75*(3), 966–983.

Valentine, J. C., Hirschy, A. S., Bremer, C. D., Novillo, W., Castellano, M., & Banister, A. (2009). *Systematic reviews of research: Postsecondary transitions. Identifying effective models and practices.* Atlanta, GA: National Research Center for Career and Technical Education. Retrieved from www.nrccte.org/sites/default/files/publication-files/valentine_postsecondary_transitions.pdf

Wordle [online word cloud generator]. (2014). www.wordle.net.

Wray-Lake, L., & Syvertsen, A. K. (2011). The developmental roots of social responsibility in childhood and adolescence. *New Directions for Child and Adolescent Development,* (134), 11–25.

CHAPTER 3

The Pathways of English Learners in Community Colleges

Persistence and Push-Out

Tasha Darbes

A report by the College Board (2008) opens with the statement that community colleges are "the Ellis Island of American higher education, the crossroads at which K–12 education meets higher education, and the institutions that give students the tools to navigate the modern world" (p. 5). Because of the influx of immigrants to the United States, community colleges are serving greater numbers of culturally and linguistically diverse students (Passel, 2011) than they have in the past. Immigrant-origin students bring a wide variety of cultural resources and linguistic practices that can impact their experiences and academic outcomes (Louie, 2009; Teranishi, C. Suárez-Orozco, & M. Suárez-Orozco, 2011). Many immigrant students may also still be in the process of acquiring full academic English proficiency, making language proficiency a pertinent issue for understanding their academic pathways (Conway, 2009; Harklau & Siegal, 2009; Kanno & Cromley, 2015).

In spite of the fact that language minority students tend to begin their higher education trajectories in 2-year colleges at higher rates than their English-dominant peers do, there is a dearth of large-scale research focusing on the unique effects of language acquisition (Kanno & Cromley, 2015; Nuñez & Sparks, 2012). Studies that have included issues of multilingual immigrant-origin students problematically ignore or conflate language with other factors such as race, ethnicity, or immigration status (Oropeza, Varghese, & Kanno, 2010). This situation has meant that there is a very incomplete picture of how the experiences of students, the processes of language acquisition in globalized spaces, and institutional policies intersect to produce differentiated academic trajectories in which linguistic minority students acquiring English may be less likely to fulfill their academic aspirations than other students (Kanno & Cromley, 2015; Razfar & Simon, 2011).

This chapter will review findings of the analyses of both quantitative and qualitative data from the Research on Immigrants in Community College (RICC) Study to better understand the unique issues and experiences of language minority students acquiring English in community college settings. After drawing on the survey data (see online appendix at www.tcpress.com for details) to review some of the characteristics of this complex population, I will explore how these students experienced their classes, the impact of gatekeeping policies such as testing and remediation, and the particular obstacles that these students faced along their academic pathways using a subset of 12 qualitative interviews with English learners (see online appendix at www.tcpress.com).

ENGLISH LEARNERS IN COMMUNITY COLLEGES: DEFINING THE POPULATION

The pathways to acquisition of academic English proficiency are increasingly complex, making it very difficult to define and understand the experiences of multilingual students. *Language minority students,* those who speak a language other than English at home, are an extremely heterogeneous group in terms of proficiencies and immigration experiences, but they also share a number of often co-occurring factors such as having low socioeconomic status (SES), being a member of the first generation of their families to go to college, and being enrolled in resource-poor schools (Kanno & Cromley, 2015). A subset of language minority students are *English learners* (ELs), students whose academic English proficiency is still developing and who may not fully benefit from mainstream instruction without language supports. Unlike public K–12 systems, higher education does not have any federally mandated or cross-institutional policies that function to consistently define, assess, or identify EL students across contexts; consequently, there is no consistency in policies or even an attempt to collect data on language learners as a separate, distinct population. Naming, categorizing, and serving the needs of these students are inherently difficult tasks and pose a challenge to conducting research (Bunch et al., 2011).

There are a number of factors that present problems when identifying students whose process of acquiring academic English proficiency interacts with their pathways through a community college. For example, the most obvious way to identify English learners would be to find those who have been placed in an English as a Second Language (ESL) class. But how does this process actually work when there are no consistent, explicit policies, assessments, demographic information, or self-identification mechanisms in place to identify English learners? When such linguistically diverse language minority students encounter open-access community colleges, they must undergo a process that involves initial screening, usually through the taking of standardized English tests, to determine whether or not they have "college-ready" language skills. Those who are found to be college ready begin their academic pathways; those who do not are divided into separate tracks that develop the skills of either native English speakers or ESL students.

This three-track model (college-ready English, remedial English, and ESL) was created in conjunction with prevalent immigration patterns and made assumptions about bilingualism and the types of instruction students need (Valdes, 1992).

This process of assessment and placement can be both particularly problematic and critical for students' future engagement (Bunch & Panyatova, 2008; Perry, Bahr, Rosin, & Woodward, 2010). For example, the assessments that community colleges use to place students into these tracks were not designed to distinguish ESL students from the general population (Curry, 2004; Llosa & Bunch, 2011), leading to serious issues of misplacement. Both Scott-Clayton (2012) and Belfield and Crosta (2012) found that using English test scores was likely to result in a "severe error rate," a finding that means that many students (Scott-Clayton estimated close to 30%) may be placed in classes that are either above or below their predicted abilities. In addition, the colleges in the study had institutional mechanisms to keep EL students out of college and instead provided students instruction in liminal, noncredit-bearing spaces such as English Language Institute or bridge programs. For these reasons, the number of students placed in a credit-bearing ESL course may only be a rough approximation of the number of students who are in the process of acquiring English and have aspirations for higher education.

RETHINKING PERSISTENCE: GATEKEEPERS AND BOUNCERS

Research has shown that as time spent in developmental or "precollege" courses increases, persistence and graduation rates decrease (Bailey, Jeong, & Cho, 2010), a finding that may signal something about the characteristics of the students (perhaps being more underprepared than others or having other risk factors for noncompletion), but that also attests to the role of these courses and tests as "gatekeepers." The effects of the length of time spent in developmental courses are multiplied for English learners. For example, a student placed in the lowest level of developmental English may spend one or two semesters taking classes before having the possibility of enrolling in college-level (credit-bearing) classes; this process will be lengthened if the student does not pass either the reading or the writing tests at any point. However, for students tracked in ESL courses, such as a more recent immigrant placed in the lowest level, completing just the ESL sequence could take three to five semesters, without taking test failure into account. Given the financial and personal impact of enrolling in courses that do not grant credit toward a degree or transfer, students facing multiple semesters of basic skills work often abandon their academic aspirations altogether (Bailey, 2009; Bailey et al., 2010).

Although particular attention has been paid to the relationship between remediation and persistence, the explanatory narratives often overlook the role that language acquisition and bilingualism may play in the experiences of immigrant students at community colleges. In fact, institutional structures such as remediation were originally designed to provide additional academic supports for math and English for a largely native English-speaking population; these policies may have different consequences when applied to a population that is in the process of acquiring English as another language. Studies have shown that students who were identified as needing ESL displayed lower rates of persistence (Hawley & Harris, 2005) and were less likely to transfer to a 4-year college (Almon, 2010; Razfar & Simon, 2011). These studies hint at the particular role that assessed linguistic competence plays in high immigrant-origin settings.

THE MULTILINGUAL CAMPUS

In order to gain an emic perspective that does not fully depend on institutional identifications, we provide a snapshot of the multilingual backgrounds of students on community college campuses derived from survey questions on self-reported proficiencies in both English and home languages. These data reveal that students attending the community colleges in this study are incredibly linguistically diverse. Of the total 644 community college students who participated in the RICC survey, half (54%; $N = 347$) reported speaking a language other than English at home. Approximately two-thirds (65.4%) of those respondents listed Spanish as their home language, reflecting the large number of Latino students in the areas these colleges serve. However, there is great diversity in the remaining third—a total of 44 languages ranging from Albanian to Yoruba and including languages from Africa, all parts of Asia, the Middle East, the Caribbean, and Europe. Bilingualism is highly valued by this population; a large number reported that speaking their home language was important (79.3%) and that they had high levels of comfort speaking both English and their home language (74.9%).

Much research takes the category of "ESL" or "English learner" as a given, an a priori condition, when in fact there is a complex interaction among language acquisition processes, institutional practices of placement, and the ways in which students perceive and develop their abilities over time. Analysis of qualitative student interviews revealed that even though most students in the sample did not explicitly self-identify using the term *ESL student*, many described their experiences of "learning English" and the accompanying characteristics that are commonly associated with being in the early stages of language acquisition in their interviews. "Learning English" refers to feeling limited with English production, speaking with an accent, the use of bilingual dictionaries and issues with first-language transference, and conscious efforts to learn the language. Ramiro, who had immigrated to the United States from Panama at the age of 16, described himself before entering college: "I didn't know anything before—not how to write, nothing, not even English." The 12 interviews that formed the qualitative sample for this chapter were all with students who described experiences learning English while attending a community college.

Although all students are confronted with potholes during the transition to higher education and beyond, English learners face particular challenges while navigating the community college systems that test, place, and provide language supports. The following sections detail the *qualitative experiences* of these English learners, especially in regard to the gatekeeping mechanisms that assessed and placed them in the remedial and "liminal" courses of the community colleges under study.

EXPERIENCES OF ENGLISH LEARNERS IN ESL CLASSES: "STUDENTS LIKE ME"

The community colleges in our sample all offered various types of ESL instruction, including noncredit ESL geared toward workplace English that offered the possibility of future transfer, "bridge" programs that offered 1 year of intensive ESL instruction combined with academic preparation, and ESL developmental courses (usually for less than full academic credit). English learners in the sample reported that at first they generally did not have negative feelings about their initial placement in an ESL course. Their reactions differed from those of English-dominant students who were placed in remedial English who generally were shocked at or resented their test failure and the subsequent delay in their college entry. In contrast, English learners believed that their ESL placement meant that they would be given a chance to acquire academic proficiencies and the tools necessary to pass the exit exams and do well in college-level courses. For example, Felix, a recent immigrant from the Dominican Republic, was placed in an ESL bridge program at Domino. He had fully anticipated this placement, explaining, "I was expecting to go to [ESL Bridge]. . . . I knew that my English writing level and my speaking level abilities were not [good] enough [for me] to be in college, so I need[ed] to improve them. So it was clear in my mind that I was going to the [ESL Bridge] Program, and then I was going to go to college."

Students placed in ESL courses reported highly positive experiences and said that these courses made them feel more confident about their abilities and their performance in the college-level courses that they took afterward. They often reported having positive or significant relationships with the faculty, whom they perceived as explicitly offering academic help. For example, Heydi, also a recent immigrant from the Dominican Republic, described her experience in the Taino ESL courses, saying, "It was very helpful for me. They [taught] me everything about English. I still, you know, have to improve my English more, but they help[ed] me a lot." In this sample, English learners who successfully transitioned took anywhere from one to six semesters to pass both reading and writing exams and be eligible for college-level English courses, a testament to their persistence and ability to progress.

Another positive aspect of ESL classes was the sense of belonging that students attached to being placed in a class with peers who were "learning English, like me." Many English learners described their ESL classes as spaces where they could receive help and did not experience fear of speaking in class. "First, in the classes, I'm an ESL student; they know that I'm just like them. A lot of them tell me if you have a question, we can help you," said Heydi. Felix also made friends while in the ESL Bridge Program—friends who continued to be his support network, as when he would email them drafts of his work to ask for feedback and corrections of his English.

These feelings of belonging could extend beyond the classroom to the college setting itself. Oscar, a Dominican student with only 2 years of U.S. residency, chose to enroll at Taino because he believed it would be a place where recent immigrants like himself would feel comfortable. He said, "Since I was recently off the boat, as people say, it was easier for me to be admitted here. I just decided to come here. Also, it has a Spanish name, so I thought the Latino representation here [would] be much larger than in other places. [I thought] I would have felt more comfortable here." Kanno and Cromley (2015) have highlighted the tendencies of ELL-identified high school students to avoid applying to 4-year colleges and their overrepresentation at 2-year colleges. However, what they see as a problem for English language learner (ELL) students in terms of their academic trajectories could in fact be a conscious strategy to choose settings they perceive will offer them a sense of belonging and language learning supports.

"I AM NOT FROM HERE": ACCENT AND INSECURITY

For some students, feelings or insecurities about their language proficiency or na-tivity became salient when they were around others, especially peers whom they identified as "English speakers" or "Americans." Students' linguistic insecurity be-came more pronounced in the presence of others, a factor that affected their class participation. Heydi, who took other classes besides ESL at Taino, said that her participation "depends of [sic] the class. ESL, I'm okay. . . . If [I'm in] another class, like psychology, I feel the pressure 'cause everybody that's in psychology know[s] English." Felix also feared speaking in front of others, saying, "I'm afraid of, like, if I say something bad, they're going to make fun of me, that kind of stuff. That's why I don't feel comfortable speaking in class."

These anxieties about their perceived lack of proficiency in speaking could also be rooted in experiences of actual shame and embarrassment in class when their fears of exposing their "bad English," and therefore exposing their other-ness, their lack of nativity and belonging, had come true. Sophal, who had im-migrated from Cambodia at age 17, related a story from her college-level English course, saying,

> I got made fun of once. I was saying something in English, and then my accent, and they were all laughing. I felt kind of stupid. . . . There was this one guy, he just basically made fun of everybody, but they all didn't take it seriously. But to me, I find it offensive because, you know, I am not from here. . . . I kind of laugh at myself, but at that one point, that hurts.

These linguistic insecurities then extended to other academic and career-related decisions. Sophal's belief that her English was not as good as that of a native speaker limited her confidence to choose certain careers. She explained, "I really love media, but for some reason something pulls me back. I am not from here, and my English is not that [good], so I think it is very competitive, so right now I'm just doing business and administration." For this reason, feelings of insecurity can arise from students' interactions with others as well as from their academic linguistic performance. These experiences affected not only their confidence in their English-language skills but also their relations with peers and their feelings of belonging since their spoken language marked them as "others" who could be the target of microaggressions (see Chapter 6).

"WHIRLPOOLING"

Although many ESL-identified students reported generally having positive experiences in their classes, there is a time limit for these positive feelings. Students who spent more than two or three semesters in ESL courses eventually became frustrated with this placement. Both Felix and Heydi experienced increasing feelings of frustration by their third semester of ESL course work—Felix was able to pass all of the tests at that point, but at the time of the interview Heydi was still awaiting the results of her fourth time taking the tests. Heydi stated that she did not want to "go back" to an ESL course after taking the courses for three semesters: "I don't want to go back. I feel everything that they gonna teach me that they *ya me lo enseñaron* [they already taught that to me]. Gonna be the same class. Now I have to work myself."

Many English learners in the sample experienced what I call "whirlpooling"—when students experience multiple test failures and therefore spend extended periods of time in remedial ESL courses. The whirlpooling pattern was especially evident among ESL students who had entered college with a low level of English proficiency and perhaps also had other issues such as lower levels of preparation in their home language or an (often undiagnosed) learning disability. Not only did these students have to repeat taking the exams, but they also were usually repeating the same ESL courses, especially the last course in the developmental sequence. For example, Noemi had come to the United States at the age of 18. At the time of her interview, she had spent 2 years in ESL—1 year in a bridge program and then two semesters in developmental ESL courses. She had just failed the English exams for the third time. Noemi was beginning to feel frustrated since she was passing her ESL classes but not passing the exams. The combination of hard work and failure made Noemi extremely stressed. Instead of seeing these results as part of a developmental language acquisition process that takes time and can only be accelerated so much through hard work, Noemi and students like her sometimes blame themselves. For example, Noemi stated that she "was lazy" and just needed to work harder. In general, students in the sample expressed their belief that hard work will yield positive results and improvement, but Noemi's story shows how sometimes "hard work doesn't pay."

In addition to paying for the same ESL courses, Noemi also faced the possibility of losing her state-based financial aid because of her repeated failure to pass the exams. New state regulations, called "Ability to Benefit," require students to raise their test scores and pass exams within a designated amount of time; if they cannot, they lose their financial aid. Noemi's time was almost up. She explained:

> They [ESL classes] affect me because I'm wasting money from financial aid, so if I don't pass that, they going to take away financial aid, then I have to pay with my own money, so I don't have money to pay it, so I'm afraid of that. . . . I worry too much.

Higher education literature generally assumes that students enter institutions being proficient in English and therefore sees students' longer time spent in remedial education as an indicator of failure, either of the remedial programs or of the students themselves. Policies that set and define limits of time spent in remedial education and of access to aid do not take into consideration the time that it takes for language acquisition to develop or what the language needs of students in later stages of acquisition are. What is sometimes interpreted as failure is in fact part of a normal acquisition process that can take an estimated 5 to 7 years (Collier, 1987), during which supports are necessary and useful. However, policies that limit access to content-rich college-level courses, enforce the results of invalid tests, and send multiple messages that students do not belong in college could be said to be more like "bouncers" pushing students out of college rather than neutral gatekeepers.

POLICY IMPLICATIONS

Seeing community colleges as linguistically diverse spaces has important implications for community college policies and practices. Kibler, Bunch, and Endriss (2011) have argued for shifting from deficit perspectives to a resource perspective when constructing interventions and policies for language minority students, in particular for those who have been educated in the United States and may not conform to the ESL category. Recommendations include providing more integration of content and language instruction, accelerating access to the mainstream college-level curriculum, and supporting transitions and informed decisionmaking.

Community colleges should make greater efforts to understand the complex nature of students' bilingual competencies and reformulate the categories currently in use. Analysis has revealed that it is the perception of a student's being an English learner, a classification that depends on many factors such as the student's proficiency level in the home language, confidence in speaking, and factors related to immigration (such as age and length of U.S. residency) that influences how students react to instructional interventions such as ESL placement. For example, ESL students may feel more comfortable in classrooms tailored to their needs and feel silenced in other classrooms in the presence of perceived "English speakers," at least during their first two semesters. These dynamics affect classroom partici-pation, and interventions such as learning communities need to be informed by an understanding of the social issues related to linguistic diversity. Unfortunately, community colleges currently do not collect data or use any information related to the home language, speaking, or immigration factors when making placement decisions and do not have any category that refers to students as bilinguals or multilinguals. The use of a bilingual confidence questionnaire (as was developed for the RICC survey) or even just using demographic information in placement decisions would ensure that course work be better aligned with student needs and perceptions.

Additionally, students in the qualitative sample expressed frustration at having to attend language remediation that lasted longer than two or three semesters; at that point any effectiveness of remedial-type instruction had worn off, especially since this instruction was largely skills focused. The implications for this finding are to remove the binaries of readiness or not ready and replace them with a system of supports that are gradually reduced as students progress. Such an approach would acknowledge the amount of time that language acquisition can take. This approach should replace punitive measures that bounce students out of college and cut off their financial aid. Supports that are offered in tandem with the general curriculum would also benefit the majority of students, not just English learners, and are the model currently favored in the K–12 system.

Last but not least are the implications for theories of persistence. Research on persistence often does not fully take language factors into account (Oropeza et al., 2010) and either focuses on race, ethnicity, or class (Gándara, Horn, & Orfield, 2005) or depends on proxy measures. In these models, persistence is seen as the result of a combination of factors that act on individual students and predict out-comes that are assumed to be the result of student choice since even the word *per-sistence* constructs the student as an agent who either persists or does not. Students who did not fit patterns of normative development—for example, students in early acquisition stages who may have taken longer than 2 years to pass standard-ized assessments—found their progress impeded by policies, and their persistence in the face of institutional obstacles led to whirlpooling. Thus, persistence was not always synonymous with progress; whirlpooling meant that students could become stuck in a remedial space because of assessment and placement practices. Therefore, *persistence* meant effort expended to overcome institutional barriers and messages of not belonging rather than being a description of an individual characteristic or situation.

Given that community colleges are important sites for the academic and social integration of immigrant-origin youth (Teranishi et al., 2011), it is imperative to understand how students respond to institutional practices that can impact their engagement and trajectories during the critical first year of attendance. Conflicting discourses on a community colleges as democratizing spaces and discourses on standards and accountability are played out in the process of assessment and place-ment, resulting in policies that delineate who belongs or does not belong in higher education (Deil-Amen, 2011). Research on remediation, assessments, and constructs related to persistence and achievement should be informed by the findings of this study that reveal the complex ways in which language, peer relations, and institutional barriers shape the trajectories and experiences of English learners.

REFERENCES

Almon, C. (2010). *English language learner engagement and retention in a community college setting.* Unpublished doctoral dissertation. Temple University, Philadelphia, PA.

Bailey, T. R. (2009). *Rethinking developmental education in community college.* New York, NY: Community College Research Center.

Bailey, T. R., Jeong, W. D., & Cho, S.-W. (2010). Student progression through developmental education sequences in community colleges (CCRC Brief #45). Community College Research Center, Teachers College, Columbia University, New York, NY.

Belfield, C., & Crosta, P. M. (2012). *Predicting success in college: The importance of placement tests and high school transcripts.* Retrieved from http://academiccommons.columbia.edu/catalog/ac:146486

Bunch, G., Endris, A., Panayotova, D., Romero, M., & Llosa, L. (2011). *Mapping the terrain: Language testing and placement for US-educated language minority students in California's community colleges.* Report prepared for the William and Flora Hewlett Foundation. Retrieved from www.escholarship.org/uc/item/31m3q6tb

Bunch, G., & Panayotova, D. (2008). Latinos, language minority students, and the construction of ESL: Language testing and placement from high school to community college. *Journal of Hispanic Higher Education, 7*(1), (2008), 6–30.

College Board. (2008). *Winning the skills race and strengthening America's middle class: An action agenda for community colleges.* New York, NY: The College Board, Center for Innovative Thought, National Commission on Community Colleges. Retrieved from professionals.collegeboard.com/data-reports-research

Collier, V. (1987) Age and rate of acquisition of second language for academic purposes. *TESOL Quarterly, 21*(4), 617–641.

Conway, K. M. (2009). Exploring persistence of immigrant and native students in an urban community college. *Review of Higher Education: Journal of the Association for the Study of Higher Education, 32*(3), 321–352.

Curry, M. J. (2004). UCLA community college review: Academic literacy for English language learners. *Community College Review, 32*(2), 51–68.

Deil-Amen, R. (2011, Fall). Beyond remedial dichotomies: Are "underprepared" college students a marginalized majority? *New Directions for Community Colleges, 2011*(155), 59–71.

Gándara, P., Horn, C., & Orfield, G. (2005). The access crisis in higher education. *Educational Policy, 19*(2), 255.

Harklau, L., & Siegel, M. (2009). Immigrant youth and higher education: An overview. In M. Roberge, M. Siegal, & L. Harklau (Eds.), *Generation 1.5 in college composition* (pp. 25–34). New York, NY: Routledge.

Hawley, T. H., & Harris, T. A. (2005). Student characteristics related to persistence for first-year community college students. *Journal of College Student Retention: Research, 7*(7), 117–142.

Kanno, Y., & Cromley, J. G. (2015). English language learners' pathways to four-year colleges. *Teachers College Record, 117*(120306), 1–46.

Kibler, A. K., Bunch, G. C., & Endris, A. K. (2011). Community college practices for U.S.-educated language-minority students: A resource-oriented framework. *Bilingual Research Journal, 34*, 201–222.

Llosa, L., & Bunch, G. (2011). *What's in a test? ESL and English placement tests in California's community colleges and implications for US-educated language minority students.* Retrieved from escholarship.org/uc/item/5qt5s496.pdf

Louie, V. (2009). The education of the 1.5 generation from an international migration framework: Demographics, diversity and difference. In M. Roberge, M. Siegal, & L. Harklau (Eds.), *Generation 1.5 in college composition* (pp. 35–49). New York, NY: Routledge.

Nuñez, A. M., & Sparks, P. J. (2012). Who are linguistic minority students in higher education? In Y. Kanno & L. Harklau (Eds.), *Linguistic minority students go to college: Preparation, access, and persistence* (pp. 110–129). New York, NY: Routledge.

Oropeza, M. V., Varghese, M. M., & Kanno, Y. (2010). Linguistic minority students in higher education: Using, resisting, and negotiating multiple labels. *Equity & Excellence in Education, 43*(2), 216–231. doi:10.1080/10665681003666304

Passel, J. S. (2011). Demography of immigrant youth: Past, present and future. *The Future of Children, 21*(1), 19–41.

Perry, M., Bahr, P. R., Rosin, M., & Woodward, K. M. (2010). *Course-taking patterns, policies, and practices in developmental education in the California Community Colleges.* Mountain View, CA: EdSource. Retrieved from www.edsource.org/iss_research _communitycollege.html

Razfar, A., & Simon, J. (2011). Course-taking patterns of Latino ESL students: Mobility and mainstreaming in urban community colleges in the United States. *TESOL Quarterly, 45*(4), 595–627.

Scott-Clayton, J. (2012). *Do high-stakes placement exams predict college success?* CCRC Working Paper No. 41. Community College Research Center, Columbia University, New York, NY. Retrieved from ezproxy.library.nyu.edu:3827/?id=ED529866

Teranishi, R., Suárez-Orozco, C., & Suárez-Orozco, M. (2011). Immigrants in community colleges. *The Future of Children, 21*(1), 153–169.

Valdes, G. (1992). Bilingual minorities and language issues in writing: Toward profession-wide responses to a new challenge. *Written Communication, 9*(1), 85–136.

CHAPTER 4

Resilience in the Face of Adversity
Undocumented Students in Community Colleges

Olivia Osei-Twumasi & Guadalupe López Hernández

> Being undocumented is a constant stressor that . . . pushes me to strive for academic excellency but also inhibits my ability to focus solely on my academic journey because of the constant need to find resources, whether [they] be scholarships or jobs, that will allow me to continue said education.
>
> —Community college participant responding to
> the UndocuScholars survey

No book on the immigrant-origin student community college experience would be complete without addressing the topic of undocumented college students. As two generations have now reached adulthood under a series of administrations that have not resolved the immigration impasse, they have found themselves growing up in the shadows of an undocumented status (Suárez-Orozco et al., 2015; Yoshikawa, Suárez-Orozco, & Gonzales, 2017). In the nation as a whole, an estimated 6% of those between the ages of 16 and 34 are undocumented (Migration Policy Institute, 2015; U.S. Census Bureau, 2018).

Nearly 65,000 undocumented students graduate from U.S. high schools every year, with many facing uncertainty about their future in higher education (Oliverez, Chavez, Soriano, & Tierney, 2006). Undocumented youth face a variety of obstacles, including being ineligible for any form of government-sponsored financial assistance and for most scholarships, being legally barred from formal employment, not being able to apply for a driver's license in most states, and living in constant danger of being deported at any time (Perez, Espinoza, Ramos, Coronado, & Cortés, 2009). Despite these challenges, some persist to attend college, with an estimated 225,000 undocumented college students currently enrolled nationwide (Suárez-Orozco et al., 2015). Research has consistently suggested that many undocumented students choose to enroll at a community college for their first higher education experience largely due to the affordable cost of the education, the ease of access to it, and their need to take remedial courses (Gonzales, 2011; Teranishi, C. Suárez-Orozco, & M. Suárez-Orozco, 2011).

In the Research on Immigrants in Community College (RICC) Study, we did not directly ask about participants' undocumented experiences for a number of reasons, including concerns about losing participants, validity of data, and multiple institutional review boards (IRBs). Since consideration of the implications of this status is essential in framing the immigrant community college student experience, we drew on other available data to examine this issue. Thus, in this chapter we bring together the relevant literature on enrollment patterns for undocumented youth and the reasons why community colleges appear to be the dominant educational pathway for them. We then compare the experiences of undocumented students at community colleges with those of their undocumented peers attending 4-year schools. Next, we compare the outcomes of undocumented students in the City University of New York (CUNY) community colleges with those of their peers who have legal status. Finally, we discuss the implications for policy and practice.

UNDOCUMENTED UNDERGRADUATES
IN COMMUNITY COLLEGES

Every year about 80% of undocumented 18-year-olds who have been in the United States for at least 5 years graduate from a U.S high school (Passel, 2003), with this group thereby achieving high school graduation rates comparable to the national average (U.S. Department of Education, 2018). However, only about 10% of undocumented high school graduates continue on to college (Gonzales, 2007; Passel, 2003), as compared with the national average of more than 60% of all high school graduates doing so (U.S. Department of Education, 2018). Undocumented students are entitled to free public primary and secondary schooling as mandated by the Supreme Court decision *Plyer v. Doe*, but this mandate does not extend beyond the K–12 level and does not address federal actions to help undocumented students pursue higher education. Furthermore, undocumented families are likely to reside in segregated neighborhoods that expose their children to poverty, violence, and underresourced schools that often fail to provide timely information about access to college (Pérez, Cortés, Ramos, & Coronado, 2010). Fear of deportation is also very prominent among undocumented students and their families. This concern can silence them from asking for help about the college application process and can lead some students to not consider college as an option (Abrego, 2011; Suárez-Orozco et al., 2015).

In what kinds of institutions do those who do continue on to college enroll? Given the precarious and often hidden nature of undocumented status, even calculating accurate estimates of the undocumented population as a whole represents a statistical challenge, as does the estimation of the total number of enrolled undocumented students. Breaking this figure down further into estimates of enrollment by college type (2-year or 4-year) presents additional difficulties and does not appear to have been done on a national level. For example, Greenman and Hall (2013) used nationally representative data and sophisticated statistical techniques to examine the educational outcomes of undocumented Mexican youth. Although the researchers demonstrated that a lack of legal status presented a significant barrier to both high school completion and college enrollment, they were unable to report on enrollment by college type due to data limitations.

Precise figures on undocumented students' enrollment patterns by institution type are hard to find at the state level as well. In Illinois, for example, some institutions intentionally avoid collecting data on students' citizenship status for fear that this information may be used to target students (S. Lopez, personal communication, August 21, 2018). However, other states have more available information. From data from two states with relatively high numbers of undocumented students—California and New York—we have learned that undocumented students enroll in community colleges at vastly disproportionate rates. For example, 80% of undocumented students in California are enrolled at a community college (California Community Colleges, 2017). Conger and Chellman (2013) report that just under two-thirds of the undocumented students who had enrolled in the CUNY system between 1999 and 2004 enrolled in one of its community colleges. These figures suggest that, compared with the enrollment patterns of lawful permanent residents and U.S. citizens, undocumented students who attend college are much more likely to enroll at community colleges than at 4-year schools.

Several qualitative studies (e.g., Abrego & Gonzales, 2010; Diaz-Strong, Gómez, Luna-Duarte, & Meiners, 2011; Gonzales, 2011; Negrón-Gonzales, 2017) have also indicated that undocumented students, particularly Latinos, are more likely to attend a community college than other types of schools. Negrón-Gonzales (2017) argues that community colleges have become the "educational home" for many undocumented students (p. 112). Consequently, researchers have cautioned against focusing on undocumented students at 4-year schools since "the vast majority of undocumented youth are either at community colleges or out of school" (Abrego & Gonzales, 2010, p. 155). Although the enrollment of outstanding undocumented students in elite private schools is often well reported (e.g., see Guerrero, 2014), these students represent only a tiny proportion of undocumented youth.

Prior research suggests that community colleges are the most likely educational port of entry for undocumented students for a number of reasons. There are a variety of systemic factors such as state and federal policies, xenophobia, and poverty that negatively impact the educational trajectories of undocumented students (see C. Suárez-Orozco, Yoshikawa, Teranishi, & M. Suárez-Orozco, 2011). Of particular concern is the limited number of financial resources for which these students can apply (Abrego, 2008; Negrón-Gonzales, 2017). Undocumented students are not eligible for federal financial aid such as Pell Grants and are often excluded from scholarships (Abrego & Gonzales, 2010). Currently, there are only five states (California, Minnesota, New Mexico, Texas, and Washington) that provide state financial aid for eligible undocumented students (National Conference of State Legislatures, 2015). Therefore, most undocumented students are forced to pay out of pocket for their educational expenses with little other available financial support (Abrego & Gonzales, 2010; Gonzales, Suárez-Orozco, & Dedios-Sanguineti, 2013). To add to these students' financial burdens, many states have policies that charge undocumented students out-of-state tuition rates that are often three times as high as in-state rates (Suárez-Orozco et al., 2015). Faced with these stark realities, a vast majority of undocumented students opt to enroll in community colleges.

Once enrolled at a community college, undocumented students often struggle to remain there due to financial strains (Negrón-Gonzales, 2017). Many of these students come from families that endure high levels of poverty (Yoshikawa et al., 2017). Consequently, these students cannot rely on their parents for financial help and furthermore feel obligated to support their families financially (Terriquez, 2015). Faced with the dilemma of how to allocate their limited resources among school expenses, personal expenses, and/or family obligations, they are often forced to take time off from attending school in order to save money (Terriquez, 2015).

A second key reason why undocumented students tend to enroll at community colleges rather than at 4-year schools is a lack of access to clear and timely information about higher education options during high school (Negrón-Gonzales, 2017). Undocumented high school students are often misinformed about their educational rights and their ability to attend college and to receive fee waivers or state financial aid (when eligible). Students receiving little or late information about the college application process often end up at community colleges, which have historically been a more accessible pathway to higher education for them with more flexible deadlines. Since many of these students are first-generation college attendees, they are especially reliant on school personnel to inform them about how to navigate the educational system (Negrón-Gonzales, 2017).

CHAPTER AIMS

Despite the fact that most undocumented students are enrolled in community colleges, there have been very few studies that have specifically examined their experiences and outcomes. Thus, the aim of this chapter is to describe the experiences and academic outcomes of undocumented community college students by using a comparative approach. We address the following two research questions:

RQ1: How do the experiences of undocumented community college students compare with those of undocumented students at 4-year schools?

RQ2: How do the academic outcomes of undocumented community college students compare with those of community college students who have a different legal status?

To answer the first question, we drew on data from the UndocuScholars survey, a national online survey of undocumented college students (Suárez-Orozco et al., 2015). This questionnaire explored participants' demographic characteristics and various aspects of their college experiences as well as their aspirations and anxieties. The sample consisted of 909 respondents, 389 (43%) of whom were community college students, and 517 (58%) of whom were studying at public or private 4-year schools (as well as three respondents who did not provide their schools' names). Students reported 52 different countries of origin, though nearly 90% were of Mexican origin. Sixty-two percent were enrolled at colleges in California, followed by 10% in Illinois, 6% in Texas, and the remainder in 31 other states. Survey respondents attended 264 schools in total, with just under half being community colleges (121 schools, 46%).

To answer the second question, we drew on administrative data from the CUNY system. During the application process, students attending CUNY schools are required to report their citizenship status and submit supporting documentation such as a current or expired visa (Conger & Chellman, 2013). During the academic year 2006–2007, 1,908 undocumented students enrolled in the CUNY system (5% of all first-time freshmen); two-thirds (66%) enrolled in one of the system's community colleges. The demography of the undocumented students was extremely varied. For the CUNY system as a whole, undocumented students reported 103 different countries of birth, with the top 10 countries in terms of number of students being Mexico, Jamaica, Trinidad and Tobago, Ecuador, Colombia, Guyana, South Korea, China, the Dominican Republic, and Poland. Just over one-third of the undocumented students were Black, a third were Hispanic, a fifth were Asian, and a tenth were White. Asian students were slightly more likely to be undocumented than students of other races were. The data revealed that 7% of the Asian students were undocumented, as compared with 5% of the Black students, 5% of the Hispanic students, and 2% of the White students.

We analyzed the two sets of data separately and reported descriptive statistics. Comparing undocumented students at 2-year and 4-year schools for RQ1, we tested for group differences using independent samples of t tests for continuous variables and chi-square tests for categorical variables. For RQ2, we compared undocumented students with lawful permanent residents as well as with U.S. citizens and used one-way ANOVAs to test for group differences. Our findings are reported next.

UNDOCUMENTED COMMUNITY COLLEGE
STUDENTS' EXPERIENCES

The UndocuScholars survey provided a unique opportunity for us to compare the experiences of undocumented students attending community colleges with the experiences of those attending 4-year schools. Although undocumented students at both types of colleges faced similar issues in some regard (such as fears surrounding their own potential deportation or the deportation of loved ones), we found that two issues in particular revealed substantial differences between undocumented community college students and their counterparts at 4-year schools: financial concerns and lack of safe spaces.

Our findings indicate that almost all undocumented students were concerned about financing their education and buying books and supplies (see Table 4.1). However, undocumented students attending community colleges had higher rates of being "extremely concerned" about these issues than did students at 4-year schools. This result appears to be related to the ways in which students fund their education at the different types of schools. More than half of the undocumented students at community colleges were funding their education through their personal resources (compared with 25% of those attending 4-year colleges who were doing so). Furthermore, while more than half of the undocumented students at 4-year schools were financing their education through grants and scholarships, only 27% of undocumented students at community colleges were doing so. Very few students at either type of school were relying on loans since undocumented students generally do not have access to formal sources of credit such as federal student loans or private bank loans.

The majority of students at both types of schools cited cost as a major factor in their school choices. Similarly, location was an important factor for most students. Relatively few students at either school type mentioned college ranking as a key factor governing their choice of school to attend. Undocumented students at 4-year schools were more likely to mention the "undocufriendly climate" as a key factor in their school choice than their peers at community colleges were. Undocumented students at community colleges were also more likely to cite the flexible schedule as a key factor influencing their college choice, possibly due to their other commitments such as paid work. Indeed, a higher percentage of students at community colleges had attended college part-time or taken a break from school, citing the need to work or financial difficulties as their reasons for doing so.

Undocumented students attending community colleges were also less likely to report having access to safe campus spaces than those attending 4-year colleges were (see Table 4.2). Approximately half of the community college participants reported having access to such campus supports, while 65 percent of students at 4-year campuses did. Unsurprisingly, the disparity was especially marked for residential life spaces (since almost all community colleges are commuter schools) and student clubs. At campuses that did have safe spaces for undocumented students, students at 4-year schools were also more likely to make use of the spaces and to report that the spaces were very or extremely important to them. Notably, when safe spaces were available, students at community colleges also reported high rates of using such spaces and noted that they found them very or extremely important.

The UndocuScholars data confirmed that financial stress and lack of access to safe spaces are issues faced by undocumented students across the board. These issues appeared to be further exacerbated for undocumented students at community colleges, however.

Table 4.1. Financial Difficulties

	2-year (n = 517)		4-year (n = 517)		Differences between school types[a]
	n	(M, SD) %	n	(M, SD) %	
Financial concerns scale	383	(3.3, 1.0)	515	(3.0, 1.0)	$t(896) = 3.61$***
% concerned about financing education[b]	383	96%	514	94%	$\chi^2(1,897) = 1.10$
% extremely concerned about financing education	383	62%	514	53%	$\chi^2(1,897) = 8.26$**
% concerned about buying books and supplies[b]	383	91%	515	89%	$\chi^2(1,898) = 1.26$
% extremely concerned about buying books and supplies	383	35%	514	25%	$\chi^2(1,898) = 11.27$***
Funding college—at least halfway through					
Family resources	380	26%	510	20%	$\chi^2(1,890) = 3.28$
Personal resources	380	54%	509	25%	$\chi^2(1,889) = 75.18$***
Grants and scholarships	374	27%	511	54%	$\chi^2(1,885) = 66.64$***
Loans	372	5%	494	3%	$\chi^2(1,866) = 1.94$

College choice—very or extremely important

Cost	387	86%	517	89%	$\chi^2(1{,}904) = 2.29$
Class size	387	27%	517	23%	$\chi^2(1{,}904) = 1.43$
Location	387	60%	516	67%	$\chi^2(1{,}903) = 5.78$*
College ranking	387	30%	517	37%	$\chi^2(1{,}903) = 4.79$*
Flexible schedule	387	60%	517	42%	$\chi^2(1{,}904) = 26.59$***
UndocuScholar-friendly climate	388	56%	516	67%	$\chi^2(1{,}904) = 11.67$***
Enrolled part-time	370	33%	499	6%	$\chi^2(1{,}869) = 103.31$***
Enrolled part-time due to need to work[c]	122	57%	30	63%	$\chi^2(1{,}15^2) = 0.45$
Have ever taken a break from school	386	19%	514	12%	$\chi^2(1{,}900) = 8.11$**
Taken a break because of financial difficulties[d]	73	70%	64	78%	$\chi^2(1{,}137) = 1.20$

Notes: [a]Independent sample *t* tests were used to check for group differences for continuous variables, and *chi*-square tests were used for categorical variables; [b]*Concerned* means slightly, somewhat, moderately, or extremely concerned; [c]Percentage of students who are enrolled part-time; [d]Percentage of students who have taken a break from school; * $p < .05$. ** $p < 0.01$. *** $p < 0.001$.

Table 4.2. UndocuScholar Safe Spaces

	2-year		4-year		Differences between school types[a]
	n	%	*n*	%	
Colleges	(*n* = 121)		(*n* = 143)		
Campuses with UndocuScholar safe spaces	121	51%	143	65%	$\chi^2(1,264) = 5.14^*$
Including					
Student clubs	121	37%	143	55%	$\chi^2(1,264) = 7.93^{**}$
Student affairs office	121	17%	143	27%	$\chi^2(1,264) = 3.86^*$
Residential life/dorm spaces	121	3%	143	13%	$\chi^2(1,264) = 10.02^{**}$
Office designated for undocumented students	121	10%	143	17%	$\chi^2(1,264) = 2.62$
Student center	121	26%	143	29%	$\chi^2(1,264) = 0.46$
Other	121	13%	143	15%	$\chi^2(1,264) = 0.12$
Students	(*n* = 389)		(*n* = 517)		
% of students with access reporting use of the safe space	176	63%	380	78%	$\chi^2(1,556) = 14.47^{***}$
% of students who used the safe space reporting that the support was very or extremely important	111	78%	296	87%	$\chi^2(1,407) = 4.40^*$

Note: [a]*Chi*-squared test used to check for group differences; * $p < .05$. ** $p < 0.01$. *** $p < 0.001$.

UNDOCUMENTED COMMUNITY COLLEGE STUDENTS' ACADEMIC OUTCOMES

Drawing on data from the CUNY system on first-time freshmen enrolling during the academic year 2006–2007, we considered how the academic outcomes of undocumented students at community colleges compared with those of their U.S. citizen and lawful permanent resident peers (see Table 4.3).

Undocumented students had somewhat more favorable outcomes than U.S. citizen students did in terms of first semester credits attempted and passed, GPA in the first semester, and cumulative GPA after six semesters and had similar outcomes when compared with those of lawful permanent residents (LPRs, or green card holders). Undocumented students were also just as likely as LPRs and more likely than U.S. citizens were to graduate from AA degree programs in 3 years or 6 years. In terms of graduating from bachelor's degree programs in 6 years, undocumented students' rates were similar to those of U.S. citizens and slightly lower than those of LPRs. The only metric on which undocumented students did not

Table 4.3. Academic Outcomes of Undocumented Students in CUNY Community Colleges

	Undocumented (n = 1,349)		LPR (n = 5,249)		U.S. citizen (n = 18,904)		Differences between legal status types[a]
	M	SD	M	SD	M	SD	
Credits attempted—Semester 1	5.9[c]	0.1	5.4b	0.1	5.6	0.0	$F(2,25499) = 4.39$*
Credits passed—Semester 1	88%[d]	0.7%	87%[d]	0.4%	77%[b,c]	0.3%	$F(2,19159) = 229.79$***
GPA—Semester 1	2.6[d]	0.0	2.5[d]	0.0	2.0[b,c]	0.0	$F(2,22666) = 356.41$***
Cumulative GPA—Semester 6	2.8[d]	0.0	2.7[d]	0.0	2.5[b,c]	0.0	$F(2,10760) = 183.93$***
AA in 3 years	10.0%[d]		11.6%[d]		8.0%[b,c]		$F(2,25499) = 34.27$***
AA in 6 years	21.1%[d]		22.1%[d]		15.1%[b,c]		$F(2,25499) = 80.98$***
BA in 6 years	8.7%		10.3%[d]		8.1%[c]		$F(2,25499) = 12.54$***

Notes: [a]One-way ANOVAs were used to check for group differences. In all cases, Bartlett's test for equal variances was significant; [b]Statistically significantly different from undocumented students; [c]Statistically significantly different from lawful permanent resident students; [d]Statistically significantly different from U.S. citizen students. Differences based on Bonferonni post hoc tests; * $p <.05$. ** $p <0.01$. *** $p <0.001$.

surpass the outcomes of U.S. citizens was the 6-year graduation time to complete a BA degree.

CHALLENGES AND RESILIENCE

We learned that undocumented students were more likely to begin their higher education voyages in community colleges. Our findings demonstrate that these students were more likely to face extremely high levels of financial stress than were their peers at 4-year schools who were better able to finance their education through scholarships and grants. We also found that undocumented students had less access to "undocufriendly" safe spaces than did their peers at 4-year schools.

Despite these challenges, we also saw evidence of these students' remarkable academic resilience. Consistent with Conger and Chellman's (2013) findings, undocumented students surpassed the outcomes of U.S. citizens at the CUNY community colleges and achieved outcomes comparable to those of immigrants with permanent lawful resident status. This result represented a remarkable achievement on the part of undocumented students given that they had little or no access to financial aid.

Some have suggested that undocumented youth who are enrolled in college may be positively selected in terms of their academic abilities (e.g., see Conger & Chellman, 2013). However, since undocumented young people face extraordinary barriers to participating in higher education, it is not clear whether those students who do enroll are superior to their counterparts who do not enroll along the dimension of academic ability. In fact, the available evidence on academic resilience among undocumented youth indicates that the key predictors of academic success in high school are, on the negative side, number of hours worked per week and, on the positive side, support systems such as involved parents and school activities as well as the extent to which the student values school (Perez et al., 2009). At the college level, access to information about scholarships is a key determinant of persistence for undocumented students, and, once again, this finding is more related to students' social capital than to their academic abilities. This result implies that many of the undocumented youth who are not enrolled in college may be just as academically able as their peers who do enroll are but perhaps may face greater barriers or have less robust support systems.

Since those who are enrolled are performing academically as well as or even better than their peers with legal status are, this finding provides a compelling argument for increasing support and lowering the barriers to college access for undocumented youth generally. Ideally, such reforms would broaden undocumented students' access not only to community colleges but also to 4-year schools. This development would be important since students who enroll as freshmen at 4-year schools tend to have far greater rates of completing bachelor's degrees than those who first attend community colleges and then transfer to 4-year colleges do (see Chapter 13).

IMPLICATIONS FOR PRACTICE AND POLICY

Taken together, our findings have implications for practice and policy. Although 4-year schools are generally substantially more expensive than community colleges are, making affordability one of the attractive qualities of community colleges (Abrego & Gonzales, 2010) for undocumented students, our results indicate, paradoxically, that undocumented students at community colleges are nevertheless experiencing higher levels of financial stress than undocumented students at 4-year schools. Community college tuition and fees (though generally much lower than those at 4-year schools) still amount to a substantial sum for low-income students with limited access to formal employment and no access to federal financial aid. Clearly, there is an urgent need for policies that address the financial stress undocumented community college students endure.

We also recommend increasing the availability of safe spaces for undocumented community college students. It is vital to create spaces where students can connect and share resources with undocumented peers and allies (Suárez-Orozco et al., 2015). These safe spaces could be undocumented centers with designated offices and advisers who can provide undocumented students with tailored information to fit their specific needs. At a minimum, campuses should support student-led organizations from which undocumented students can seek academic and emotional support (Suárez-Orozco et al., 2015). Furthermore, community colleges should provide training for school personnel about the rights and challenges of undocumented students. College-level administrators, including financial aid officers, play a vital educational role in facilitating the positive trajectories of undocumented community college students (Nienhusser, 2014). They should be well informed about the ways in which state and institutional policies can best be implemented to achieve the maximum benefit for these students (Suárez-Orozco et al., 2015). College campuses must strive to understand and meet the needs of this all-too-often invisible student population.

From a policy point of view, lowering the barriers for undocumented youth to pursue higher education would be beneficial. As has been argued elsewhere (Abrego & Gonzales, 2010; Diaz-Strong et al., 2011), there is a pressing need for policies to regularize the status of undocumented students. Doing so could make these young people eligible for the same financial supports that their peers enjoy and allow them to work legally while attending college, reducing their financial pressures. Additionally, after graduation they would be able to productively utilize the workplace advantages of having a college degree. This outcome would be beneficial not only for the well-being of these students and their families but also for the prosperity of our nation. In a context in which an aging baby boomer generation is putting strains on the Social Security system as its members move into retirement (Tweedy, 2018) and large numbers of U.S. companies are facing shortages of skilled workers (Holzer, 2015), we should invest in all of our young people, including those who are American in every way but on paper.

REFERENCES

Abrego, L. J. (2008). Legitimacy, social identity, and the mobilization of law: The effects of Assembly Bill 540 on undocumented students in California. *Law & Social Inquiry*, 33(3), 709–734.

Abrego, L. J. (2011). Legal consciousness of undocumented Latinos: Fear and stigma as barriers to claims-making for first- and 1.5-generation immigrants. *Law & Society Review*, 45(2), 337–370.

Abrego, L. J., & Gonzales, R. G. (2010). Blocked paths, uncertain futures: The postsecondary education and labor market prospects of undocumented Latino youth. *Journal of Education for Students Placed at Risk*, 15(1–2), 144–157.

California Community Colleges. (2017). *Supporting undocumented students.* Retrieved September 20, 2018, from www.cccco.edu/Portals/1/supporting-undocumented-students .pdf

Conger, D., & Chellman, C. C. (2013). Undocumented college students in the United States: In-state tuition not enough to ensure four-year degree completion. *Education Finance and Policy*, 8(3), 364–377.

Diaz-Strong, D., Gómez, C., Luna-Duarte, M. E., & Meiners, E. R. (2011). Purged: Undocumented students, financial aid policies, and access to higher education. *Journal of Hispanic Higher Education*, 10(2), 107–119.

Gonzales, R. G. (2007). Wasted talent and broken dreams: The lost potential of undocumented students. *Immigration Policy in Focus*, 5(13), 1–11.

Gonzales, R. G. (2011). Learning to be illegal: Undocumented youth and shifting legal contexts in the transition to adulthood. *American Sociological Review*, 76(4), 602–619.

Gonzales, R. G., Suárez-Orozco, C., & Dedios-Sanguineti, M. C. (2013). No place to belong: Contextualizing concepts of mental health among undocumented immigrant youth in the United States. *American Behavioral Scientist*, 57(8), 1174–1199.

Greenman, E., & Hall, M. (2013). Legal status and educational transitions for Mexican and Central American immigrant youth. *Social Forces*, 91(4), 1475–1498.

Guerrero, D. (2014). *I told Harvard I was an undocumented immigrant. They gave me a full scholarship.* Retrieved August 12, 2018, from www.washingtonpost.com/posteverything/wp/2014/09/24/i-told-harvard-i-was-an-undocumented-immigrant-they-gave-me-a-full-scholarship/?utm_term=.41182fdc1114

Holzer, H. (2015). *Job market polarization and US worker skills: A tale of two middles.* Washington, DC: Economic Studies, The Brookings Institution.

Migration Policy Institute. (2015). Profile of the unauthorized population: United States. Washington, DC: Migration Policy Institute. Retrieved August 2, 2018, from www .migrationpolicy.org/data/unauthorized-immigrant-population/state/US

National Conference of State Legislatures. (2015). *Undocumented student tuition: Overview.* Washington, DC: National Conference of State Legislatures. Retrieved September 27, 2018, from www.ncsl.org/research/education/undocumented-student-tuition-overview.aspx

Negrón-Gonzales, G. (2017). Constrained inclusion: Access and persistence among undocumented community college students in California's Central Valley. *Journal of Hispanic Higher Education*, 16(2), 105–122.

Nienhusser, H. K. (2014). Role of community colleges in the implementation of postsecondary education enrollment policies for undocumented students. *Community College Review*, 42(1), 3–22.

Oliverez, P. M., Chavez, M. L., Soriano, M., & Tierney, W. G. (2006). The college & financial aid guide for: AB540 undocumented immigrant students. Center for Higher Education Policy Analysis, University of Southern California.

Passel, J. S. (2003). *Further demographic information relating to the DREAM Act.* Washington, DC: The Urban Institute.

Perez, W., Espinoza, R., Ramos, K., Coronado, H. M., & Cortes, R. (2009). Academic resilience among undocumented Latino students. *Hispanic Journal of Behavioral Sciences, 31*(2), 149–181.

Pérez, W., Cortés, R. D., Ramos, K., & Coronado, H. (2010). "Cursed and blessed": Examining the socioemotional and academic experiences of undocumented Latina and Latino college students. *New Directions for Student Services, 2010*(131), 35–51.

Suárez-Orozco, C., Katsiaficas, D., Birchall, O., Alcantar, C. M., Hernandez, E., Garcia, Y., . . . Teranishi, R. T. (2015). Undocumented undergraduates on college campuses: Understanding their challenges and assets and what it takes to make an undocufriendly campus. *Harvard Educational Review, 85*(3), 427–463.

Suárez-Orozco, C., Yoshikawa, H., Teranishi, R., & Suárez-Orozco, M. (2011). Growing up in the shadows: The developmental implications of unauthorized status. *Harvard Educational Review, 81*(3), 438–473.

Teranishi, R. T., Suárez-Orozco, C., & Suárez-Orozco, M. (2011). Immigrants in community colleges. *The Future of Children, 21*(1), 153–169.

Terriquez, V. (2015). Dreams delayed: Barriers to degree completion among undocumented community college students. *Journal of Ethnic and Migration Studies, 41*(8), 1302–1323.

Tweedy, J. (2018). Social insecurity: A proposal to reform the United States Social Security retirement system. *Indiana International & Comparative Law Review, 28*, 129.

U.S. Census Bureau. (2018). *Monthly national population estimates by age, sex, race, Hispanic origin, and population universe for the United States: April 1, 2010 to December 1, 2018.* Retrieved August 2, 2018, from www.census.gov/data/datasets/2017/demo/popest/nation-detail.html

U.S. Department of Education, National Center for Education Statistics. (2018). *Public high school graduation rates.* Retrieved July 13, 2018, from nces.ed.gov/programs/coe/indicator_coi.asp

Yoshikawa, H., Suárez-Orozco, C., & Gonzales, R. G. (2017). Unauthorized status and youth development in the United States: Consensus statement of the society for research on adolescence. *Journal of Research on Adolescence, 27*(1), 4–19.

Part II

THE ROLE OF COMMUNITY COLLEGE SETTINGS

CHAPTER 5

Classroom Engagement in Community Colleges

Moving Beyond Student and Instructor Dimensions to a Dynamic Settings Approach

Stacey Alicea & Carola Suárez-Orozco

Educational researchers, developmental scientists, and policymakers concur that classroom processes are crucial for both student engagement and achievement outcomes (Pascarella & Terenzini, 2005; Pianta & Hamre, 2009). However, despite large bodies of research on the relevance of classroom environments from pre-K through secondary education (Crombie, Pyke, Silverthorn, Alison, & Piccinin, 2003; Pianta & Allen, 2008), there is a dearth of empirical research focusing specifically on classroom processes in higher education and more specifically on such processes in community colleges. Unlike their campus-residing peers, community college students often face multiple competing life and school obligations, limiting their time available to participate in extracurricular activities or take advantage of campus services (Saenz et al., 2011; Teranishi, C. Suárez-Orozco, & M. Suárez-Orozco, 2011). Thus, what happens in the classrooms may constitute the bulk of community college student experiences, making it critical to understand these settings.

Classroom engagement is defined as "what happens in classrooms" (Lawson & Lawson, 2013). Classroom transactions among the various individuals within in the classroom—between instructors and students and between and among students—are central to classroom engagement. Research in elementary and secondary schools has established that well-performing classrooms tend to be high in emotional support, instructional quality, and organization; these characteristics are, in turn, related to learning (Pianta, La Paro, & Hamre, 2008). In higher education, evidence has established that *student engagement* broadly defined is critical for college completion and transfer (Harper & Quaye, 2009; Kuh, Cruce, Shoup, Kinzie, & Gonyea, 2008; Pascarella & Terenzini, 2005). Empirically, much less is known about how specifically *classroom* engagement may function. Previous cross-sectional data using student self-reports (Deil-Amen, 2011) and qualitative classroom studies (Cox, 2009) offer some insights into how postsecondary classrooms may shape student outcomes in community colleges. Although these studies have provided evidence of meaningful links between student- and teacher-driven factors in classrooms for student outcomes, they have failed to systematically explore the patterns of these relationships for immigrant-origin community college students.

CLASSROOM INTERACTIONS

Classrooms involve multiple actors dynamically interacting over a sustained period of time in order to achieve certain goals (Pianta & Allen, 2008; Tseng & Seidman, 2007). During repeated interactions, institutional norms become established, leading to varying kinds of organizational climates (Sarason & Klaber, 1985).

Using systematic classroom observations, Pianta and Allen (2008) have found that relationships between teachers and students, as well as cooperative peer relationships and the positive classroom interactions that result from these relationships, are linked to motivation and engagement for elementary and high school students. Extant higher education literature also provides support for the crucial importance of student–teacher relationships (Pascarella & Terenzini, 2005) and peer relationships (Booker, 2007) for supporting learning. Studies suggest that when students are meaningfully challenged in ways that scaffold their learning in supportive relational environments, they are more likely to be both socially and academically integrated in college (Nelson Laird, Chen, & Kuh, 2008).

Within the higher education literature, *student engagement* (aka *integration* and *involvement*) is broadly described as "the time and energy students invest in educationally purposeful activities and the effort institutions devote to using effective educational practices" (Kuh et al., 2008, p. 5). Notably, while the K–12 conceptualization of engagement focuses largely on what occurs *within the classroom*, the higher education use of the concept includes processes that occur across the campus both outside and inside the classroom (Kuh et al., 2008; Tinto, 1993). Indeed, higher education theories developed to explain student outcomes suggest that demographic variables (e.g., being in the first generation to attend college and socioeconomic status) and academic preparation (e.g., academic English skills, entrance scores, study skills) interact with factors at the institutional setting level (in and out of the classroom) in ways that lead to an array of academic outcomes (e.g., grades, persistence, and likelihood to graduate or transfer) (Tinto, 1993).

CHAPTER AIMS

Classrooms have received little attention in research on community colleges. In this analysis focusing on immigrant-origin students, we sought to explore the role of classroom engagement in classroom contexts using a systematic observational strategy. In this chapter, we begin by outlining the key dimensions of engagement

Figure 5.1. Empirical Model of Classroom Engagement in Community Colleges

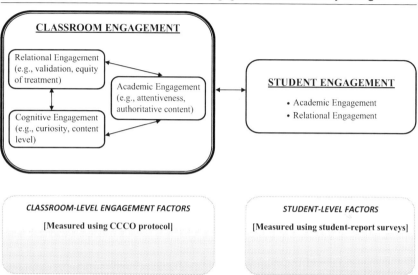

as they have been articulated in the previous literature. We then consider whether there is a relationship between student-reported classroom engagement (i.e., the old standard in the field) and observed classroom-level engagement measured by using the Community Colleges Classroom Observation (CCCO) tool, a qualitatively grounded quantitative measure that taps specific *observable* behavioral and interactional indicators across three primary dimensions of classroom engagement—academic, relational, and cognitive (see Figure 5.1)—and student-level variables gathered by the Research on Immigrants in Community College (RICC) Study data collection team (see online appendix for details). Lastly, we make the case for why observing classrooms and paying attention to practices in classrooms are important for all community college students but particularly for immigrant-origin students.

ENGAGEMENT WITHIN THE CLASSROOM DEFINED

Extant literature in higher education generally mirrors concepts found in the primary and secondary school literatures although these domains have been more deeply researched in K–12 education (Lawson & Lawson, 2013). Figure 5.2 provides a conceptual model that integrates domains of engagement at both the classroom and the student levels and links them to related student outcomes (Alicea, Suárez-Orozco, Singh, Darbes, & Abrica, 2016).

Academic engagement, intentional activities related to involvement in courses such as attending classes, participating in class, doing reading assignments,

**Figure 5.2. Integrated Model of Engagement Domains and Student Outcomes from
the K–12 and Higher Education Literatures**

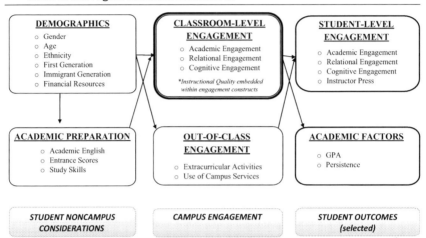

studying for tests, and turning in assignments, is predictive of both grades and
persistence (Kuh et al., 2008; Robbins et al., 2004; Svanum & Bigatti, 2009).

Relational engagement (aka *social belonging, social integration, inclusion,* and
involvement) is the degree to which students feel supported by and connected
to their peers, their instructors, or their college's personnel (Bensimon, 2007).
Relationships play a crucial role in serving to build confidence and encourage students to redouble their efforts when motivation fails (Bensimon, 2007; Hurtado &
Carter, 1997). The concept of a student's relatedness to "school peers, teachers, and
the school overall" in the K–12 literature has been variably referred to as *affective/
emotional engagement* (Finn & Zimmer, 2012; Fredricks, Blumenfeld, & Paris, 2004;
Voelkl, 2012) as well as *relational engagement* (Suárez-Orozco, Pimentel, & Martin,
2009).

Cognitive engagement is the degree to which students "think deeply about
ideas and concepts" (Lawson & Lawson, 2013, p. 5) and are curious about and
interested in what they are learning (Suárez-Orozco, Pimentel, & Martin, 2009).
The National Survey of Student Engagement (NSSE) assesses constructs of *deep
learning* (the way faculty promote higher order thinking, analysis, and integration
of learning) and *academic challenge* (higher order thinking skills) (NSSE, 2006).
Qualitative approaches to observing processes related to cognitive engagement
have primarily been concerned with the role of the instructor in promoting cognitive engagement (Grubb, 1999). "Instructor press" in K–12 literature (Lee & Smith,
1999) posits that quality and type of instruction are key to cognitive development
and learning academic content. Other higher education work has theorized effective teaching practices and their connection to student learning as evidenced
by students reading widely, integrating knowledge, discussing ideas with others,

and applying knowledge to real-world situations (Pascarella & Terenzini, 2005; Ramsden, 2003).

WHY COLLEGE CLASSROOMS MATTER

Although disjointed, the literature on college classrooms points to these contexts as critical to many positive student outcomes. Students' perceptions of their class-room experiences as they relate to instructor-driven practices and quality have been linked to the development of a number of student outcomes, including cognitive development, knowledge acquisition, skill development, education-al goal setting, development of interpersonal skills, and greater involvement in educational activities (Cabrera et al., 2002; Pascarella, Salisbury, & Blaich, 2011; Pascarella & Terenzini, 2005), as well as to student persistence (Braxton, Bray, & Berger, 2000; Tinto, 1997). Qualitative studies support these findings. In two ob-servational studies of community college classrooms, researchers suggested that student engagement depended primarily on the instructor's practices and teach-ing skills rather than on the mode of instruction (i.e., lecture-based versus collab-orative) (Cox, 2009; Grubb, 1999).

Similarly, research has established links between interactions with faculty and a host of overlapping positive student outcomes, including gains in social self-confidence and leadership skills (Lundberg & Schreiner, 2004; Sax, Bryant, & Harper, 2005). Faculty practices within classrooms such as interacting with students and challenging students academically have been shown to increase the levels of reported student engagement (Nelson Laird, Chen, & Kuh, 2008), highlighting the importance of instructor expectations and relationships for promoting overall engagement in higher education classrooms.

Other scholars suggest that it is also important to consider a more dynamic view of student engagement that includes peer interaction. For example, Fassinger (1997) found that examining classrooms as social groups with their own particular characteristics was more strongly associated with student engagement than exam-ining individual student or instructor characteristics alone. Peers have the potential to be both direct and indirect contributors to the classroom climate. For instance, students with shared attributes, experiences, and ideologies may be more likely to trust and emotionally support one another. Conversely, classrooms with sets of stu-dents who do not interact in respectful ways toward one another may promote a set of classroom norms that contribute to decreased classroom relational and aca-demic engagement. Peer interactions have been associated with improved learning outcomes in community college contexts in particular (Booker, 2007).

To date, the higher education research has largely considered 4-year college contexts, in particular instructor practices and how students experience faculty, neglecting both community colleges and the dynamic nature of classroom en-gagement. Yet the populations that community colleges serve, community college missions, and community colleges' structural characteristics are all substantively different from those of 4-year institutions (Bailey & Morest, 2006). Given that classrooms are the primary and most proximal settings where learning takes place for students (Blumenfeld, 1992; Pianta & Allen, 2008), it is essential that we gain a more nuanced understanding of how community college classrooms engage community college students in learning.

OBSERVING CLASSROOM ENGAGEMENT: THE METHOD

Data presented in this chapter focus on the analyses of classroom engagement assessed using the Community College Classroom Observation (CCCO) protocol specially designed for the RICC study (see details below) and also draw on student survey data (see online appendix for details).

The development of the CCCO protocol was grounded in our review of the extant higher education student engagement literature; our ethnographic, focus-group findings; CLASS-S methodology; and the Community College Survey of Student Engagement (CSSSE) student and teacher survey constructs (Alicea et al., 2016). The CCCO protocol assessed three primary dimensions of classroom engagement: academic engagement, relational engagement, and cognitive engagement (see Figure 5.1). Each engagement dimension is composed of items that reflect interactions theoretically and empirically related to the respective dimension. Items were placed along a scale with behaviorally anchored descriptors of types of interactions among all members in the class (i.e., student–student, student–teacher) on a continuum from 1 (low engagement) to 5 (high engagement). Classroom observers completed item ratings on all dimensions for each observational segment (see online appendix for details).

This sample was drawn from 60 classrooms across the three participating community college campuses in the New York City metropolitan area, including 17 developmental/ remedial, 29 general education, and 14 vocational/elective classrooms. The CCCO was evaluated using survey data from 313 students nested in these classrooms that were observed by the research team. After classroom observations had been completed, all students in the classrooms were invited to participate in the online survey.

Classroom observations were conducted by highly trained multiracial/ethnic researchers during regularly scheduled class times. In order to ensure high levels of inter-rater reliability, all members of the research team who participated in data collection underwent rigorous CCCO protocol training (see online appendix for training details). Observers followed strict, structured coding guidelines for each of the observed segments. Observers conducted 20-minute observational segments that included 12 minutes of observation and 8 minutes of scoring. The number of observation segments was based on the length of each class. All observers rated items across observation segments simultaneously and independently for the length of an entire class period. Lead rater scores were used to calculate mean scores for scales; however, 96% of observations were double-coded to ensure reliability of observations given the measure's novelty. Inter-rater reliability was assessed as the degree to which two coders were within one point of each other's scores (La Paro, Pianta, & Stuhlman, 2004). Inter-rater reliability across all classroom scale items was 0.90.

Students nested in observed classrooms reported on their perceptions of their classroom environment along three dimensions that mirrored those of the classroom-level engagement constructs. These dimensions were used to test the overall construct validity of the CCCO protocol. All student-level measures were included in our two-level confirmatory factor analysis (CFA) model (see online appendix).

RELATIONSHIPS BETWEEN CLASSROOM-LEVEL ENGAGEMENT AND STUDENT-LEVEL ENGAGEMENT

Examining classroom engagement (at the ecological level of the classroom) in contrast with student engagement (at the individual level) as it relates to student outcomes is clearly a novel method in higher education. Lawson and Lawson (2013) argue that in order to adequately address student engagement, the field of inquiry should be broadened to include the dynamic ways in which student engagement functions in the context of ecological systems. Although the literature on engagement clearly recognizes the features of classrooms that link to positive student outcomes, surprisingly little quantitative work has been done to systematically elucidate ways in which classroom processes shape classroom engagement and, in turn, student engagement (Lawson & Lawson, 2013). To date, the best approximation of classroom process has come in the form of qualitative research and student perceptions of aspects of the classroom experience.

We sought to extend important work conducted at the primary and secondary levels (Pianta, La Paro, & Hamre, 2008) by attending to the ecological structure of community college settings serving diverse students. Our approach considered classrooms as the unit of analysis rather than aggregating student reports of classroom engagement—the current norm in engagement research. This approach allowed for the study of classroom ecologies as indicators of engagement in addition to student and teacher variables of interest. Importantly, this strategy allowed us to focus on observable classroom interactions among all members of the class (i.e., between students and students and between students and instructors) (Tseng & Seidman, 2007) across a wide range of types of community college classrooms.

Classrooms observed had relatively high levels of academic engagement in which the majority of the members of the class were on task for the majority of the class period. Cognitive and relational engagement were lower in comparison with academic engagement, and there was evidence of inconsistency in these domains such that some but not all members of classes may have been cognitively and/or relationally engaged for some but not all of the class session. Students nested in classrooms also reported feeling strongly that their peers were academically and relationally engaged and that instructor press was strong, meaning that instructors were attuned to students' learning needs in class (see online appendix).

We were most interested in testing whether classroom engagement variables correlated with students' perceptions of peer academic engagement, instructor press, and peer relational engagement in their observed classrooms. Several important findings emerged from this work. First, our results indicated that our model was an excellent fit for the data (see online appendix for details), providing empirical support for the way in which we were conceptualizing relationships between our classroom-level and student-level engagement domains.

Second, we found that classrooms with higher levels of CCCO academic engagement were more likely to have students in the class report perceiving their peers as being more behaviorally engaged. Thus, there was consistency between our standardized observation protocol and what students reported about their own classmates' observable behaviors of being prepared for class and participating in class activities. This finding extends the extant K–12 behavioral engagement literature and the higher education academic engagement literature such that it provides empirical support for classroom-level academic engagement as a predictor of student-level behavioral engagement, which has to date been suggested by qualitative work on engagement (Cox, 2009).

Third, classrooms with higher levels of CCCO cognitive engagement were more likely to have students in the class report perceiving that their instructors were sensitive to the academic needs of students in their class. Instructor press in the context of instruction in the classroom has been theoretically linked to student-level cognitive engagement (Corno & Mandinach, 1983; Pintrich & Schrauben, 1992). Thus, this finding aligns with qualitative work done in college classrooms that promotes engagement as a dynamic process (Cox, 2009) influenced by more than mode of instruction (Grubb, 1999). Further, numerous empirical studies focusing on student reports of engagement have linked students' perceptions of instructional quality to cognitive development and knowledge accrual (Pascarella et al.; Pascarella, Seifert, & Whitt, 2008).

Fourth, we expected that students who attended classes in which we observed high levels of relational engagement would be more likely to report their peers as being connected to one another; however, this supposition was not the case. Research in higher education suggests that a classroom climate shaped by peer interactions characterized as trusting and emotionally supportive promotes norms that contribute to relational engagement for students (Booker, 2007). However, our analysis relied on students' reports of their own relational engagement rather than on reports of how relationally engaged they perceived their peers to be. It may be that students are well attuned to their own relational engagement but may not be particularly well equipped to report on that of their peers. In contrast, trained observers had been taught to consider many ways of observing indicators of relational engagement between class members. Future work should compare student self-reported relational engagement with observed relational engagement in order to tease apart these relationships. Interestingly, students' perceptions of peer academic engagement significantly predicted their perceptions of peer relational engagement, suggesting that classrooms where students think their peers are academically engaged may be places where students are more likely to experience their peers as being relationally engaged.

DISCUSSION

Although extensive literature has linked student reports of classroom engagement to student motivation and learning outcomes (Reeve, 2012; Skinner & Pitzer, 2012), there has been a dearth of research in higher education that systematically examines these dynamic processes at the classroom level. Engagement researchers have called for expansion of research in this area that explicitly focuses on factors external to the student (Eccles & Wang, 2012; Lawson & Lawson, 2013; Wentzel, 2012). To address this gap, we studied classroom ecologies as indicators of engagement in concert with student and teacher variables of interest. Our analyses yielded three distinct but interrelated classroom-level engagement domains—academic engagement, cognitive engagement, and relational engagement—which, when taken together, are thought to holistically represent classroom engagement.

Our results revealed that community college students held mixed views of how engagement played out in their classes. Students perceived that their peers were academically engaged in the tasks of learning and that their course instructors were committed to their students' learning needs while they simultaneously acknowledged that their peers demonstrated *low to moderate levels of cognitive and relational engagement in class*. The CCCO also predicted students' perceptions of engagement in class in ways that would be expected based on existing literature and demonstrated construct validity. In classrooms with high levels of observed academic engagement, students were also more likely to perceive that their peers were likewise so engaged. In classrooms with reported high levels of cognitive engagement, students also reported that they perceived that their instructors were sensitive to the academic needs of their students (Lawson & Lawson, 2013).

Turning to practice and policy implications, we found that the CCCO protocol has promise as a tool for both researchers and practitioners seeking to address the needs of increasingly diverse student populations in higher education. Because our analysis focused on classroom engagement in community colleges serving large numbers of low-income immigrant-origin students, the CCCO may be particularly well suited to schools serving these populations. The CCCO also focuses on classrooms as the unit of analysis rather than simply aggregating student self-reports of engagement—the current norm in engagement research. This approach expands the study of engagement variables beyond those of student and teacher to include classroom ecology as an engagement indicator. With this additional information, researchers and practitioners can broaden their focus of engagement research in higher education, moving beyond the current practice of examining instructor quality to a more dynamic setting-level approach that considers transactions among all members of the classroom.

Within the complex and multifaceted crisis of low graduation and high transfer rates, community colleges must move beyond the current practice of focusing largely on instructor quality as the main lever in student outcomes to a more dynamic approach that considers setting and classroom-level engagement. Attending to this need, the CCCO could inform evidence-based teaching (Groccia & Buskist, 2011) by providing educators and administrators with a classroom engagement assessment tool that could be linked to instructor professional development and coaching interventions, similar to what K–12 scholars have already achieved (Pianta & Allen, 2008; Pianta & Hamre, 2009), to address unsatisfactory engagement levels. Such a model would allow community college educators to focus on both social interactions that can bolster relational engagement and academic and instructional strategies that can increase academic and cognitive engagement for the whole class.

For researchers, the CCCO provides an additional tool to assess unique variation in student outcomes that may be associated with classrooms as a distinct ecology. Such information can elucidate areas for further study and possible intervention. For example, researchers can use the CCCO to examine correlations between classroom-level engagement domains and other student outcomes of interest long studied in the higher education literature, such as student engagement, GPA, credit accrual, attendance, degree completion, persistence, and a number of psychosocial outcomes.

Most importantly, educators and intervention researchers alike can utilize the CCCO as an improvement science tool to inform rapid intervention implementation and feedback loops to determine whether targeted efforts are effective (Bryk, Gomez, Grunow, & LeMahieu, 2015). Specifically, the CCCO's design allows for deep engagement in an improvement process that involves identifying key areas for intervention within classroom engagement domains, planning and implementing change initiatives, determining whether targeted efforts are effective, and building on successes or failures and course correcting as needed. Coupling the CCCO with an improvement science framework can lead to a deeper understanding of community college classrooms, thereby increasing the quality of classroom engagement practices and processes for all.

Understanding how classroom ecologies function in ways that support (or may fail to support) growing numbers of immigrant-origin students in community colleges represents an important but currently missed opportunity. The CCCO is an innovative strategy to support the enhancement of classrooms as supportive learning environments for immigrant-origin students and their native-born counterparts.

REFERENCES

Alicea, S., Suárez-Orozco, C., Singh, S., Darbes, T., & Abrica, E. J. (2016). Observing classroom engagement in community college: A systematic approach. *Educational Evaluation Policy Analysis, 34*(4), 757–782. doi:10.3102/0162373716675726

Bailey, T., & Morest, V. S. (Eds.). (2006). *Defending the community college equity agenda.* Baltimore, MD: Johns Hopkins University Press.

Bensimon, E. M. (2007). The underestimated significance of practitioner knowledge in the scholarship on student success. *The Review of Higher Education, 30*(4), 441–469. doi:10.1353/rhe.2007.0032

Blumenfeld, P. C. (1992). Classroom learning and motivation: Clarifying and expanding goal theory. *Journal of Educational Psychology, 84*(3), 272. doi:10.1037/0022-0663.84.3.272

Booker, K. C. (2007). Perceptions of classroom belongingness among African American college students. *College Student Journal, 41*(1), 178–186.

Braxton, J. M., Bray, N. J., & Berger, J. B. (2000). Faculty teaching skills and their influence on the college student departure process. *Journal of College Student Development, 41*(2), 215–227.

Bryk, A. S., Gomez, L. M., Grunow, A., & LeMahieu, P. G. (2015). *Learning to improve: How America's schools can get better at getting better.* Cambridge, MA: Harvard Education Press.

Cabrera, A. F., Crissman, J. L., Bernal, E. M., Nora, A., Terenzini, P. T., & Pascarella, E. T. (2002). Collaborative learning: Its impact on college students' development and diversity. *Journal of College Student Development, 43*(1), 20–34.

Corno, L., & Mandinach, E. B. (1983). The role of cognitive engagement in classroom learning and motivation. *Educational Psychologist, 18*(2), 88–108.

Cox, R. D. (2009). *The college fear factor: How students and professors misunderstand one another.* Cambridge, MA: Harvard University Press.

Crombie, G., Pyke, S. W., Silverthorn, N., Alison, J., & Piccinin, S. (2003). Students' perceptions of their classroom participation and instructor as a function of gender and context. *The Journal of Higher Education, 74*(1), 51–76. doi:10.2307/3648264

Deil-Amen, R. (2011). Socio-academic integrative moments: Rethinking academic and social integration among two-year college students in career-related programs. *The Journal of Higher Education, 82*(1), 54–91.

Eccles, J. S., & Wang, M. (2012). Part I commentary: So what is student engagement anyway? In S. L. Christenson, A. L. Reschly, & C. Wylie (Eds.), *Handbook of research on student engagement* (pp. 133–145). New York, NY: Springer.

Fassinger, P. A. (1997). Classes are groups: Thinking sociologically about teaching. *College Teaching, 45*(1), 22–25. doi:10.1080/87567559709596184

Finn, J. D., & Zimmer, K. S. (2012). Student engagement: What is it? Why does it matter? In S. L. Christenson, A. L. Reschly, & C. Wylie (Eds.), *Handbook of research on student engagement* (pp. 97–131). New York, NY: Springer.

Fredricks, J. A., Blumenfeld, P. C., & Paris, A. H. (2004). School engagement: Potential of the concept, state of the evidence. *Review of Educational Research, 74*(1), 59–109. doi:10.3102/00346543074001059

Groccia, J. E., & Buskist, W. (2011). Need for evidence-based teaching. *New Directions for Teaching and Learning, 2011*(128), 5–11. doi:10.1002/tl.463

Grubb, W. N. (1999). *Honored but invisible: An inside look at teaching in community colleges.* New York, NY: Routledge.

Harper, S. R., & Quaye, S. J. (2009). *Student engagement in higher education: Theoretical perspectives and practical approaches for diverse populations.* New York, NY: Routledge.

Hurtado, S., & Carter, D. F. (1997). Effects of college transition and perceptions of the campus racial climate on Latino college students' sense of belonging. *Sociology of Education, 70*(4), 324–345. doi:10.2307/2673270

Kuh, G. D., Cruce, T. M., Shoup, R., Kinzie, J., & Gonyea, R. M. (2008). Unmasking the effects of student engagement on first-year college grades and persistence. *The Journal of Higher Education, 79*(5), 540–563. doi:10.1353/jhe.0.0019

La Paro, K. M., Pianta, R. C., & Stuhlman, M. (2004). The classroom assessment scoring system: Findings from the prekindergarten year. *The Elementary School Journal, 104*(5), 409–426.

Lawson, M. A., & Lawson, H. A. (2013). New conceptual frameworks for student engagement research, policy, and practice. *Review of Educational Research, 83*(3), 432–479. doi:10.3102/0034654313480891

Lee, V. E., & Smith, J. B. (1999). Social support and achievement for young adolescents in Chicago: The role of school academic press. *American Educational Research Journal, 36*(4), 907–945.

Lundberg, C. A., & Schreiner, L. A. (2004). Quality and frequency of faculty-student interaction as predictors of learning: An analysis by student race/ethnicity. *Journal of College Student Development, 45*(5), 549–565. doi:10.1353/csd.2004.0061

National Survey of Student Engagement (NSSE). (2006). *Engaged learning: Fostering success for all students.* Bloomington: Indiana University Center for Postsecondary Research.

Nelson Laird, T. F., Chen, D., & Kuh, G. D. (2008). Classroom practices at institutions with higher-than-expected persistence rates: What student engagement data tell us. *New Directions for Teaching and Learning, 2008*(115), 85–99. doi:10.1002/tl.327

Pascarella, E. T., Salisbury, M. H., & Blaich, C. (2011). Exposure to effective instruction and college student persistence: A multi-institutional replication and extension. *Journal of College Student Development, 52*(1), 4–19. doi:10.1353/csd.2011.0005

Pascarella, E. T., Seifert, T. A., & Whitt, E. J. (2008). Effective instruction and college student persistence: Some new evidence. *New Directions for Teaching and Learning, 2008*(115), 55–70. doi:10.1002/tl.325

Pascarella, E. T., & Terenzini, P. T. (2005). *How college affects students: A third decade of research* (Vol. 2). San Francisco, CA: Jossey-Bass.

Peña, E. V., Bensimon, E. M., & Colyar, J. E. (2006). Contextual problem defining: Learning to think and act from the standpoint of equity. *Liberal Education, 92*, 48–55.

Pianta, R. C., & Allen, J. P. (2008). Building capacity for positive youth development in secondary school classrooms: Changing teacher interactions with students. In M. Shinn & H. Yoshikawa (Eds.), *Toward positive youth development: Transforming schools and community programs* (pp. 21–39). Oxford, UK: Oxford University Press.

Pianta, R. C., & Hamre, B. K. (2009). Conceptualization, measurement, and improvement of classroom processes: Standardized observation can leverage capacity. *Educational Researcher, 38*(2), 109–119. doi:10.3102/0013189x09332374

Pianta, R. C., La Paro, K. M., & Hamre, B. K. (2008). *Classroom assessment scoring system.* Baltimore, MD: Paul H. Brookes.

Pintrich, P. R., & Schrauben, B. (1992). Students' motivational beliefs and their cognitive engagement in classroom academic tasks. In D. H. Schunk & J. L. Meece (Eds.), *Student perceptions in the classroom* (pp. 149–183). Hillsdale, NJ: Erlbaum.

Ramsden, P. (2003). *Learning to teach in higher education.* London, UK: Routledge Falmer.

Reeve, J. (2012). A self-determination theory perspective on student engagement. In S. L. Christenson, A. L. Reschly, & C. Wylie (Eds.), *Handbook of research on student engagement* (pp. 149–172). New York, NY: Springer.

Robbins, S. B., Lauver, K., Le, H., Davis, D., Langley, R., & Carlstrom, A. (2004). Do psychosocial and study skill factors predict college outcomes? A meta-analysis. *Psychological Bulletin, 130*(2), 261. doi:10.1037/0033-2909.130.2.261

Saenz, V. B., Hatch, D., Bukoski, B. E., Kim, S., Lee, K. H., & Valdez, P. (2011). Community college student engagement patterns: A typology revealed through exploratory cluster analysis. *Community College Review, 39*(3), 235–267.

Sarason, S. B., & Klaber, M. (1985). The school as a social situation. *Annual Review of Psychology, 36*(1), 115–140. doi:10.1146/annurev.psych.36.1.115

Sax, L. J., Bryant, A. N., & Harper, C. E. (2005). The differential effects of student-faculty interaction on college outcomes for women and men. *Journal of College Student Development, 46*(6), 642–657. doi:10.1353/csd.2005.0067

Skinner, E. A., & Pitzer, J. R. (2012). Developmental dynamics of student engagement, coping, and everyday resilience. In S. L. Christenson, A. L. Reschly, & C. Wylie (Eds.), *Handbook of research on student engagement* (pp. 21–44). New York, NY: Springer.

Suárez-Orozco, C., Pimentel, A., & Martin, M. (2009). The significance of relationships: Academic engagement and achievement among newcomer immigrant youth. *The Teachers College Record, 111*(3), 712–749.

Svanum, S., & Bigatti, S. M. (2009). Academic course engagement during one semester forecasts college success: Engaged students are more likely to earn a degree, do it faster, and do it better. *Journal of College Student Development, 50*(1), 120–132. doi:10.1353/csd.0.0055

Teranishi, R. T., Suárez-Orozco, C., & Suárez-Orozco, M. (2011). Immigrants in community colleges. *The Future of Children, 21*(1), 153–169.

Tinto, V. (1993). *Leaving college: Rethinking the causes and cures of student attrition* (2nd ed.). Chicago, IL: University of Chicago Press.

Tinto, V. (1997). Classrooms as communities: Exploring the educational character of student persistence. *The Journal of Higher Education, 68*(6), 599–623. doi:10.2307/2959965

Tseng, V., & Seidman, E. (2007). A systems framework for understanding social settings. *American Journal of Community Psychology, 39*(3–4), 217–228.

Voelkl, K. E. (2012). School identification. In S. L. Christenson, A. L. Reschly, & C. Wylie (Eds.), *Handbook of research on student engagement* (pp. 193–218): New York, NY: Springer.

Wentzel, K. (2012). Part III commentary: Socio-cultural contexts, social competence, and engagement at school. In S. L. Christenson, A. L. Reschly, & C. Wylie (Eds.), *Handbook of research on student engagement* (pp. 479–489). New York, NY: Springer.

CHAPTER 6

The Prevalence and Relevance of Microaggressions in Community College Classrooms

Carola Suárez-Orozco, Saskias Casanova, Margary Martin,
Dalal Katsiaficas, & Sukhmani Singh

Across college classrooms, the question of whether or not microaggressions may matter for students has swept across the research and social imagination. Microaggressions have been defined as "brief and commonplace daily verbal, behavioral, or environmental indignities, whether intentional or unintentional, that communicate hostile, derogatory, or negative . . . slights and insults" (Sue et al., 2007, p. 271) toward individuals of underrepresented status. Though discounted by some as inconsequential (Lukianoff & Haidt, 2015), there is mounting evidence that subtle microaggressions have negative emotional, cognitive, and behavioral implications for their victims (Sue, 2010c). They are often delivered carelessly without thought, and while the intent of the person initiating the microaggression may not have consciously been to render harm, the victim often reports that she or he felt distinctly uncomfortable afterward (Solórzano, Ceja, & Yosso, 2000; Sue, 2010b; Sue et al., 2007).

Microaggressions have been documented in a number of settings, including workplaces (Deitch et al., 2003; Sue, 2010b) and clinical practices (Johnston & Nadal, 2010; Sue et al., 2007) as well as educational settings (Minikel-Lacoque, 2013; Sue, 2010c). In education, most of the research has focused on 4-year college settings and has been presented from the target's point of view (Lau & Williams, 2010; Solórzano et al., 2000). This research has largely been retrospective in nature, with targets reporting their memories of how microaggressions have affected them (Lau & Williams, 2010). In this chapter, we share findings from the Research on Immigrants in Community College (RICC) Study that captured covert microaggressions in vivo, shedding light on how microaggressions occur in community college classrooms.

MICROAGGRESSIONS: AN ELUSIVELY TOXIC BIAS

Initially, the theory of *racial* microaggression was introduced as a form of enduring bias encountered by African Americans (Pierce, 1974, 1995). Pierce argued that, in the post–civil rights era, these denigrations were the most fundamental remaining form of racism (1974) and that the cumulative burden of bearing these ongoing indignities was damaging to individuals' self-confidence and health (1995). Although, arguably, *overt* forms of racism and discrimination have declined since the civil rights era, *covert* racism and implicit biases have remained intractable (Devos & Banaji, 2005; Dovidio & Gaertner, 1996). In recent years, the concept of *microaggressions* delivered by someone of relative power or privilege has been extended to other underrepresented or devalued groups, including *Latinos* (Minikel-Lacoque, 2013; Rivera, Forquer, & Rangel, 2010), *Asian Americans* (Lin, 2010), *women* (Capodilupo et al., 2010), *LGBT populations* (Nadal, Rivera, & Corpus, 2010), *religious minorities* (Nadal, Issa, Griffin, Hamit, & Lyons, 2010), *individuals of low socioeconomic status* (Smith & Redington, 2010), and *people with disabilities* (Keller & Galgay, 2010), among others.

Microaggressions are by their very nature elusive. The sting of the words as well as the actions generally seem trivial to the initiator, who often does not recognize either his or her own position of privilege or the repeated similar prior incidents that the target may have encountered (Solórzano et al., 2000; Sue, Capodilupo, Nadal, & Torino, 2008). Typically, the initiator delivers the comment without forethought, does not consider it to have been ill-intentioned, and perceives the target to be overly sensitive if the person reacts negatively to it (Kohli & Solórzano, 2012; Sue, 2010b, 2010c; Sue et al., 2007). The reality of the victim's experience may be called into question (Sue et al., 2008) without recognition of the victim's cumulative burden and fatigue from ongoing questioning of the legitimacy of such occurrences (Smith, Allen, & Danley, 2007; Sue, 2010a).

There is a notable and emerging body of evidence demonstrating the negative associations between microaggressions and an array of emotional, cognitive, and behavioral outcomes. Anxiety, depression, and anger are all associated with exposure to microaggressions (Sue, 2010c). At least two forms of cognitive distraction and disruption of attention arise following microaggressive events— an attempt to make meaning of the event (did that *really* just happen?) (Sue, 2010c) and the activation of a stereotype threat (do I have to prove myself as a member of my group *yet again?*). Behavioral disruptions following a microaggressive event can lead to an individual's disengagement resulting from feeling disempowered or initiated as an act of protest (Sue, 2010c). In addition to the immediate effects, there are the cumulative effects of continuous "othering" and questioning of one's social belongingness (Kohli & Solórzano, 2012; Pierce, 1995; Sue, 2010a).

MICROAGGRESSIONS IN EDUCATIONAL SETTINGS

As educational settings increasingly serve students from a broad variety of backgrounds and social circumstances, microaggressions on campuses are of growing concern. Several studies in education have illuminated this phenomenon. In a seminal study using focus group interviews, Solórzano et al. (2000) linked microaggressions to "self-doubt and frustration as well as isolation" (p. 69) for African American college students. In a retrospective study of grades K through 12 experiences, students of color recalled microaggressions that specifically targeted their names (Kohli & Solórzano, 2012). In a case study of six Latino students attending a primarily majority-serving college, participants voiced their frustration over their disempowerment following covert microaggressions (Minikel-Lacocque, 2013). Thus, emerging research suggests that microaggressive interactions are linked to "a hostile and invalidating learning environment" (Sue, 2010b, p. 235).

Most research on microaggressions in educational settings has primarily been qualitative in nature, based on small samples participating in focus groups or interviews (Lau & Williams, 2010). This research has been mostly retrospective in nature, asking participants to reflect on their past experiences—with overremembering and underremembering as well as misremembering being possible biases (Lau & Williams, 2010). This body of research to date has shed important light on targets' experiences of this phenomenon. However, a gap in the field has been the lack of observation of the effects of microaggressions in "real-life settings" as they occur (Lau & Williams, 2010, p. 319).

Although most of the work on microaggressions has taken place in 4-year college settings (Lau & Williams, 2010), community colleges represent an interesting learning context for the study of microaggressions. They are at the midway point between 4-year institutions and public high schools. As institutions of higher education, community colleges share some structural similarities with 4-year college settings; however, as open-access, affordable, second-chance settings, community colleges also serve a broad array of racial/ethnic minority students and fewer socioeconomically advantaged students, as is the case in public high schools (Bailey, 2009; Bailey & Morest, 2006). Community college students are often subjected to negative racialized stereotyping of intellectual inferiority (Jain, Herrera, Bernal, & Solórzano, 2011; Rhoads & Valadez, 1996). Consequently, community colleges are an important context in which to consider microaggressions.

CHAPTER AIMS

In this chapter we explore ways of observing and recording real-time covert microaggressions in community college classrooms, drawing from the RICC study. This chapter also utilizes data from microaggression (MA) observations collected as part of a structured classroom observation protocol during Phase 1. Microaggressions were documented as part of the classroom observation by using a specially designed protocol (see Alicea, Suárez-Orozco, Singh, Darbes, & Abrica, 2016) and online appendix for details of the methodology. As part of that study, we wanted to document the kinds of classroom climates that immigrant-origin students were experiencing. Excellent work has been done ethnographically in this regard in community colleges. We wanted to extend that work by doing systematic observations of classrooms. Although structured classroom observations have been made in K–12 research, they have not been similarly conducted in community college classrooms (Pianta & Hamre, 2009). Thus, we set out to develop a systematic protocol that could be replicated across classrooms by a team of graduate research assistants. Given that the settings we were observing served students from a broad variety of backgrounds and social circumstances, we thought it was very important to capture whether or not microaggressions occurred during instruction as an important aspect of the classroom climate.

Our conceptualization of microaggressions was influenced by both sociological (e.g., Solórzano et al., 2000) and psychological (e.g., Sue et al., 2007) perspectives. The sociological view uses critical race theory to frame researchers' work in this field (Solórzano et al., 2000). Since immigrant-origin students in contemporary society are "otherized" in a variety of ways that include race, undocumented status, and accent and language as well as poverty (Suárez-Orozco, Tseng, & Yoshikawa, 2015; Viruell-Fuentes, Miranda, & Abdulharim, 2012), we used an intersectionality framework (Cole, 2009; Syed, 2010) in our approach to this research. Hence, we assumed that MAs could be initiated and perpetrated according to various social categories and that these categories would be jointly associated. Therefore, we set out to capture a wide array of observed microaggressions as they occurred, including, but not limited to, racial microaggressions, and then analyzed them for intersectionality. Lastly, whereas we recognize that many MAs are highly subjective events (Solórzano et al., 2000; Sue et al., 2008), we expected that at least some of these events would be observable and that the field would be advanced by such observation (Lau & Williams, 2010).

Here we consider these questions: To what *extent* do microaggressions emerge across campuses and classroom types? What *types* of microaggressions are delivered in diverse community college classrooms? *Who* are the initiators and who are the targets of microaggressions?

THE EXTENT OF MICROAGGRESSIONS

At least one microaggression (MA) was identified in 17 classrooms (28.3%) of the 60 classrooms observed. Further, in 14 of these classrooms in which MAs were observed, these events occurred more than once (ranging from 2 to 10 times during the same class session). Thus, a total of 51 MAs was recorded for the 17 classrooms in which microaggressions had been detected.

The 51 MAs were observed most frequently on the two campuses that served predominantly racial/ethnic minority students: 11.8% of the MAs occurred

Table 6.1. Microaggression Occurrences in Observed Classrooms by
        Course Type

Course type	CIMA occurrence	
	Total classes observed	Classes with at least one CIMA
Remedial	17 (28.3%)	7 (41.2%)
General education	29 (48.3%)	7 (24.1%)
Vocational	14 (23.3%)	3 (21.4%)
Total	60 (100%)	17 (28.3%)

at Oakmont in contrast with 35.3% observed at Domino and 52.9% at Taino, ($\chi2_{(2,51)} = 13.1, p < .001$). Furthermore, of the 60 classrooms, MAs were observed in 41.2% of all remedial classrooms as compared with MAs observed in only 24.1% of all general education classrooms and 21.4% of all vocational classrooms (see Table 6.1). Given the relatively small sample size, we could not confidently calculate statistical significance among course types to see if campuses differed; nonetheless, these findings suggest that MAs disproportionately occurred in remedial courses relative to their occurrences in general education and vocational courses.

TYPES OF MICROAGGRESSIONS

Four predominant categories emerged from the analyses: intelligence ($N = 30$), cultural/racial ($N = 12$), gendered ($N = 4$), and intersectional ($N = 5$) MAs.

Intelligence-Related Microaggressions

Sue (2010a) has described "ascription of intelligence" as MAs that are intended to demean a person's intellectual competence by questioning the individual's intelligence based on her or his group membership. A classic example would be asking a woman how she became so good at math (the underlying assumption being that women cannot do math). In the context of our analysis, the intelligence-type MAs were also expressed as a challenge to the student's college identity. This questioning of intelligence and competence occurred frequently during our observations; this type of MA was the most frequently witnessed one, happening in 59% ($N = 30$) of observed MAs ($\chi2_{(3,51)} = 34.1, p < .001$).

The following example from a general education math course illustrates intelligence belittling:

> After collecting quizzes from students, the instructor states, "Now you've got to show your work." He asks a young Latino male to come to the board

to solve a problem. The student attempts to solve the problem but gets the wrong answer. The professor states, "You need to do it like you are in kindergarten; that way you make no mistakes, right? Write this 17 times [he writes '17 times' on the board]—Right, Javier"? Expressionless, Javier[1] looks at the board.

In another example of an intelligence-related microaggression, one observed in a remedial math class, a teacher says to his Latina student, "I'm assuming, Leticia, that problem you will do Eeny, meeny, miny, moe, right?"

Cultural/Racial Microaggressions

Cultural MAs overtly disparage the assumed cultural backgrounds of the victims and can send messages that certain groups are inferior. This situation might occur, for example, by stereotyping or pathologizing based on a person's culture or race (Sue, 2010a). These cultural/racial MAs expose biases that reflect cultural or racial stereotypes. We observed cultural/racial MAs that victimized a person's country of origin, immigrant status, ethnicity/race, and linguistic or socioeconomic background:

In a student-to-student exchange, a Latino student approaches a table with several students from a variety of origins. Jokingly, he says, "You're spying, man!" A white female with a strong accent looks offended and responds seriously, "Yeah, Eastern Europeans—we're all spies." The two students exchange hard looks before returning to their work.

In a remedial English class, an Asian student encounters a language-based MA when the instructor, while going over a homework assignment, randomly calls on him to answer a question. When he does not respond immediately, the instructor yells, "English Channel!" at the student. The student flushes, does not respond, and is silent for the duration of the class.

In another example, another instructor in a remedial English course asks her class, "Have any of you ever visited a prison?" As some students raise their hands, the professor continues, "Better yet, have any of you been to prison?" As students share their experiences with the prison system, the professor insists, "Use I statements."

In this incident, the instructor makes assumptions about the criminal experiences of her community college students that she is unlikely to have made if she had been teaching middle- or upper-class students.

Gendered Microaggressions

Gendered MAs refer to gendered roles, sexuality, sexual objectification, or sexual orientation (Sue, 2010a). We observed nine gendered MAs, five of which occurred in combination with either culture- or intelligence-based MAs.

In the following example from a philosophy class, the male instructor reinforces negative stereotypes of women:

> "Anyone know somebody beautiful?" A male student responds, "I know someone beautiful. She is an exotic dancer . . ." The instructor continues the gendered discourse by adding, "I'm in love with a stripper." The class laughs in response. . . . Later, the instructor asserts, "Beauty is power. Who uses it more?" Most of the students answer, "Women." Continuing with this discussion, the instructor calls on a male student by name and elicits the response "Women."

The instructor here brings up the topic of beauty, which the students turn into a gendered conversation focusing on stereotypes of women. The instructor encourages this line of discussion rather than steering it back to neutral ground and in so doing, perpetuates gendered stereotypes.

Intersectional Microaggressions

Individuals can identify with multiple social groupings. An individual's intersectional identity may result from a combination of groups to which the person belongs, some of which may be marginalized (Purdie-Vaughns & Eibach, 2008), such as being Black, Dominican, and female. On several occasions, we noted that multiple identities were overtly targeted in the same MA. We coded intersectional MAs as those that conveyed biases against a combination of a victim's gender, intelligence, and/or culture. Of the five MAs typed as multiple/intersecting, two involved culture/race and gender; two targeted intelligence and gender; and one combined intelligence, gender, and culture/race.

An example of an intersecting-type MA targeting both race and gender was observed in a remedial English class described as having 13 students of color in a group of 17:

> The White instructor started to speak about Thomas Jefferson and his relationship with his slave Sally Hemings. A Black male student asked, "He raped her?" The instructor disagreed, saying, "He had three or four children with her." The student then asked, "Oh, so he had a relationship with her?" The instructor replied, "He was an honorable guy. He bought her a sandwich." [The instructor] grinned, evoking what seemed to be uncomfortable laughter from the students in the class.

In this case the instructor conjured up an example from history of an exploited Black slave woman. When a Black student suggested the possibility of abuse, the instructor quickly dismissed the likelihood by (1) suggesting that Jefferson was "honorable," (2) maintaining that it does not follow that additional children would be born after a rape, and (3) making light of the matter by equating the provision of a "sandwich" with some kind of courtship.

WHO INITIATES MICROAGGRESSIONS, AND WHO ARE THE TARGETS?

Instructors were most frequently the initiators of the MAs recorded ($n = 45$; $\chi2_{(1, 51)} = 29.82$, $p < .001$). The majority of the instructors' MAs (41 out of 45) were directed at a specific student (e.g., the intelligence MA described earlier), though some were undirected, with no specific victim (e.g., the prison cultural/racial MA noted previously). Significantly, the six MAs initiated by students were never directed at an instructor. Most of the student-initiated MAs targeted other students.

Microaggressions occurred most often in remedial classrooms (see Table 6.1 above) where the majority of faculty members were White (see Table 6.2 below). Although the literature predominantly considers MAs perpetuated by members of the majority on members of underrepresented groups, we found that a diverse range of instructors across the gender, age, and ethnicity/race spectrum initiated microaggressions.

IN SUM

Each microaggression, like a toxic raindrop, falls corrosively into learning environments (Meyer, 2003; Suárez-Orozco et al., 2015; Sue, 2010c). A large body of the existing literature on microaggressions has articulated the negative cumulative effects of MAs on individual well-being across a variety of domains of functioning in a number of settings (Sue, 2010a, 2010b), though there are remaining debates in the field around measurement, terminology, and outcomes, among other concerns (see Littlefield, 2017). With this research we have contributed to an understanding of the field by developing both an observational strategy not subject to self-reporting and a methodology to systematically capture this phenomenon in classroom environments.

Our novel research approach took on the challenge of capturing microaggressions as they occurred during class sessions (Lau & Williams, 2010). Rather than exclusively burdening the victims with the responsibility of reporting these incidents retroactively, we trained observers to recognize events and capture them as they occurred. Although we cannot claim random sampling, by collecting

Table 6.2. Instructor Characteristics by Course Type

Instructor characteristic	General education (n = 29) (48.3%)		Vocational (n = 14) (23.3%)		Remedial (n = 17) (28.3%)		Total (N = 60) (100%)	
	n	%	n	%	n	%	n	%
Faculty in all 60 observed classrooms								
Female	17	58.6	8	57.1	11	64.7	36	60.0
Asian	6	20.7	1	7.1	1	5.9	8	13.3
Black	5	17.2	1	7.1			6	10.0
Latino	3	10.3	2	14.3	2	11.8	7	11.7
White	14	48.3	9	64.3	13	76.5	36	60.0
Unclear/unknown	1	3.4	1	7.1	1	5.9	3	5.0
Faculty in 17 classrooms where microaggressions occurred								
Female	3	42.9	1	33.3	5	71.4	9	52.9
Asian	2	28.6	1	33.3			3	17.6
Black	2	28.6	1	33.3			3	17.6
Latino	1	14.3					1	5.9
White	2	28.6	1	33.3	6	85.7	9	52.9
Unclear/unknown					1	14.3	1	5.9

observations from several types of campuses and a range of classrooms, we attempted to represent a variety of classrooms and subject areas. Although just a snapshot, our findings provide evidence that classroom interpersonal microaggressions are pervasive—occurring in nearly 30% of the community college classrooms that we observed.

We found that while cultural/racial and gendered microaggressions were uniquely observed, the most frequent types of microaggressions witnessed were those that attacked the intelligence and competence of students (Sue et al., 2007). Strikingly, these intelligence- and competence-related microaggressions were observed in the institutions with the highest concentrations of racial/ethnic minority students. As we consider this finding, it is useful to draw on both critical race theories (Solórzano, 1998) and intersectionality theories (Cole, 2009; Syed, 2010). For visible racial/ethnic minority students, race is a central feature of their educational experiences (Solórzano, 1998). Further, students are also concurrently members of multiple subordinate groups and experience stereotyping and expectations on any number of levels. When stereotyping and microaggressions occur, the attribution of a category that is the cause for stereotyping may not necessarily be obvious (Cole, 2009; Syed, 2010). Nonetheless, expectations and stereotypes are a daily part of students' experiences.

Community colleges, which primarily serve low-income students from traditionally underserved backgrounds, are settings that have been documented as having low expectations of their students (Jain et al., 2011; Rhoads & Valadez, 1996). We found that instructors were far more likely to initiate microaggressions than students were, reflecting power dynamics in the classroom (Sue et al., 2008). The comments made by instructors were often sarcastic and laced with their obvious frustration with students (Cox, 2009). Most often, the microaggressions were directed at a specific student rather at the class as a whole. Many of the observed microaggressions served to convey a sense of the teacher's low expectations of students (Weinstein, 2002). The kinds of classroom interactions that we observed, especially those that happened over time and across numerous classroom settings, have the potential to reinforce stereotype vulnerability (Aronson & Inzlicht, 2004), undermine academic self-concept (Bong & Skaalvik, 2003), and activate stereotype threat (Steele, 1997) for its victims. This development is deeply concerning since students representing a variety of backgrounds and social circumstances will increasingly continue to be present in every classroom.

Both Sue (2010c) and Solórzano et al. (2000) have hypothesized that negative cognitive and emotional as well as behavioral implications follow a person's having been subjected to microaggressions. We witnessed numerous microaggressions that undermined student intelligence in these classrooms serving students from diverse backgrounds. Our research provides a window for observing the embodiment of low instructor expectations in the form of microaggressions and provides insight into how they may act as a powerful undertow contributing to poor performances of community college students (Riley & Ungerleider, 2012).

NOTES

Details on the data collection and analytic strategies are available in the original extended version of this manuscript, which appeared in the *Educational Researcher*: "Toxic Rain in the Classroom: Classroom Interpersonal Microaggressions," by C. Suárez-Orozco, S. Casanova, M. Martin, D. Katisaficas, V. Cuellar, S. Dias, and N. Smith, 2015, *Educational Researcher, 44*(3), 151–160.

1. All names used in this chapter are pseudonyms.

REFERENCES

Alicea, S., Suárez-Orozco, C., Singh, S., Darbes, T., & Abrica, E. (2016). Observing classroom engagement in community college: A systematic approach. *Educational Evaluation and Policy Analysis, 38*(4), 757–782.

Aronson, J., & Inzlicht, M. (2004). The ups and downs of attributional ambiguity: Stereotype vulnerability and the academic self-knowledge of African American college students. *Psychological Science, 15*(12), 829–836.

Bailey, T. (2009). *Rethinking developmental education in community college* (Policy Brief, Vol. 40). New York, NY: Community College Research Center.

Bailey, T. R., & Morest, V. S. (Eds.). (2006). *Defending the community college equity agenda.* Baltimore, MD: Johns Hopkins University Press.

Bong, M., & Skaalvik, E. M. (2003). Academic self-concept and self-efficacy: How different are they really? *Educational Psychology Review, 15*(1), 1–40.

Capodilupo, C. M., Nadal, K. L., Corman, L., Hamit, S., Lyons, O. B., & Weinberg, A. (2010). The manifestations of gender microaggressions. In D. W. Sue (Ed.), *Microaggressions and marginality: Manifestations, dynamics, and impacts* (pp. 193–216). Hoboken, NJ: Wiley.

Cole, E. R. (2009). Intersectionality and research in psychology. *American Psychologist, 64*(3), 170–180.

Cox, R. (2009). *The college fear factor: How students and professors misunderstand one another.* Cambridge, MA: Harvard University Press.

Deitch, E. A., Barsky, A., Butz, R. M., Chan, S., Brief, A., & Bradley, J. C. (2003). Subtle yet significant: The existence and impact of everyday racial discrimination in the workplace. *Human Relations, 56*(11), 1299–1324.

Devos, T., & Banaji, M. R. (2005). American = White? *Journal of Personality and Social Psychology, 88*(3), 447–466.

Dovidio, F. J., & Gaertner, S. L. (1996). Affirmative action, unintentional racial biases, and intergroup relations. *Journal of Social Issues, 52*(4), 51–75.

Jain, D., Herrera, A., Bernal, S., & Sólorzano, D. (2011). Critical race theory and the transfer function: Introducing a transfer receptive culture. *Community College Journal of Research and Practice, 35*(3), 252–266.

Johnston, M. P., & Nadal, K. L. (2010). Multiracial microaggressions: Exposing monoracism in everyday life and clinical practice. In D. W. Sue (Ed.), *Microaggressions and marginality: Manifestations, dynamics, and impacts* (pp. 123–144). Hoboken, NJ: Wiley.

Keller, R. M., & Galgay, C. E. (2010). Microaggressive experiences of people with disabilities. In D. W. Sue (Ed.), *Microaggressions and marginality: Manifestations, dynamics, and impacts* (pp. 241–268). Hoboken, NJ: Wiley.

Kohli, R., & Solórzano, D. (2012). Teachers, please learn our names! Racial microaggressions and the K–12 classroom. *Race, Ethnicity, & Education, 15*(4), 441–462.

Lau, M. Y., & Williams, C. D. (2010). Microaggression research: Methodological review and recommendations. In D. W. Sue (Ed.), *Microaggressions and marginality: Manifestations, dynamics, and impacts* (pp. 313–336). Hoboken, NJ: Wiley.

Lin, A. I. (2010). Racial microaggressions directed at Asian Americans: Modern forms of prejudice and discrimination. In D. W. Sue (Ed.), *Microaggressions and marginality: Manifestations, dynamics, and impacts* (pp. 85–104). Hoboken, NJ: Wiley.

Littlefield, S. O. (2017). Microaggressions: Strong claims, inadequate evidence. *Perspectives on Psychological Science, 12*(1), 138–169.

Lukianoff, G., & Haidt, J. (2015). The coddling of the American mind. *The Atlantic Review*. Retrieved from www.theatlantic.com/magazine/archive/2015/09/the-coddling-of-the-american-mind/399356

Meyer, I. H. (2003). Prejudice, social stress, and mental health in lesbian, gay, and bisexual populations: Conceptual issues and research evidence. *Psychological Bulletin, 129*(5), 674–697.

Minikel-Lacocque, M. (2013). Racism, college, and the power of words: Microaggressions reconsidered. *American Educational Research Journal, 50*(3), 432–465.

Nadal, K. L., Issa, M. A., Griffin, K. E., Hamit, S., & Lyons, O. B. (2010). Religious microaggressions in the United States: Mental health implications for religious minority groups. In D. W. Sue (Ed.), *Microaggressions and marginality: Manifestations, dynamics, and impacts* (pp. 287–312). Hoboken, NJ: Wiley.

Nadal, K. L., Rivera, D. P., & Corpus, M. J. H. (2010). Sexual orientation and transgender microaggressions: Implications for mental health and counseling. In D. W. Sue (Ed.), *Microaggressions and marginality: Manifestations, dynamics, and impacts* (pp. 217–240). Hoboken, NJ: Wiley.

Pianta, R. C., & Hamre, B. K. (2009). Conceptualization, measurement, and improvement of classroom processes: Standardized observation can leverage capacity. *Educational Researcher, 38*(2), 109–119.

Pierce, C. (1974). Psychiatric problems in the Black minority. In S. Arieti (Ed.), *American handbook of psychiatry* (pp. 265–282). New York, NY: Basic Books.

Pierce, C. (1995). Stress analogs of racism and sexism: Terrorism, torture, and disaster. In C. Willie, B. Rieker, B. Kramer, & B. Brown (Eds.), *Mental health, racism, and sexism* (pp. 277–293). Pittsburg, PA: University of Pittsburg Press.

Purdie-Vaughns, V., & Eibach, R. P. (2008). Intersectional invisibility: The distinctive advantages and disadvantages of multiple subordinate-group identities. *Sex Roles, 59*(5–6), 377–391.

Rhoads, R. A., & Valadez, J. R. (1996). *Democracy, multiculturalism, and the community college: A critical perspective* (Vol. 5). New York, NY: Taylor & Francis.

Riley, T., & Ungerleider, C. (2012). Self-fulfilling prophecy: How teachers' attributions, expectations, and stereotypes influence the learning opportunities afforded Aboriginal students. *Canadian Journal of Education, 35*(2), 303–333. Retrieved from blade2.vre.upei.ca/ojs/index.php/cje-rce/article/view/406

Rivera, D. P., Forquer, E. E., & Rangel, R. (2010). Microaggressions and the life experience of Latina/o Americans. In D. W. Sue (Ed.), *Microaggressions and marginality: Manifestations, dynamics, and impacts* (pp. 59–84). Hoboken, NJ: Wiley.

Smith, L., & Redington, R. M. (2010). Class dismissed: Making the case for the study of classist microaggressions. In D. W. Sue (Ed.), *Microaggressions and marginality: Manifestations, dynamics, and impacts* (pp. 269–286). Hoboken, NJ: Wiley.

Smith, W. A., Allen, W. R., & Danley, L. L. (2007). "Assume the position. . . . You fit the description": Psychosocial experiences and racial battle fatigue among African American male college students. *American Behavioral Scientist, 51*(4), 551–578.

Solórzano, D. G. (1998). Critical race theory, race and gender microaggressions, and the experience of Chicana and Chicano scholars. *International Journal of Qualitative Studies in Education, 11*(1), 121–136.

Solórzano, D. G., Ceja, M., & Yosso, T. (2000). Critical race theory, racial microaggressions, and campus racial climate: The experiences of African American college students. *Journal of Negro Education, 69*(1), 60–73. Retrieved from www.jstor.org/stable/2696265

Steele, C. M. (1997). A threat in the air: How stereotypes shape intellectual identity and performance. *American Psychologist, 52*(6), 613–629. doi:10.1037/0003066X.52.6.613

Suárez-Orozco, C., Casanova, S., Martin, M., Katisaficas, D., Cuellar, V., Dias, S., & Smith, N. (2015). Toxic rain in the classroom: Classroom interpersonal microaggressions. *Educational Researcher, 44*(3), 151–160.

Suárez-Orozco, C., Tseng, V., & Yoshikawa, H. (2015). *Intersecting inequality: Research to reduce inequality for immigrant-origin children & youth.* New York, NY: W. T. Grant Foundation. Retrieved from www.wtgrantfoundation.org/post/111903703827/intersecting-inequalities-research-to-reduce

Sue, D. W. (Ed.). (2010a). *Microaggressions and marginality: Manifestations, dynamics, and impacts.* Hoboken, NJ: Wiley.

Sue, D. W. (2010b). *Microaggressions in everyday life: Race, gender, and sexual orientation.* Hoboken, NJ: Wiley.

Sue, D. W. (2010c). Microaggressions, marginality, and oppression: An introduction. In D. W. Sue (Ed.), *Microaggressions and marginality: Manifestations, dynamics, and impacts* (pp. 3–24). Hoboken, NJ: Wiley.

Sue, D. W., Capodilupo, C. M., Nadal, K. L., & Torino, G. C. (2008). Racial microaggressions and the power to impose reality. *American Psychologist, 63*(4), 277–279.

Sue, D. W., Capodilupo, C. M., Torino, G. C., Bucceri, J. M., Holder, A. M. B., Nadal, K. L., & Esquilin, M. (2007). Racial microaggressions in everyday life: Implications for clinical practice. *American Psychologist, 62*(4), 271–286.

Syed, M. (2010). Disciplinarity and methodology in intersectionality theory and research. *American Psychologist, 65*(1), 61–62.

Viruell-Fuentes, E. A., Miranda, P. Y., & Abdulrahim, S. (2012). More than culture: Structural racism, intersectionality theory, and immigrant health. *Social Science & Medicine, 75*(12), 2099–2106.

Weinstein, R. (2002). *Reaching higher ground: The power of expectations in schooling.* Cambridge, MA: Harvard University Press.

CHAPTER 7

The Use of Out-of-Class Time on Campus of Immigrant-Origin Students

Olivia Osei-Twumasi, Carola Suárez-Orozco, Edwin Hernandez, Monique Corral, & Janet Cerda

> Why would you want to do research on students' experiences in community college settings? Our students hardly spend any time on campus.
>
> —College administrator, RICC study

Within the higher education literature, a "tangled web of [interrelated] terms" (Wolf-Wendel, Ward, & Kinzie, 2009, p. 407), including *engagement, involvement,* and *integration,* has been used when considering both institutional and student dimensions to explain student success and persistence. In each of the following theories, the amount of *time* invested in a variety of campus activities has been thought to play an important role in student outcomes.

Engagement theory suggests that at the institutional level providing well-considered opportunities for students to invest their time (both academically and socially) and to utilize spaces (such as the library, tutoring center, or gym) on campus is important. At the student level, considering how and in what ways students spend their time is important (Kuh, Kinzie, Cruce, Shoup, & Gonyea, 2006). Research has shown that institutions can influence students' engagement by providing enhanced support services, an effort that results in improved student outcomes (Saenz et al., 2011).

Addressing related issues in his *theory of involvement,* Alexander Astin (1984, 1999) states that a student's having positive experiences with faculty, peers, and work is important for enhancing cognitive and affective development as well as for learning, academic performance, and retention (Astin, 1984). Using Astin's categories, researchers have considered what motivates students to become involved on campus when they are not in class, utilizing as a proxy for engagement the amount of time they spend interacting with faculty and peers, working, and engaging in other on-campus activities (Saenz et al., 2011).

Similarly, Vincent Tinto's (1993) *integration theory* argues that dedicating time to engaging with social and intellectual communities helps students receive support and feel a sense of membership, factors that are vital for student retention. Tinto's model has been widely applied to predict the persistence rather than the departure of mainstream students at 4-year institutions (e.g., see Pascarella & Terenzini, 2005).

However, given the changing demographics on college campuses, scholars have questioned the applicability of Tinto's theory to non-White, nontraditional student populations (Tierney, 1992). Some scholars have argued that Tinto's model employs an assimilationist framework that suggests that minority students integrate into the dominant White culture of American society at the cost of their heritage cultures or that it identifies students' external commitments (such as family, work, and friends outside of school) as barriers to academic commitments and goals without recognizing them as potential sources of strength and motivation (Rendon, Jalomo, & Nora, 2000; Tierney, 1992).

AN INTEGRATIVE CONCEPTUAL MODEL

Drawing on the aforementioned literature and building on seminal research in the field, we developed a conceptual model that could serve to explain both what may contribute to the use of time on campus and the role of time in student outcomes (see Figure 7.1).

Student Noncampus Considerations

Students bring with them a set of demographic, academic, and other characteristics—*student noncampus considerations* such as immigrant generation, academic skills, and family responsibilities—when they arrive on campus. Research has indicated differences in students' levels of involvement according to demographic characteristics (e.g., see Greene, Marti, & McClenney, 2008). Furthermore, various studies have examined the ways in which family responsibilities, commuting, academic preparation, and financial difficulties impact students' academic engagement and outcomes (see Chapter 1 and Hernandez et al. [in press] for a literature review). Therefore, the ways in which immigrant-origin students negotiate external influences in college are important for their engagement and success.

Campus Engagement

In the middle of Figure 7.1 are *campus engagement* factors. Time spent on campus should include a consideration of *productive class time* (which would include not only the hours spent in class but also the quality of the interactions and instruction in class) (Alicea, Suárez-Orozco, Singh, Darbes, & Abrica, 2016). In addition, time spent outside of class in community colleges (as in 4-year colleges) is likely

Figure 7.1. Integrative Theoretical Model of Use of Time by Community College Immigrant-Origin Students

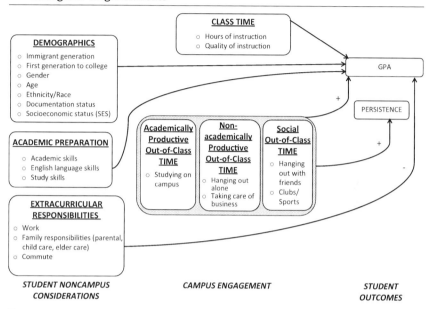

divided among *academically productive out-of-class time* (which may be linked to better academic outcomes), *social out-of-class time* (which may be linked to affective attachment to the campus and potentially to persistence), and *nonacademically productive out-of-class time* (which may consist of time spent taking care of student- or campus-related business [i.e., financial aid, registrar's office] or time spent alone) that may be necessary but is not directly linked to better academic or social outcomes.

Although time spent on campus studying or using campus resources may be tangibly linked to grades, the social expenditures are more likely associated with affective connection and affiliation, which in turn are more likely connected to longer term persistence (Hurtado & Carter, 1997). A large-scale survey study based on University of California undergraduates specifically examined the use of student time. It divided time use into three separate *time binaries* and then examined their relationship to academic outcomes (Brint & Cantwell, 2010). These binaries were (1) study versus nonstudy time, (2) active (e.g., volunteering or exercising) versus passive (e.g., watching TV or playing video games) time, and (3) connecting (hanging out with peers on campus) versus separating (being alone or off campus) time. Not surprisingly, after controlling for previous academic achievements, socioeconomic status (SES), and psychosocial stress, time focused on studying was most predictive of academic conscientiousness as well as of grades. Social time had a weak connection to conscientiousness but not to grades, and there was no relationship to grades for any of the other factors with the exception of work, which was negatively associated with grades (Brint & Cantwell, 2010). This study sheds some light on the tangible importance of the concrete dimensions of time spent on campus, but it is limited in its applicability to community colleges since it is based on students in a network of competitive 4-year public institutions.

In addition, research has demonstrated that time spent making use of student services on campus is a strong indicator of engagement (Saenz et al., 2011), in part shifting the responsibility to institutions to create more opportunities for student engagement. An important point here is that *quality of time* (or how time is spent)—not just length of time spent—matters.

Student Outcomes

Student outcomes typically include grades and persistence. Research has shown that community college students are more at risk of leaving college early and not persisting than are students at 4-year schools (Handel, 2007; Ma & Baum, 2016). Therefore, exploring how these students use their time on campus is important to better understand how to enhance their success.

CHAPTER AIMS

In the higher education literature, student engagement as measured by time spent on campus (e.g., studying on campus and using services there) has been related to the academic success (Harper & Quaye, 2015; Kuh et al., 2006; Wolf-Wendel et al., 2009) of traditional college students. Thus, this research sought to consider the role of time spent on campus by immigrant-origin students attending community colleges—a growing nontraditional demographic in these settings (Teranishi, C. Suárez-Orozco, & M. M. Suárez Orozco, 2011).

The purpose of this analysis was to quantify how much time immigrant-origin community college students reported spending on campus and to explore the links between use of time and academic outcomes. We have used our conceptual model as a framework; given our available data, however, we were not able to test every factor presented in the conceptual model. Nonetheless, we aim to illuminate a number of elements and put in place a foundation that may generate ideas for future studies on immigrant-origin students enrolled at community colleges. Drawing on the survey and GPA administrative data from the Research on Immigrants in Community College (RICC) Study (see online appendix), our research questions included the following:

> **RQ1a.** How much time do students report spending on campus doing what activities? **RQ1b.** What is the demographic variation in these patterns (according to immigrant generation, ethnicity/race, and gender)?

RQ2. What factors predict how much *overall time* immigrant-origin students spend on campus?

RQ3. What is the effect of *academically productive time* spent on campus on GPA for immigrant-origin students?

SPENDING TIME ON CAMPUS

First, we drew on survey data (see Table 7.1 for a description of the survey sample) to examine whether immigrant-origin community college students spent considerable time on campus outside of class and contemplated the distinctions among academically productive, nonacademically productive, and social out-of-class time. One notable finding was that the community college students in our sample spent substantial amounts of quality time on campus (see Table 7.2). Our finding contrasts with the common belief expressed by the community college administrator

Table 7.1. Participant Demographic Description Table

		All students		Immigrant-origin students	
		n	%	*n*	%
Immigration Generation	1st	213	33%	212	44%
	2nd	275	43%	274	56%
	3rd +	150	23%	n/a	n/a
	Missing	6	1%	n/a	n/a
Gender	Male	292	45%	223	46%
	Female	350	54%	262	54%
	Missing	2	0%	1	0%
Race	Hispanic	250	39%	212	44%
	Black	172	27%	127	26%
	White	81	13%	35	7%
	Asian	58	9%	54	11%
	Other or mixed	77	12%	58	12%
	Missing	6	1%	–	–
Age	18–19	275	43%	214	44%
	20–21	211	33%	155	32%
	22–25	156	24%	117	24%
	Missing	2	0%	–	–

Table 7.2. Use of Time and Campus Resources

n	Time in class (hours) 629		Time outside class (total hours) 631		Academically productive time (hours) 629		Social time (hours) 631		Nonacademically productive time (hours) 631		No. of services used (on average) 642	
	M	SD	M	SD	M	SD	M	SD	M	SD	M	SD
All students	12.5	6.7	9.2	7.7	3.5	4.7	4.0	5.3	3.5	5.0	3.3	2.4
1st generation	14.0	6.9	10.7	8.0	5.2	8.8	4.3	5.6	4.0	5.4	3.4	2.5
2nd generation	11.4	6.3	8.5	7.6	3.4	7.2	3.8	4.9	3.1	4.7	3.5	2.5
3rd+ generation	12.1	6.5	8.7	7.4	3.4	5.7	4.0	5.5	3.4	5.1	3.0	2.2
Black	12.9	7.5	9.9	7.2	3.8	5.9	4.4	5.2	3.8	5.1	3.3	2.3
White	13.1	6.3	7.8	7.3	3.7	7.6	3.6	5.5	2.6	4.8	2.5	2.1
Latinx	12.2	6.3	9.3	7.9	4.5	9.1	3.9	5.4	3.9	5.3	3.6	2.5
Asian	12.7	6.0	11.1	8.5	5.2	7.1	4.1	5.1	4.2	5.2	3.5	2.4
Other	11.6	6.5	8.0	7.6	2.7	4.5	3.8	5.1	2.1	3.8	3.3	2.7
Male	12.9	6.8	9.8	7.7	4.0	7.5	4.7	5.6	3.6	5.2	3.1	2.4
Female	12.1	6.6	8.8	7.7	4.1	7.5	3.4	4.9	3.4	4.9	3.6	2.4
Taino	12.7	7.3	10.0	8.3	4.8	9.1	4.5	6.1	4.8	6.1	3.9	2.7
Domino	12.1	6.0	8.4	7.4	3.4	6.4	3.5	4.9	3.0	4.5	3.2	2.3
Oakmont	12.7	6.8	9.6	7.5	4.0	7.1	4.1	5.0	2.9	4.4	3.0	2.3

Note: Academically productive time on campus included time spent "studying on campus." Social time included time spent "hanging out with friends" and "participating in a club or sport." Nonacademically productive time included time spent "hanging out alone" and "taking care of business." The average number of services used in the past semester refers to the internship office, the tutoring center, the academic advising office, the registrar's office, the transfer office, the financial aid office, the health center, the security center, the counseling center, and other site-specific centers.

in this chapter's opening statement and in prior research that has suggested that community college students spend a minimal amount of time on campus due to their work and family responsibilities (Astin, 1999). We found that despite students' external commitments, the average amount of time that they spent on campus outside of class was 9.2 hours a week—a considerable amount of time. Furthermore, fewer than one-sixth (16%) of students reported having spent no time on campus outside of class in the previous week while a third had spent more than 10 hours on campus outside of class.

We tested for demographic differences concerning time. We found statistically significant differences across immigrant generations. Despite the external commitments of work and family responsibilities that first- and second-generation immigrant-origin students might experience (Tseng, 2004), our findings document that first-generation immigrant-origin students spent more academically productive time (studying) on campus than later generations did. Furthermore, when examining gender differences, we found that males spent more time socializing on campus (e.g., hanging out with friends, being involved in clubs and sports) than did their female peers. Our findings also demonstrate that Latinx students, particularly those at Taino, used more services than their White peers did. This result may in part be due to the fact that the community colleges we studied were making particular efforts to strategically engage their Latinx students. Students choosing to spend their out-of-class time on campus in academically productive ways and in making use of campus services thus might be a reflection of both student needs and responsive campus programming.

To underscore this point, we found statistically significant differences among participant responses from the three community college campuses. Taino students spent the most time on campus outside of class and used the greatest number of services on average while students at Domino spent the least amount of time on campus. Notably, Taino has historically been a Hispanic-serving institution that expends considerable effort to provide culturally relevant programming for its students while Domino pays little attention to this dimension of service provision. Previous empirical research has demonstrated the significance of the role of institutions in the ways in which they provide spaces for students to engage and thrive on their respective college campuses (Bowen & Bok, 2000; Perez & McDonough, 2008). Research has shown that not all learning environments are the same—from the number of allocated resources, to the organization of learning opportunities, to the services provided for students to engage in those activities that will benefit them, to name a few (Kuh, Kinzie, Schuh, & Whitt, 2010). Our findings contribute to the literature not only by focusing on community college students but also by specifically focusing on immigrant-origin students as they describe the available opportunities and the limitations of their respective campus out-of-class settings.

Having established that the community college students surveyed were, on average, spending substantial amounts of out-of-class time on campus, we then used multiple regression analysis to explore factors that predict time spent on campus specifically for immigrant-origin community college students. We found that peer relationships as well as time spent helping parents and commute time had a positive impact on time spent on campus outside of class. On the other hand, attending the Domino campus had a negative effect (see Table 7.3). Thus, our analysis reveals that immigrant-origin students who spent more time helping their parents also spent longer periods of time on campus than other students did. This finding is contrary to those of previous research that have suggested that family demands might make it difficult for students to remain on campus and engage with the school community (Tseng, 2004). Perhaps high levels of external commitments to the family may be related to students' seeking quiet spaces on campus where they can complete their readings and assignments. Although family responsibilities may make it more challenging for students to spend discretionary time on campus, immigrant-origin students are likely to need to use their campus time efficiently and to seek out spaces on campus that are conducive to studying.

Furthermore, similar to the findings of previous research that peer relationships may contribute to engagement (Astin, 1984; Rendon et al., 2000; Saenz et al., 2011), our findings indicate the importance of peer relationships to students' spending more time on campus outside of class in community college settings. One possible explanation may be that students who develop peer relationships on campus may be encouraged by these peers to remain on campus (Astin, 1984; Rendon et al., 2000; Saenz et al., 2011).

Our findings also demonstrate that immigrant-origin students with long commutes are more likely than other students to spend time on campus and utilize services offered there. This situation probably occurs because students with long commutes opt to stay on campus when they have long gaps in their class schedules. College administrators should be aware that commuter students in particular may be spending large amounts of time on campus and should consider providing quiet spaces (apart from the library) where students can study.

Finally, we analyzed the influence of out-of-class time spent on campus on GPA. We started by examining the correlation between GPA and each of the different categories of time. Total time spent outside of class, social time, and nonacademically productive time were not significantly correlated with GPA, but academically productive time (studying on campus) was positively and statistically significantly correlated with GPA. Results from a multiple regression analysis of the factors that predict GPA are shown in Table 7.4. These results confirm that using out-of-class time in academically productive ways (like studying at the library) did contribute to GPA. This finding aligns with previous research on students at 4-year colleges that has found that it is not just the time that students spend on campus but also the quality of the ways in which that time is spent that matter for academic success (Brint & Cantwell, 2010).

Table 7.3. Hierarchical Regression Predicting Time Spent on Campus Outside of Class

Variable	Model 1			Model 2			Model 3		
	B	SE B	β	B	SE B	β	B	SE B	β
Constant	5.16	4.33		1.57	4.68		-3.11	4.72	
Age	0.18	0.21	0.04	0.18	0.20	0.04	0.32	0.20	0.08
Female	-1.22	0.75	-0.08	-1.06	0.74	-0.07	-0.87	0.73	-0.06
Asian	3.45	1.78	0.14	2.34	1.78	0.09	2.18	1.76	0.09
Black	2.95	1.55	0.17	2.23	1.54	0.13	1.96	1.51	0.11
Latinx	1.68	1.49	0.11	1.14	1.48	0.07	0.89	1.46	0.06
Other	0.64	1.70	0.03	0.03	1.70	0.00	0.00	1.67	0.00
First generation	1.54*	0.76	0.10*	1.70*	0.75	0.11*	1.32	0.75	0.08
Taino	-0.64	1.04	-0.04	-0.80	1.03	-0.05	-1.16	1.02	-0.07
Domino	-2.17*	0.88	-0.14*	-2.04*	0.87	-0.13*	-2.35**	0.87	-0.15**
Peer relationships				1.37**	0.44	0.16**	1.15**	0.43	0.13**
Instructor relationships				-0.48	0.51	-0.05	-0.55	0.51	-0.05
Services used				0.28	0.15	0.09	0.21	0.15	0.07
Commute time							0.20**	0.06	0.14**
Work time							-0.01	0.03	-0.01
Parent help							0.09	0.04	0.12**
Time in class							0.09	0.06	0.08
$R2$	0.051			0.082			0.128		
F	2.554**			3.187**			3.877**		
$\Delta R2$	0.051			0.031			0.046		

$* p < .05, ** p < .01$

Table 7.4. Hierarchical Regression Predicting Cumulative GPA

Variable	Model 1 B	SE B	β	Model 2 B	SE B	β
	Model predicting cumulative GPA					
	Model 1			**Model 2**		
Constant	1.15	0.53		1.58**	0.53	
Age	0.07**	0.02	0.15**	0.06**	0.02	0.14**
Female	0.01	0.09	0.01	0.00	0.08	0.00
Asian	−0.30	0.20	−0.11	−0.33	0.20	−0.12
Black	−0.56**	0.17	−0.30**	−0.57**	0.17	−0.31**
Latinx	−0.58**	0.17	−0.35**	−0.60**	0.16	−0.36**
Other	−0.50**	0.19	−0.20**	−0.49**	0.19	−0.20**
First generation	0.19*	0.08	0.11*	0.17*	0.08	0.10*
Taino	−0.22	0.12	−0.12	−0.21	0.12	−0.11
Domino	−0.36	0.10	−0.22**	−0.34**	0.10	−0.20**
Study skills	0.15	0.06	0.14**	0.14*	0.06	0.12*
Work time	0.00	0.00	−0.04	0.00	0.00	−0.03
Parent help	0.00	0.00	−0.02	0.00	0.00	−0.04
Commute time	0.00	0.00	−0.01	0.00	0.00	−0.02
Academically productive time				0.02**	0.00	0.15**
R^2		0.134			0.153	
F		4.306**			4.657**	
Δ R^2		0.134			0.019	

* $p <.05$, ** $p <.01$

IMPLICATIONS FOR PRACTICE

The received knowledge is that community college students spend little time on campus outside of class, partly because of long commutes and family responsibilities. However, this study has shown that community college students are in fact spending substantial amounts of out-of-class time on campus—around 9 hours per week on average. Interestingly, this situation is especially so for students with long commutes and high levels of family commitments. This finding speaks to other scholars' calls for the need "to move beyond knowing that students are busy and have many responsibilities" to investigating how family responsibilities and students' engagement on campus can complement each other (Rios-Aguilar & Kiyama, 2017, p. 5). We also found differences among the three campuses in terms of time spent on campus and services used. These variations may be an indication of successful responsive programming on the part of certain campuses. It is important to highlight our finding that when immigrant-origin community college students' use of on-campus time is productive, this endeavor leads to better grades. Hence, community college administrators need to be aware that their students are in fact using and relying on campus spaces. Therefore, these administrators should strive to provide spaces that engage and anchor immigrant-origin students within the campus and should provide the kind of on-campus programming that will enhance their success.

REFERENCES

Alicea, S., Suárez-Orozco, C., Singh, S., Darbes, T., & Abrica, E. J. (2016). Observing classroom engagement in community college: A systematic approach. *Educational Evaluation and Policy Analysis, 38*(4), 757–782.

Astin, A. W. (1984). Student involvement: A developmental theory for higher education. *Journal of College Student Personnel, 25*(4), 297–308.

Astin, A. W. (1999). Student involvement: A developmental theory for higher education. *Journal of College Student Development, 40*(5), 518–529.

Bowen, W. G., & Bok, D. (2000). *The shape of the river: Long-term consequences of considering race in college and university admissions.* Princeton, NJ: Princeton University Press.

Brint, S., & Cantwell, A. (2010). Undergraduate time use and academic outcomes: Results from the University of California undergraduate experiences survey 2006. *Teachers College Record, 112*(9), 2441–2470.

Greene, T. G., Marti, N. C., & McClenney, K. (2008). The effort-outcome gap: Differences for African American and Hispanic community college students in student engagement and academic achievement. *Journal of Higher Education, 79*(5), 513–539.

Handel, S. J. (2007). Second chance, not second class: A blueprint for community-college transfer. *Change: The Magazine of Higher Learning, 39*(5), 38–45.

Harper, S. R., & Quaye, S. J. (2015). Making engagement equitable for students in U.S. higher education. In S. R. Harper & S. J. Quaye (Eds.), *Student engagement in higher education: Theoretical perspectives and practical approaches for diverse populations* (2nd ed., pp. 1–14). New York, NY: Routledge.

Hernandez, E., Suárez-Orozco, C., Cerda, J., Osei-Twumasi, O., Corral, M., Garcia, Y., . . . Ruedas-Gracia, N. [in press]. Immigrant origin students in community college: How do they use their time on campus? *Teachers College Record.*

Hurtado, S., & Carter, D. F. (1997). Effects of college transition and perceptions of the campus racial climate on Latino college students' sense of belonging. *Sociology of Education, 70*(4), 324–345. doi:10.2307/2673270

Kuh, G. D., Kinzie, J., Cruce, T. M., Shoup, R., & Gonyea, R. M. (2006). *Connecting the dots: Multi-faceted analyses of the relationships between student engagement results from the NSSE, and the institutional practices and conditions that foster student success.* Bloomington: Center for Postsecondary Research, Indiana University.

Kuh, G. D., Kinzie, J., Schuh, J. H., & Whitt, E. J. (2010). *Student success in college: Creating conditions that matter.* San Francisco, CA: Jossey-Bass.

Ma, J., & Baum, S. (2016). Trends in community colleges: Enrollment, prices, student debt, and completion. New York, NY: The College Board.

Pascarella, E. T., & Terenzini, P. T. (2005). *How college affects students: A third decade of research* (Vol. 2). San Francisco, CA: Jossey-Bass.

Perez, P. A., & McDonough, P. M. (2008). Understanding Latina and Latino college choice: A social capital and chain migration analysis. *Journal of Hispanic Higher Education, 7,* 249–265.

Rendon, L. I., Jalomo, R. E., & Nora, A. (2000). Theoretical consideration in the study of minority student retention in higher education. In J. M. Braxton (Ed.), *Rethinking the departure puzzle: New theory and research on college student retention* (pp. 127–156). Nashville, TN: Vanderbilt University Press.

Rios-Aguilar, C., & Kiyama, J. M. (2017). Introduction: The needs for funds of knowledge approach in higher education contexts. In J. M. Kiyama & C. Rios-Aguilar (Eds.), *Funds of knowledge in higher education: Honoring students' cultural experiences and resources as strengths* (pp. 3–6). New York, NY: Routledge.

Saenz, V. B., Hatch, D., Bukoski, B. E., Kim, S., Lee, K. H., & Valdez, P. (2011). Community college student engagement patterns: A typology revealed through exploratory cluster analysis. *Community College Review, 39*(3), 235–267.

Teranishi, R. T., Suárez-Orozco, C., & Suárez Orozco, M. M. (2011). Immigrants in community colleges. *The Future of Children, 21*(1), 153–169.

Tierney, W. G. (1992). An anthropological analysis of student participation in college. *The Journal of Higher Education, 63*(6), 603–618.

Tinto, V. (1993). *Leaving college: Rethinking the causes and cures of student attrition* (2nd ed.). Chicago, IL: University of Chicago Press.

Tseng, V. (2004). Family interdependence and academic adjustment in college: Youth from immigrant and U.S.-born families. *Child Development, 75*(3), 966–983.

Wolf-Wendel, L., Ward, K., & Kinzie, J. (2009). A tangled web of terms: The overlap and unique contribution of involvement, engagement, and integration to understanding college student success. *Journal of College Student Development, 50*(4), 407–428.

CHAPTER 8

Immigrant-Origin Community College Students' Help-Seeking Orientation and Use of Counseling Services

Sandra I. Dias

Young adulthood is an age of particular vulnerability for mental health challenges as nearly three quarters of lifetime psychiatric disorders emerge during adolescence and early adulthood (Kessler et al., 2005). College campuses across the country are seeing an increase in serious psychological issues such as depression, suicidal ideation, and alcohol abuse (Kitzrow, 2003). In an annual report by the Center for Collegiate Mental Health (2014), more than half of students indicated a current concern related to anxiety. Untreated mental illness is a growing concern for campuses across the country, with significant implications for academic success, productivity, substance use, and social relationships (Hunt & Eisenberg, 2010). As such, an increasing number of students are seeking counseling services on these campuses (Kitzrow, 2003).

Yet despite the availability of a wide range of professional services, many young adults, in particular, suffering from mental health problems, do not seek formal/professional help—a dilemma known as the "service gap" (Cramer, 1999, p. 381). This gap is particularly salient for ethnic minority populations and individuals of immigrant origin (Harris, Edlund, & Larson, 2005). Extensive research at 4-year universities has demonstrated that although the majority of college students are aware of the mental health counseling services available to them via the counseling centers on campus, more than half of the students who used such services sought them outside of the university (Eisenberg, Golberstein, & Gollust, 2007). Moreover, research conducted with ethnic and minority emerging adult students attending 4-year universities shows that they do not avail themselves of counseling services in significant numbers when compared with the practices of their White peers (Ayalon & Young, 2005). Cultural barriers—including language barriers, adherence to cultural values, the stigma of mental health problems, and cultural distrust—have influenced immigrant, ethnic, and racial minority emerging adult students' help-seeking perceptions and experiences (American Psychological

Association [APA], 2012; Ayalon & Young, 2005; Loya, Reddy, & Hinshaw, 2010; Nickerson, Helms, & Terrell, 1994).

Research at 4-year universities has demonstrated the importance of institutional environments, including the counseling center, in contributing to students' academic and social integration as well as to their overall mental well-being (Yosso, Smith, Ceja, & Solórzano, 2009). Although community college students spend considerably less time in their school settings than students at 4-year universities do, increasing evidence indicates that these settings, particularly their counseling centers, are "sites of opportunities" (Weis & Fine, 2000) that could provide the immigrant-origin emerging adult student population and ethnic minority students with readily available low-cost mental health services. Counseling service centers are a crucial component in the mission of community colleges and are an example of preventive services particularly directed toward aiding the transition, persistence, and academic achievement as well as the overall mental well-being of emerging adults in college (Eichler & Schwartz, 2010). Counseling centers provide services for a broad range of concerns, including "multicultural and gender issues, career and developmental needs, life transitions, stress, and violence" (Archer & Cooper, 1998, p. 13).

The literature on the psychological challenges of immigration such as depression, anxiety, acculturation stress, and substance abuse is abundant and increasing (APA, 2012). However, very little research has focused on immigrant emerging adulthood and the relationships among this developmental phase, the unique factors experienced by this population, and the mental health or the help-seeking orientation of this group. Further, there has been a dearth of research at 2-year colleges and community colleges examining their students' use of counseling services.

This chapter sought to shed light on how immigrant-origin students are utilizing the counseling centers at community college campuses as well as on what services are being utilized and for what reasons.

IMMIGRANT EMERGING ADULTHOOD AND MENTAL HEALTH

Young adult immigrants go through unique processes related to the vulnerable identity-forming transitional stage of life they are in. Along with the so-called normal developmental challenges of emerging adulthood, they are faced with the stress of assimilating into the host country's culture while remaining loyal to their original culture (see Chapter 2). In addition to facing these challenges, young adults and their immigrant parents acculturate at different paces, what Mollenkopf, Waters, Holdaway, and Kasinitz (2005) describe as being "suspended between the 'old country' ways of their parents and the American subcultures in which they are growing up" (p. 455). All these factors certainly constitute sources of family conflict as well as conflicts with peers and are added stressors that may affect young immigrant adults' mental health as well as their help-seeking orientation.

In some ways immigrant young adults differ from nonimmigrants in their transition to adulthood. About half (49%) of first-generation young adults migrate to the United States on their own, leading to vast differences in their transitions to adulthood and their transitional needs (Rumbaut & Komaie, 2010). As such, first-generation immigrant emerging adults stand out because of their greater propensity to have already completed the five major conventional transitions to adulthood—leaving home, finishing school, entering the work force, getting married, and having children (Rumbaut & Komaie, 2010). In contrast, the U.S.–born, second-generation immigrant emerging adults are the least likely to have transitioned through these conventional markers (not only when compared with first-generation immigrant emerging adults but also when compared with their mainstream U.S. peers).

Although there is diversity within ethnicities and races, second-generation immigrants are the most likely to be living at home with their parents, to be employed and helping to support their family, and to be pursuing a higher degree and the least likely to be married or have children (Rumbaut & Komaie, 2010). These differences are particularly important when understanding emerging adulthood and its intersection with mental health since the prevailing view is that social constraints and life choices in school, employment, finances, access to health care, and interpersonal spheres serve to "forge directions or pathways that for some youth involve opportunity and growth but for others involve risk and dysfunction" (Gore & Aseltine, 2003, p. 371).

Nevertheless, there are factors that safeguard first-generation immigrant emerging adults and reduce negative impacts on their mental well-being, and these should be recognized. These factors consist of (1) help-seeking behaviors such as relying on social supports, including family support, within their new communities; (2) socioeconomic status, including education and employment; (3) cognitive attributes such as expectations about and attitudes toward acculturation (positive or negative); and (4) the degree of tolerance and overall acceptance of cultural diversity in the host society (Lipsicas & Mäkinen, 2010).

HELP-SEEKING DURING EMERGING ADULTHOOD

National and international scholars and research attest to "young people's reluctance to seek professional mental health care" (Rickwood, Deane, & Wilson, 2007, p. 35). Moreover, research with Asian Americans has shown that the underutilization of services and the "high level of illness severity for those who eventually enter the mental health care system" (Zhang, Snowden, & Sue, 1998, p. 318) are due to students' reluctance to seek services rather than to a lack of need. Although many factors contribute to the low rate of services usage, in order to best understand the patterns, we need to examine the help-seeking orientation of minority and immigrant groups and comprehend differences that may exist by developmental stage, generational status, racial/ethnic group, and gender.

Although much research has been conducted to understand what impedes young adults from seeking formal help, particularly in the context of university/college campuses, most of this research has focused on a person's reluctance to seek treatment from the standpoint or perspective that the young adult knows that such help exists (Rickwood et al., 2007). Very little research has focused on understanding what college students know about their college campus's counseling centers or mental health services and how they obtained that information.

A study conducted by Yorgason, Linville, and Zitzman (2008) with 266 undergraduate university students (84% identified as Caucasian) showed that only 32% of the respondents reported having been adequately informed about the university counseling center or mental health services. In addition, 30% had heard of the services but knew nothing specific about them or about their function. For those students who were aware of their university's mental health services, the top three sources of information were friends or fellow students, advertisements on campus, and the school website (Yorgason et al., 2008). Furthermore, the study revealed that the top two reasons why students did not use the services were lack of time and lack of knowledge about services. These studies highlight the importance of universities and colleges finding better ways to inform students about mental health services on campus.

Last, models accounting for help-seeking behaviors consider the decision to seek help as the end result of a sociocultural process (Loya et al., 2010; Stanton-Salazar, Chávez, & Tai, 2001) heavily influenced by preexisting attitudinal beliefs about mental illness and its treatment, acculturation levels, language barriers, and social identities and by obstacles such as stigma and financial barriers.

CHAPTER AIMS

The focus of this mixed-methods analysis was to understand and describe the several dimensions of the help-seeking orientation of immigrant-origin emerging adult community college students (limited to those between the ages of 18 and 25 and equally distributed by gender) at three urban northeastern community colleges. This approach included providing greater insight into (1) the utilization rates of counseling-center support services at each of the three schools, (2) the help-seeking orientation of immigrant-origin emerging community college students, and (3) the cultural barriers to help-seeking. Additionally, this chapter explored whether there were differences according to immigration generational status.

The analyses in this chapter drew from the Research on Immigrants in Community College (RICC) Study (see online appendix for details of methodology). The quantitative part of this chapter draws on data of 644 student survey responses collected during Phase 2 while the qualitative part draws on 60 semi-structured interviews with immigrant-origin students (20 from each campus) collected during Phase 3. Emerging adulthood theory (Arnett, 1998, 2006) and cultural barrier theory (Zhang et al., 1998) were used throughout the chapter as a framework for understanding the factors that may facilitate or serve as barriers in this population's help-seeking.

UTILIZATION OF COUNSELING CENTER

Of the entire quantitative sample ($n = 644$), 74% of the participants responded, "I have not used this resource" in the past semester while the remaining 26% responded, "I have used this resource" ($n = 167$). Further, the overall results indicate that utilization rates for the counseling-center support services across the three campuses are generally low and quite uniform, with 25% utilization at Taino, 23% utilization at Domino, and 30% at Oakmont. Last, the utilization rates are also generally low for this population across generations, with 25% of first generation, 28% of second generation, and 23% of third generation or higher students utilizing services.

Help-Seeking Orientation

After we deleted 185 cases containing missing values, data from 459 participants were analyzed. The overall mean results from a help-seeking orientation scale (see online appendix for details) indicate that participants' willingness to seek formal help (i.e., seeking help at the counseling center) was unlikely. The sample as a whole relied on informal help-seeking behaviors (e.g., handling the problem themselves or asking family or friends for help) to solve the problems presented. The only exception was related to this population's willingness to seek formal help for financial problems.

Barriers to Formal Help-Seeking

The overall mean results from a six-item scale generated to capture cultural barriers to help-seeking (see online appendix) reveal that, contrary to what might be expected after reviewing the literature, this sample of immigrant-origin emerging adult community college students did not feel more constrained by cultural barriers than peers from other generations did when it came to formal help-seeking.

Knowledge and Utilization of the Counseling Center

Of the 60 students who participated in the semistructured interviews, 56% ($n = 33$) reported having some knowledge of the counseling center and its functions at their respective community college campuses while 44% reported having no knowledge or awareness of the counseling center or its services. Three subthemes emerged during the in-depth analysis of participants' interview responses about their understanding and use of counseling services at their community colleges.

"There to help you if you need something." Half ($n = 17$, 52%) of the participants said that the counseling center on their campus was available to help if they
needed something. That "something," however, was generally not elaborated on
and did not reflect their own experience seeking help for themselves on a matter. A
first-generation Latina's response illustrates this point well: "I guess I have no idea.
I mean, I am assuming it is a college, so there's academic counseling or maybe even
counseling in terms . . . of . . . personal problems, school problems, . . . something
along that line."

Academic advisement. In more than a third of the responses ($n = 13$, 39%),
perceptions of and familiarity with the role of the counseling center and its functions were based on students' firsthand experiences specifically utilizing academic
advisement. A second-generation Latino male responded: "The counseling? You
mean like the adviser? I have no idea. I know there's an adviser, the student adviser
that helps you pick your classes. That pretty much is it because I only went one
time."

Therapeutic knowledge. The least frequently occurring theme ($n = 3$, 5%),
therapeutic knowledge, reflected a more traditional knowledge of the counseling center's role based on a more therapeutic/counseling orientation in which the
professional acts as a facilitator to help a student better understand and resolve a
particular concern (Archer & Cooper, 1998). A second-generation Black female
responded: "I only used [the counseling center] once. . . . It was helpful, but I just
stopped [going] because I've been able to use outside resources. . . . I've seen [rep-
resentatives] on campus, and they'll give out flyers and say, 'Come to the counseling center if you want somebody to talk to, academicwise or whatever.'"

Help-seeking orientation. If participants responded that they had not sought
out help from the counseling center, they were asked if they would consider doing
so. Similar to the response patterns of students who had used these services on
campus, these analyses revealed that 85% ($n = 34$) of participants would choose
to rely on *informal* help while only 15% ($n = 6$) reported that they would seek out
formal help. Further, 37.5% ($n = 15$) reported they would seek help from a friend,
followed by 22.5% ($n = 9$) who would seek it from family members. Another 10%
($n = 4$) stated that they would handle the problem on their own, with only one
person reporting that he or she would seek out professional help (2.5%).

BARRIERS TO FORMAL HELP-SEEKING

Congruent with the survey findings, the interview participants also reported a low
use of the campus counseling center; 67% ($n = 40$) of the participants who took
part in the semistructured interviews said that they had not used the counseling
center at their respective community college campuses. These participants were

asked to explain why they had not sought formal help at the counseling center. Three themes emerged from these analyses:

Not Knowing About Counseling Centers

Not knowing about the counseling center or its services was one of the most frequently stated reasons given by interviewees (40%, $n = 16$). A first-generation Black female responded: "I don't know anything about . . . the counseling center." When asked why she was not aware of it, she continued, "I have no clue. . . . They don't advertise it much. I mean, how I am supposed to know? That information is not easy to find. You have to call a whole bunch of numbers to find out who to speak to, who is the right person that I speak to, and stuff like that. Or you have to go on the website and hunt that person down."

Need for Autonomy

These young adults' sense of autonomy or their belief that they did not need any help or that they could solve problems on their own also was frequently noted (40%, $n = 16$). This view was exemplified by a second-generation Latino male's comment: "Because, you know, I live my life, so I don't need counseling, so I never really thought to ask [about it]. At least, I think I don't need counseling. . . . I mean, I don't have problems that I think are a problem that I [need to] talk to someone [whose] job [is to listen] . . . because one of the things is [that] I always like to settle my own problems. . . . If I can't fix my problems, . . . what can I do? So I try my best to fix it myself. You know . . . independent!"

Turning to Interpersonal Networks Rather Than Counseling Services

Participants explained that they were most likely to seek help from people in their social support circle with whom they already had well-established relationships. A first-generation Latino male stated: "My relatives, my family. They are people I can rely on, people I can trust, people I know actually care about me." A second-generation Latina explained why she relies on her parents: "I know that they are always there and [that] they care about me, so I don't really think I can go to anyone else and tell them about my personal problems. . . . I know [my parents] can understand because we've pretty much gone . . . not through the same thing, but they would understand what I am going through."

Several participants noted that in order to feel comfortable seeking help, they would need to feel a sense of commonality with the person from whom they sought help. Such commonality often took the form of being the same age or sharing a culture. A second-generation Latino male explained why he sought help from a friend: "I'm comfortable with a friend. I'm more comfortable, so that's why I'm going to speak to him first and then to the counselor." A second-generation Latina reported seeking help from her sister and her best friend: "I feel like since they are around my age—even though that is kind of not smart because they won't really know what to tell me—I feel more comfortable around them. They actually probably do [find themselves in] the same situations I do, and they listen, and I feel like they understand, and they know what I am going through, and they maybe know what to say to me to make me feel better."

Further, several participants noted that they needed to know the help giver well and to feel cared for by the person before they could trust the person enough to engage in self-disclosure (20%, $n = 8$). A second-generation Black female highlighted the need for interpersonal relationships well when she reported: "I don't have a personal connection with them. . . . I'm only going to confide in someone that I'm close with or someone that relatively knows me or my family because then she or he would be more prone to understand my situation. . . . I like to keep my business and personal stuff separate."

IN SUM

The findings suggest that immigrant-origin emerging adult community college students rarely avail themselves of the counseling center services at their respective campuses. Across the three campuses, utilization rates for the counseling center services were generally low, with approximately one quarter of the survey sample and approximately one-third of the interview sample reporting having used these services. These findings are consistent with previous national and international research that has attested to "young people's reluctance to seek professional mental health care" (Rickwood et al., 2007, p. 35).

Previous scholarship has suggested that cultural barriers (i.e., fear of stigma associated with mental health and its treatment, vulnerability to self-disclosure, financial barriers, and level of acculturation) were the likely reason for low usage among diverse young adults (Deane & Chamberlain, 1994; Loya et al., 2010; Zhang et al., 1998). Contrary to previous research that has found that higher levels of acculturation increase help-seeking behaviors and coping responses among immigrant groups (Crandall, Senturia, Sullivan, & Shiu-Thornton, 2005; Snowden & Yamada, 2005; Yoshihama, 2001), in this chapter, no significant differences in utilization rates emerged based on immigrant generational status. The first generation was no less likely to use services than second- or third-generation participants were. Instead, our analysis demonstrated that all groups' utilization rates were low.

Consistent with a recent finding by Yorgason et al. (2008), in this sample a lack of awareness about the counseling center or its services emerged as the primary barrier to usage. Most students did not know about the services available on their campus. Further, although nearly 40% of the interview participants knew that the counseling center provided academic advisement, most students were not aware of the array of other services that these centers provide. Consistent with the findings of a report by the American Psychological Association (2012), this chapter found that "lack of knowledge of available mental health services" (p. 66) contributed significantly to the help-seeking behaviors of immigrant-origin emerging adult community college students.

A further reason gleaned from this chapter's findings that explains why students do not use the counseling center services had to do with young adults' need for autonomy (e.g., "I don't need help"). Consistent with recent findings by Wilson, Rickwood, Bushnell, Caputi, and Thomas (2011) and Rickwood, Deane, Wilson, and Ciarrochi (2005), this chapter's results show that emerging adults' need for autonomy, independence, and self-reliance as part of the stage of development in which they find themselves has an impact on their perception or belief that "they can or should solve their own problems" (Wilson et al., 2011, p. 30) and as such may influence the help-seeking orientation of this group and their willingness to seek formal help via mental health services.

Moreover, although the participants expressed their need for autonomy as a barrier to formal help-seeking, the findings reveal that students rely heavily on seeking help from family and/or friends. Overall, participants reported being far more likely to rely on informal help-seeking (i.e., handling the problem on their own or asking for help from family or friends) to solve problems with which they were presented (e.g., problems with family, a romantic partner, or school or a "personal" problem) than to seek counseling center advice. Prior research in college environments has demonstrated that ethnic minority students are less likely to seek professional psychological help (Bin Sheu & Sedlacek, 2004), particularly if they believe that they can or should be able to solve the problem on their own (Wilson et al., 2011). Our analysis found that participants were much more likely to seek campus counseling service help if they had a financial problem rather than one of a personal nature. Thus, our findings suggest that these participants' willingness to seek formal help was problem dependent.

The chapter's findings also indicate that the reason that participants tended to choose an informal source (i.e., family or friends) when seeking help, especially for more personal problems, was related to their desire and expectation to have a help giver who would know them well, relate to them in an intimate matter, and care for them through an interpersonal relationship. This choice was also related to their need to be able to trust their help giver as well as their need to feel comfortable with that person, particularly if they felt that the help giver had encountered similar experiences. This finding highlights the fact that although the literature informs us that emerging adult students are in the stage of development of "self-focus" (Arnett, 2006), immigrant-origin emerging adults have a strong desire for connection and interdependence and hold collectivistic cultural ideas of responsibility for themselves and for others (e.g., family members helping other family members, friends who have had similar experiences assisting other friends) (Tseng, 2004), particularly when seeking help and navigating new situations such as those encountered at a community college. This finding is also consistent with those of previous research that have shown that developmentally, the early adult years are strongly focused on the establishment and evolution of intimate relationships, distinguishing emerging adults from adolescents (Wilson et al., 2011).

FUTURE RESEARCH

Future research should consider investigating how students with higher levels of knowledge about counseling center support services acquire that knowledge and examine how that knowledge relates to their willingness to seek formal help and, how it varies from the attitudes of those students who do not seek formal help at the counseling center. In addition, a future longitudinal study following an emerging adult cohort from age 18 until age 25 to further explore whether and/or how their help-seeking orientation might change as each year passes could provide a developmental lens for further understanding as well as parcel out the relationship and/or impact of this developmental phase and need for autonomy on their attitudes, perceptions, and behaviors regarding seeking help.

Although past research has primarily focused on cultural barriers (i.e., attitudinal beliefs about mental illness and its treatment, acculturation levels, language barriers, and mistrust of therapists) (Loya et al., 2010; Stanton-Salazar et al., 2001), the need for interpersonal relations is a strong determinant of the help-seeking orientation of immigrant-origin emerging adults and may influence their willingness to seek formal help at their community college's counseling center. As such, future research needs to pay far greater attention to understanding the role of emerging adulthood as a developmental phase as well as understanding cognitive processes, including the need for interpersonal relations, self-efficacy (confidence in one's ability to perform a new behavior) (Bandura, 1977), behavioral capability (the skills and knowledge necessary to perform the behavior), outcome expectancy (a strong belief in the value of the expected outcomes of the new behavior) (Baronowski, Perry, & Parcel, 1997), and help-seeking intentions, all of which may drive the help-seeking behaviors of ethnically diverse immigrant-origin emerging adult community college students.

IMPLICATIONS FOR PRACTICE

There are important implications related to this chapter's findings for community college administrators and educators but more importantly for counseling center personnel such as the center's director or mental health counselors regarding their responsibility in ensuring access to information and educating students about the various services offered within this support environment so that students are more likely to seek help. One way that community colleges can reach a broad range of students despite having limited personnel and budgets is through integrative care related to preventive programming outreach. Doing so means strengthening student mental health services across campuses in a bottom-up fashion through integrative preventive work by training professors to identify mental health problems and to provide students with information about mental health and treatment. It also involves supporting student peer groups to provide outreach to students in need and supporting educational programs to raise community awareness of mental health issues and to help community members recognize common mental health problems and connect students with appropriate services (Barreira & Snider, 2010).

REFERENCES

American Psychological Association (APA). (2012). *Crossroads: The psychology of immigration in the new century. Report of the APA Presidential Task force on Immigration.* Retrieved from www.apa.org/topics/immigration/report.aspx

Archer, J., Jr., & Cooper, S. (1998). *Counseling and mental health services on campus: A handbook of contemporary practices and challenges.* San Francisco, CA: Wiley.

Arnett, J. J. (1998). Learning to stand alone: The contemporary American transition to adulthood in cultural and historical context. *Human Development, 41,* 295–315. doi:10.1159/000022591

Arnett, J. J. (2006). Emerging adulthood: Understanding the new way of coming of age. In J. J. Arnett & J. J. Tanner (Eds.), *Emerging adults in America: Coming of age in the 21st century* (pp. 3–19). Washington, DC: American Psychological Association.

Ayalon, L., & Young, M. A. (2005). Racial group differences in help-seeking behaviors. *The Journal of Social Psychology, 145,* 391–403. doi:10.3200/SOCP.145.4.391-404

Bandura, A. (1977). Self-efficacy: Toward a unifying theory of behavioral change. *Psychological Review, 84,* 191–215. Retrieved from citeseerx.ist.psu.edu/viewdoc/download?doi=10.1.1.315.4567&rep=rep1&type=pdf

Baronowski, T., Perry, C., & Parcel, G. (1997). How individuals, environments, and health behavior interact. In L. Glanz & P. Rimer (Eds.), *Health behavior and health education* (2nd ed., pp. 153–178). San Francisco, CA: Jossey-Bass.

Barreira, P., & Snider, M. (2010). History of college counseling and mental health services and role of community mental health model. In J. Kay & V. Schwartz (Eds.), *Mental health care in the college community* (pp. 21–31). Oxford, UK: Wiley-Blackwell.

Bin-Sheu, H., & Sedlacek, W. E. (2004). An exploratory study of help-seeking attitudes and coping strategies among college students by race and gender. *Measurement and Evaluation in Counseling and Development, 37,* 130–142. Retrieved from web.ebscohost.com/ehost/pdfviewer/pdfviewer?sid=c9dfbe24-01c0-428e-af7c-2c560385e78d%40sessionmgr4004&vid=2&hid=4114

Center for Collegiate Mental Health. (2014). Annual report 2014. Publication No. STA 15–30.

Cramer, K. M. (1999). Psychological antecedents to help-seeking behavior: A reanalysis using path modeling structures. *Journal of Counseling Psychology, 46,* 381–387. doi:0022-0167/99/$3.00

Crandall, M., Senturia, K., Sullivan, M., & Shiu-Thornton, S. (2005). "No way out": Russian-speaking women's experiences with domestic violence. *Journal of Interpersonal Violence, 20,* 941–958. doi:10.1177/0886260505277679

Deane, F. P., & Chamberlain, K. (1994). Treatment fearfulness and distress as predictors of professional psychological help-seeking. *British Journal of Guidance and Counseling, 22,* 207–217. doi:10.1080/03069889408260315

Eichler, R. J., & Schwartz, V. (2010). Essential services in college counseling. In J. Kay and V. Schwartz (Eds.), *Mental health care in the college community* (pp. 57–94). West Sussex, UK: Wiley-Blackwell.

Eisenberg, D., Golberstein, E., & Gollust, S. E. (2007). Help-seeking and access to mental health care in a university student population. *Medical Care, 45*, 594–601. Retrieved from www-personal.umich.edu/~daneis/papers/hmpapers/help-seeking%20—%20 MC%202007.pdf

Gore, S., & Aseltine, R. H., Jr. (2003). Race and ethnic differences in depressed mood following the transition from high school. *Journal of Health and Social Behavior, 44*, 370–389. Retrieved from www.jstor.org/stable/1519785

Harris, K. M., Edlund, M. J., & Larson, S. (2005). Racial and ethnic differences in the mental health problems and use of mental health care. *Medical Care, 43*, 775–784. Retrieved from www.jstor.org/stable/3768295

Hunt, J., & Eisenberg, D. (2010). Mental health problems and help-seeking behavior among college students. *Journal of Adolescent Health, 46*(1), 3–10.

Kessler, R. C., Berglund, P., Demler, O., Jin, R., Merikangas, K. R., & Walters, E. E. (2005). Lifetime prevalence and age-of-onset distributions of DSM-IV disorders in the National Comorbidity Survey Replication. *Archives of General Psychiatry, 62*, 593–602.

Kitzrow, M. A. (2003). The mental health needs of today's college students: Challenges and recommendations. *NASPA Journal, 41*(1), 167–181.

Lipsicas, C. B., & Mäkinen, I. H. (2010). Immigration and suicidality in the young. *Canadian Journal of Psychiatry, 55*, 274–281. Retrieved from ezproxy.library.nyu.edu:2148 /psycinfo/docview/366245581/fulltextPDF/13B0A3D F468E6234D2/1?accountid=12 768

Loya, F., Reddy, R., & Hinshaw, S. P. (2010). Mental illness stigma as a mediator of differences in Caucasian and South Asian college students' attitudes toward psychological counseling. *Journal of Counseling Psychology, 57*, 484–490. doi:10.1037/a0021113

Mollenkopf, J., Waters, M. C., Holdaway, J., & Kasnitz, P. (2005). The ever winding path: Ethnic and racial diversity in the transition to adulthood. In R. A. Settersten, F. F. Fursternberg, & R. G. Rumbaut (Eds.), *On the frontier of adulthood: Theory, research, and public policy* (pp. 225–255). Chicago, IL: University of Chicago Press.

Nickerson, K. J., Helms, J. E., & Terrell, F. (1994). Cultural distrust, opinions about mental illness, and Black students' attitudes toward seeking psychological help from White counselors. *Journal of Counseling Psychology, 41*(3), 378–385. doi:0022-0167/94/$3.00

Rickwood, D. J., Deane, F. P., & Wilson, C. J. (2007). When and how do young people seek professional help for mental health problems? *Medical Journal of Australia, 187*, S35–S39. Retrieved from www.mja.com.au/journal/2007/187/7/when-and-how-do -young-people-seek-professional-help-mental-health-problems?0=ip_login_no_cache %3D04b491ab15554b57582bba49c860b161

Rickwood, D. J., Deane, F. P., Wilson, C. J., & Ciarrochi, J. (2005). Young people's help-seeking for mental health problems. *Australian e-Journal for the Advancement of Mental Health (AeJAMH), 4*, 1–34. Retrieved from www.auseinet.com/journal/vol4iss3suppl /rickwood.pdf

Rumbaut, R. G., & Komaie, G. (2010). Immigration and adult transitions. *The Future of Children, 20*(1), 43–66. Retrieved from futureofchildren.org/_futureofchildren/pub lications/docs/20_01_03.pdf

Snowden, L. R., & Yamada, A. M. (2005). Cultural differences in access to care. *Annual Review of Clinical Psychology, 1*, 143–166. doi:10.1146/annurev.clinpsy.1.102803.143846

Stanton-Salazar, R. D., Chávez, L. F., & Tai, R. H. (2001). The help-seeking orientations of Latino and non-Latino urban high school students: A critical-sociological investigation. *Social Psychology of Education, 5,* 49–82. Retrieved from dx.doi.org/10 .1023/A:1012708332665

Tseng, V. (2004). Family interdependence and academic adjustment in college: Youth from immigrant and US-born families. *Child Development, 75,* 966–983. doi:10.1111/j.1467-8624.2004.00717.x

Weis, L., & Fine, M. (Eds.) (2000). *Construction sites: Excavating race, class, gender, and sexuality spaces for and by youth.* New York, NY: Teachers College Press.

Wilson, C. J., Rickwood, D. J., Bushnell, J. A., Caputi, P., & Thomas, S. J. (2011). The effects of need for autonomy and preference for seeking help from informal sources on emerging adults' intentions to access mental health services for common mental health disorders and suicidal thoughts. *Advances in Mental Health, 10,* 29–38. doi:10.1080/13284200701870954

Yorgason, J. B., Linville, D., & Zitzman, B. (2008). Mental health among college students: Do those who need services know about and use them? *Journal of American College Health, 57,* 173–181. doi:10.3200/JACH.57.2.173-182

Yoshihama, M. (2001). Immigrants-in-context framework: Understanding the interactive influence of socio-cultural contexts. *Evaluation and Program Planning, 24,* 307–318. doi:10.1016/j.bbr.2011.03.031

Yosso, T. J., Smith, W. A., Ceja, M., & Solórzano, D. G. (2009). Critical race theory, racial microaggressions, and campus racial climate for Latina/o undergraduates. *Harvard Educational Review, 79,* 659–690. Retrieved from ezproxy.library.nyu.edu:2108/psycinfo /docview/212300985/fulltextPDF/13B0A164490DDC9315/1?accountid=12768

Zhang, A. Y., Snowden, L. R., & Sue, S. (1998). Differences between Asian and White Americans' help-seeking and utilization patterns in the Los Angeles area. *Journal of Community Psychology, 26,* 317–326. doi:10.1002/(SICI)1520-6629(199807)26:4<317::AID -JCOP2>3.0.CO;2-Q

Part III

THE IMPORTANCE OF RELATIONSHIPS IN COMMUNITY COLLEGES

CHAPTER 9

Immigrant-Origin Community College Students' Experiences with Faculty

Relational Agency or Relational Helplessness?

Carola Suárez-Orozco, Natacha M. Cesar-Davis, & Alfredo Novoa

Faculty and student relationships have been associated with greater levels of student attainment, satisfaction with the college experience, and persistence (Astin, 1993; Tinto, 1997). Although studies have investigated individual and contextual factors associated with the interaction among students and faculty within 4-year institutions, we know much less about the nature of these connections within community colleges (Wirt & Jaeger, 2014). In addition, much of the research on 4-year institutions has not studied student–instructor relationships among historically underserved populations (Chang, 2005). Further, few studies have explored the qualitative perspective of students' relational experiences with their community college faculty.

Relational engagement is the degree to which students feel supported by and connected to their instructors, their college's personnel, and their peers (see Alicea and Suárez-Orozco, Chapter 5). Institutional agents on campus, particularly faculty relationships, can play a crucial role in building confidence and encouraging students to redouble their efforts when motivation fails (Dowd, Pak, & Bensimon, 2013; Hurtado & Carter, 1997). A growing body of evidence indicates that student–faculty relationships and interactions, in particular, have a number of both direct and indirect benefits for students (see Chapter 12) by providing avenues for belonging and identity development, specific instructional feedback and information, and forms of social capital relevant to college and postcollege experiences (Hurtado & Carter, 1997; Stanton-Salazar, 2011). Research suggests that students' relationships with instructors contribute to their academic engagement, academic achievement, and retention as well as to their well-being (Barbatis, 2010; Deil-Amen, 2011; Umbach & Wawrzynski, 2005).

The quality of engagement (Tinto, 2006) has been more widely studied in traditional 4-year student populations (Astin, 1993; Lawson & Lawson, 2013; Wirt & Jaeger, 2014) but remains underexplored in community college settings (Deil-Amen, 2015). Faculty and student interaction has been associated with greater levels of student attainment, satisfaction with the college experience, and low attrition (Astin, 1993; Barnett, 2011). Although studies have investigated the individual and contextual factors associated with the interaction of students and faculty within the 4-year context, we know much less about the nature of these connections within community colleges (Wirt & Jaeger, 2014). In addition, much of the research at 4-year institutions has not focused on interactions between faculty and historically underserved populations (Chang, 2005).

Community colleges tend to serve high-need populations. They also typically have fewer available resources than most 4-year colleges do (Bailey, Jaggars, & Jensen, 2015). In addition, many community colleges depend on an adjunct faculty workforce (Wyles, 1998). Furthermore, immigrant-origin students often concurrently juggle multiple responsibilities with their academic commitments (see Chapter 2). As a result, there is considerable evidence that there may be limited opportunities for optimal student–faculty relationships to flourish on community campuses (Chang, 2005; Hagedorn, Maxwell, Rodriguez, Hocevar, & Fillpot, 2000). Although there has been limited research on student–faculty relationships at community colleges, there is a growing body of evidence indicating their importance (Alicea, Suárez-Orozco, Singh, Darbes, & Abrica, 2016; Deil-Amen & Rosenbaum, 2003).

Research on such student–faculty interactions has focused on the role of these relationships in strengthening the college-going identity of students and their integration into these institutions. It has also examined faculty members' validation and encouragement as mediating factors in students' persistence. These findings show that student–faculty relationships take place in a fusion of social and academic interactions that originate in the classroom. Overall, the research points to how students' relationships with faculty help them develop a sense of belonging to an institution and negotiate the fears that they may have that stem from past educational experiences (Cox, 2010; Hurtado & Ponjuan, 2005). Past research on student–faculty interactions at the community college level has been limited because it often has not disaggregated students—that is, it has presented student experiences as uniform without distinguishing their demographic characteristics.

A study by Barnett (2011) centered on the relationship between the academic validation of community college students and the degree to which these student–faculty relationships predict students' persistence at these institutions. According to this study, higher levels of faculty validation predicted students' academic integration; factors such as caring instruction were some of the most significant predictors. Additionally, higher levels of faculty validation predicted students' statements, particularly those of Latinx and African American students, that they would return to continue their schooling. Deil-Amen (2011) conducted a study interviewing a large diverse group of students; its findings suggest that institutional actors like faculty members play a significant role in their students' adaptation and integration into the college environment. More specifically, interactions with faculty provide social and informational benefits to students, enhancing their sense of belonging, college identity, and college competence (Deil-Amen, 2011). Students identified their preferred interactions with faculty as ones in which faculty demonstrated approachability, flexibility, and availability.

Cox (2010) examined the role of faculty members in mediating the fears and anxieties students experience when enrolling in and attending community colleges. She found that despite students' feeling compelled to enroll in community colleges to fulfill their educational and career aspirations, most of them experienced and expressed fear while in classrooms. Their fear of failure had the potential to undermine their educational and professional goals (Cox, 2010). Her study found that professors who maintained high expectations for students by assigning them college-level work, provided explicit instructions for every assignment and resolved to have a personal relationship with students, helped reduce their instances of failure. Additionally, faculty who actively addressed students' fears at the beginning of class and provided high levels of validation throughout the duration of the course stood out to students.

Although research on student–faculty relationships in community colleges has been sparse, it is evident that there are variations in levels of student–faculty relationships (from low to high) and that higher levels of successful interactions matter for better educational outcomes. There is also some evidence from research at 4-year campuses suggesting that marginalized students are less likely to form close relationships with instructors (Berardi, 2012; Museus & Ravello, 2010; Rios-Aguilar & Deil-Amen, 2012; Tinto, 1993). Furthermore, it is evident that students bring with them different relational experiences, particularly those related to receiving support, and vary in terms of their comfort levels when engaging with and seeking out support from instructors (Karabenick, 2004). Some research suggests that these variations are connected to cultural and class differences in norms and expectations (Collier & Morgan, 2008; Lareau & Cox, 2011). The role of students' characteristics in influencing their relationships with instructors has yet to be explored in the community college setting. Another area that has been overlooked in seeking to understand students' own experiences is the ways in which their actual interactions with faculty compare with their expectations for such interactions in order to inform institutional culture and pedagogical practice.

CHAPTER AIMS

This chapter examines how immigrant-origin students with contrasting levels of relational engagement attending community colleges perceive "positive" and "negative" experiences and how they describe what a "good" relationship with a faculty member is. Our intent is to give voice to this growing sector of the community college population and provide insights that could shape more responsive pedagogical practice. Our research questions included the following: How do students describe their *positive experiences* with faculty? How do they describe their *negative experiences* with faculty? How does each of these groups of students describe *what a good relationship* with a faculty member should be? Considering each of the faculty experiences (positive, negative, and ideal), in what ways do the perceptions of students who scored high on the relational engagement self-report measure contrast or overlap with those of students who reported low levels of relational engagement?

DRAWING FROM RICC

Data for this chapter were drawn from the Research on Immigrants in Community College (RICC) Study that explored the relationships between the classroom and campus environments and indicators of success such as academic engagement and performance, focusing on immigrant-origin students (see online appendix for details). The relational engagement responses and demographic data draw on the student survey responses collected during Phase 2, while the qualitative part of this chapter draws on 60 semistructured interviews with students (20 from each campus) collected during Phase 3. Each interview lasted between 45 and 90 minutes, and all were recorded and transcribed verbatim. To enhance the reliability of the data collection, a team of interviewers used a standardized interview format and script (Babbie, 2004).

During the course of our interviews, we asked participants to reflect on both their positive and negative experiences with faculty during their time taking courses and to provide their views of what a good relationship with a faculty member should be like. For the qualitative analyses, we compared the responses of immigrant-origin students who reported high levels of relational engagement with the responses of those who reported low levels in order to gain insights into their experiences with faculty (Lieber, 2009). The data for the qualitative analysis came from a subset of 28 students who self-reported among the highest and lowest levels of relational engagement on the survey questionnaire. This selection process was made by ranking, from lowest to highest, the 60 interviewees' survey responses with the student–faculty relational engagement composite variable (Cronbach's Alpha= .92). We then selected for analysis those participants who provided the lowest ($N = 15$) and highest ($N = 13$) scores on relational engagement. Participants' average age was 20 ($SD = 2.2$). See Table 9.1 for additional demographic information about this sample.

A team of three researchers qualitatively analyzed the interviews by first employing a hybrid deductive and inductive coding approach (Fereday & Muir-Cochrane, 2006). After the emerging first cycle codes were reviewed, categories were further coalesced into fewer themes and subthemes (Saldaña, 2015). To enhance the reliability of the coding of the data, coders were similarly trained and underwent two rounds of reliability analysis wherein disagreements were discussed and resolved.

Table 9.1. Demographic Characteristics of Qualitative Sample by
Relational Engagement Level

Characteristic		% Low (*n* = 15)	% High (*n* = 13)
Gender	Female	73.3	23.1
	Male	26.7	76.9
Race and ethnicity	Asian	6.7	23.1
	Black	46.7	15.4
	Latinx	33.3	53.9
	White	13.3	7.7
Immigrant generation	First	46.7	38.5
	Second	53.3	61.5

POSITIVE EXPERIENCES WITH FACULTY

When participants were asked to reflect on positive faculty experiences, several themes emerged. Some noted that faculty with whom they had had a positive experience had attended to their practical learning needs; others mentioned that their instructors had been attuned to socioemotional and relational issues.

Low Relationally Engaged Participants' Perspectives

Several low relationally engaged participants said that they appreciated some faculty members' attention to their learning needs. For example, Tyona,[1] a 19-year-old first-generation Jamaican-origin student, said that she appreciated her instructor's focus on teaching for students' comprehension of the material:

> [He would] go over the information with us and explain it in a way that [applied] to something that we knew in our current lifestyle. He didn't just say, "OK, this is from this textbook; we are discussing this today" and read everything from the textbook or everything from his teaching plan. He would give us the information and say, "OK, discuss it in small groups; then we are going to come together as a group [to] tell me what you think." It is nice to be able to voice how we are absorbing the information so [that] when I give [my response], I can know that . . . I am learning [the material] the right way or doing the right thing.

Likewise, Mahlia, a 22-year-old first-generation Philippine-origin student, noted that she liked receiving tangible feedback and being prompted to do deeper work: "I guess you could say my library professor [provides] . . . really good input on some of our work [by saying], 'Maybe you could explain this a little bit more.'" Similarly, Destin, a 22-year-old second-generation Jamaican-origin student, mentioned that his professor's keeping him informed of his class progress helped him. He described a professor who,

> in the middle of the semester, . . . let you know if you were on track to pass or if you were [going] to fail. If you were on track to fail, you could start making sure to get on track. Some professors wouldn't do that . . . so you [would be] clueless [about your class standing].

Other students who were on the less-engaged end of the spectrum stated that they appreciated teachers who made their classes interesting and who were also helpful in their approach to teaching. For example, 18-year-old Russian-born Nikolai described the effort and care demonstrated by one of his instructors:

> He'd crack corny math jokes and stuff like that. . . . Not even after every lesson [but] after every problem we did on the board, . . . he would always ask, "Does anybody have any questions?" He wouldn't just leave it up to the students to ask questions. He would always ask us. . . . I knew he wanted to help. He was actually there to help us.

Highly Relationally Engaged Participants' Perspectives

Similarly, participants who reported high relational engagement appreciated animated instruction. Ron, a 19-year-old Chinese-origin second-generation student, told in great detail about his best instructor:

> He was a great storyteller. . . . I actually looked forward to that class. . . . People were never absent. Everyone enjoyed going to class. . . . You could see [his passion] on his face. He was loving his career. [His enthusiasm] radiated from him. And we really enjoyed learning from this guy. And then, . . . since we're paying more attention, he wants to teach more. And since he wants to teach more, you want to learn more. [His approach] creates a very powerful, positive feedback, which is key in life. . . . Treat people like people, I guess.

Students who were highly relationally engaged were also quite detailed in their responses concerning other aspects of their experiences with good instruction. Several of them spoke of how instructors with whom they had had positive experiences made themselves available to them in a variety of ways. For example, Jessica, a 19-year-old Honduran-origin second-generation student, explained:

> [At] every class [this instructor is] telling us when he's in his office, so if anybody wants to stop by and talk about an essay that they are about to

write, he'll give us pointers about how to write it. . . . After we hand in our essays, he emails us our grades and tell us why he gave us the grade. He'll tell us what we need to work on the next time we write an essay.

Nineteen-year-old Alvaro, a second-generation Dominican-origin student, spoke of a teacher whom he described as "nice":

If we ever needed her for help or anything, she always asked us to stay after class or go to her office. . . . She also [held] group sessions after the classes, so basically if you didn't have a class next or if you wanted more help, she would take the time to stay after class and . . . actually go over [the material] in further detail, explain more about it . . . , so [that] was very helpful.

In addition, Alvaro noted that this teacher

would help me out, show me the ropes . . . so that I didn't look like a fool in front of everybody. . . . [She would] take the time to actually show me what to do, [tell me about] programs that I could take to improve, [and give me] books to read that would help me build up my vocabulary, . . . so she actually helped [me] a lot.

Several students who reported high relational engagement expressed their appreciation not only for the tangible and practical ways in which instructors had supported them but also for the ways in which they had provided socioemotional support. One simple way was to take the time to get to know them. Nineteen-year-old Dominican-born Jhony, for example, told the interviewer that he appreciated the fact that his instructor had learned about his new students early on:

[The math teacher] knew that I was not from [the United States]. . . . At the beginning of the class, [he] gives [students] a paper with all the requirements and all the information, and there is [a place] on the paper [asking], "Tell me about yourself, tell me what your goals are, and tell me about what is a struggle and what is difficult for you," so he [will know your situation].

In some cases, these social supports involved deep listening and the provision of emotional support. Janice, a 25-year-old second-generation Irish-American, commented,

Professor Pedroza was an emotional support to me. She let me be myself in a way I couldn't be with my other professors. . . . She had complete confidence in me; . . . she was very reassuring and very comforting. . . . I could just be honest with her. . . . I was honest with her when I was frustrated with how we were learning in class; and I was like "I'm not gonna get this; I'm not gonna pass."

On rare occasions, students with high levels of relational engagement described the development of mentoring relationships when faculty made the effort to know them. Silvino, a 19-year-old Cape Verdean–origin first-generation student, talked about how a special instructor reached out to him, changing his initial academic trajectory:

> It developed through my trying in his class but not succeeding, and then he [said], "Well, I see you are really good with this topic due to what is occurring, but I see some lack of test scores." . . . [I was] still joining the college movement, the college vibe toward education. . . . I wasn't really all there such as focus and school. That occurred first semester, and then second semester he [said], "Well, we should keep in touch." And then I joined the club he was advising so [that] I could get to see [him] a little bit more, talk to him about what went down through my years, and then he signed me up [so that he could be] my mentor.

NEGATIVE EXPERIENCES WITH FACULTY

Students who reported both low and high levels of relational engagement were able to clearly describe their negative experiences with faculty. Broadly, students' concerns were in the following areas: teachers who invested little of themselves in their teaching, teachers who were condescending or unfair toward students, and those who employed inadequate teaching methods.

Perspectives of Participants with Low Relational Engagement

The complaint of teachers not investing in their students was mentioned with disconcerting frequency. Sergei, an 18-year-old first-generation Russian, noted:

> Nobody really knows who you are. . . . You are just another student to most teachers. . . . I feel like at least 70 percent of the teachers really just don't care. They go [to their jobs] just to earn their paychecks. . . . Like my first semester math teacher. He really could care less if you understood or not. He'd just go there, teach, leave. Immediately. He would leave before the students [did]. And he was never really there for extra help or anything like that. Never really offered it. One time a week—I guess that's probably because they made him. And I don't know if he ever did test corrections; he never did homework corrections. Go there, teach, give a test, leave. And that's it.

One way that students felt this lack of concern was demonstrated by a teacher's sticking too closely to materials in the textbook. Ronica, a 19-year-old first-generation Jamaican, explained:

When [a lot of instructors] are teaching the material, . . . they teach either verbatim from the book or from whatever notes they have, and they don't really try to apply [the material]. . . . They are just so stuck on it being, well, it is in the book like this, I am going to tell it to you like this, . . . this is what it is, you study it this way because that is what it is. . . . It is nice to be able to [tell] how we are absorbing the information so [that] when I give it back . . . , I can know that . . . I am learning it the right way, or I am doing the right thing.

Some students felt that their community college instructors made their low expectations all too evident. Paula, a 25-year-old Colombian-born student, said about one of her teachers:

She would yell at us even when no one was really talking. It was like [we would ask] [whispered], "Hey, what did she say?" [She would respond,] "SHUT UP." Her teaching style was just like dealing with kindergartners. She didn't treat us like adults at all.

Other students complained that faculty communicated their disdain for them along with unclear expectations. Ronica, a 20-year-old second-generation Jamaican-origin student, commented:

Nothing was good enough for this lady. [I could] rewrite the paper three times, and she'd still tell me, "It's not good enough. I need more. I want more. . . . Her expectations . . . [were] just a little too high. . . . She [had] taught at . . . some top-notch school, and . . . [her attitude was] "This is beneath me." . . . She gave everyone that kind of a vibe. . . . It's just like you didn't even want to be [in her] class; you just did it to get by.

Similarly, Abigay, a 19-year-old first-generation Jamaican female, recalled her clear memory of being treated condescendingly when she stayed after class to ask an instructor a question:

I can't remember exactly what I asked . . . , and he just stood there and looked at me and [said], "Do you want to ask that question again?" . . . I looked back at him [and replied], "How else can I ask you the question?" He [answered], "Just think about it." And I was like, "You know what; I am just leaving," and I just left.

Instructors' disconnection from and in some cases even disdain for their students create an atmosphere of distrust and anomie and discourage students from seeking help. Indeed, such interactions lead to a kind of relational helplessness for some students.

Highly Relationally Engaged Participants' Perspectives

Many of the students who reported being highly relationally engaged also reported having had negative experiences with instructors. The themes that emerged for
these students were similar to those for students with low relational engagement.

For example, Martin, a 19-year-old Dominican-American, felt that too many
instructors were "just there to get their paychecks":

> Certain teachers do treat students with respect, . . . [but] a majority of other
> teachers . . . wouldn't bother. They are just there to get their paychecks like
> everybody else; then [they] just walk out. Most of the teachers won't bother
> to ask you if you need additional help. . . . They will kind of tell you [that
> you] will have to figure that out on your own.

Others noted that many of their instructors came to class poorly prepared.
Janice, a 25-year-old Irish-American, told us:

> Most of our teachers . . . were able to contribute to what was on the
> slides. . . . Even if they used slides that [had been] made by the textbook
> manufacturing company, which many of them did, they would contribute
> tremendously to what content was there, or they would have at least read the
> slides before class. [However, one teacher] mispronounced things left, right,
> and center. She didn't know . . . what was coming up on the next slide. She
> was just very unprepared all the time.

Juan, a 19-year-old second-generation Dominican-American, spoke for many
of his classmates who found it disconcerting that some of their instructors were
unwilling to invest in their classroom relationships:

> My math teacher . . . gave off a vibe that he wasn't there to help you. He
> would teach the class, he [would] do everything, and then he [would
> say,] "OK, I will see you next class." That was it. When he first came into
> the classroom and introduced himself, he basically didn't even introduce
> himself; he just said, "This is my name," and then he went straight into the
> lessons. . . . He noticed that a lot of people were failing, . . . but he [would]
> always just say, "Oh, there is always tutoring."

Notably, students with high overall relationship engagement scores still reported having poor instructional experiences, many involving issues of unfair
treatment. For example, Willy, a 19-year-old Chinese-American, described one of
his instructors:

> I think he was kind of racist because there were also a couple of [other]
> Asians in class, and they were picked on a lot by [him]. . . . We [Asians

would] always get yelled at even though . . . during group work [others] would chat a little. . . . When it was the Hispanics, it seemed like he [was] scared of them.

A highly engaged 24-year-old Ecuadorian-American, Steven, related a disconcerting incident between an instructor and another student:

[The instructor was] kind of . . . condescending to [a student] in front of the class [because the student had] walked in late on the first day, and I understand that [he was annoyed]. But . . . I don't think you need to do that, especially if you're just getting to know a student.

In addition, other highly engaged students spoke about the importance of agency in reaching out to faculty members. As Edvard, a 19-year-old first-generation Cape Verdean, explained:

If you don't get to know [teachers], they will just treat you like any other [student]. . . . Think about them having . . . 90 students, and only 10 of them interact with the professor, talk to [him]. You have a better chance of doing [well] in class [if] you know the professor. You could ask him [for] help any time . . . [because] you know him. If you don't [ask for help], you are most likely . . . a person who just [doesn't] know him, and you are just left off the edge if you ever need any help.

A "GOOD" FACULTY RELATIONSHIP

One of the interview questions asked students to reflect on what a good student–faculty relationship should be like. This, combined with the other questions, led to responses that provide insights into what immigrant-origin students explicitly want from their instructors.

In particular, students who had low relational engagement and who may have had histories of poor relationships with instructors were sensitive to being patronized. A 19-year-old first-generation Jamaican student asked for simple respect in her interactions: "I don't want to feel stupid whenever I go to speak with the professors. They tend to talk down to students as if we are not going to understand, as if we are children. . . . You don't have to talk down to me, like saying, 'No, don't do that.'" Similarly, James, a 22-year-old second-generation Trinidadian, asserted the importance of receiving fair treatment from instructors: "A good professor [is] someone who is understanding, someone who helps you succeed in the course that [he is] teaching. . . . He is not looking to favor you, but he is not looking to fail you, [either], because there are some professors who are looking for a way to make you fail."

Both students with self-reported high and students with self-reported low relational engagement tended to have remarkably consistent views about what they thought a good community college student–instructor relationship should provide to support student success. Many noted that it was important for faculty to be invested in a student–instructor relationship. Haeckl, a 19-year-old male Cape Verdean student with high relational engagement, remarked that instructors should get to know basic things about their students. For example, he said they should "know your first name from the attendance [roster]—my name is very hard to pronounce." Sylvie, an 18-year-old first-generation Haitian with low self-reported relational engagement, emphasized the importance of being courteous in interactions: "Being respectful of each other and respecting [a person's] need when she asks you for something. You don't make fun of her—[either] the student or the professor." Joaquin, a 19-year-old second-generation male of Dominican origin with high relational engagement, mentioned the value of available and helpful faculty: "It would be nice for them to actually be more involved with their students, to actually take the time to do some one-on-ones with their students. I know that there may be a lot of students in a class. . . . Not everybody may need the help, but if a certain student does need help, I believe [instructors] should be there to help her out." Eighteen-year-old Russian-born Nikolai, who reported low relational engagement, summed things up by saying: "I would forcefully make all of the[m] more interested in the students."

Students also made practical suggestions about ways that instructors could help students. One key issue that frequently emerged was the importance of availability and having an open-door policy. Both high and low relationally engaged students spoke of their frustration with not being able to get in touch with many of their instructors and their appreciation when they could connect with those who were available. As Tyona, a 19-year-old second-generation Jamaican, explained:

> I would say a professor who leaves his door open to students and gives us multiple ways to contact him [is essential] because there are some professors who will [say], "OK, this is my office hour; come at such and such a time," but you go there and they are never there. So . . . what is the point of giving me your office hour [time] if you are not going to be there? . . . I should be able to feel comfortable going to my professor and talking about something that I don't understand.

Students also provided pedagogical advice. One key recommendation was that instructors be interesting. As Jaime, a Dominican-origin 18-year-old second-generation male with low relational engagement, explained: "Good ones are, like, funny professors—you know, like really interesting professors; they talk about themselves, and they really like teaching the class with enthusiasm." Also, a common response across engagement types was the importance of faculty's striving to foster learning in terms of both relationships with students and course content. Highly relationally engaged 19-year-old Alvaro, a second-generation Dominican-origin student, said he would like "teachers who will actually be there, like [for a] . . . one-on-one relationship, but who also . . . [will help] you understand what they are trying to teach you—not . . . a teacher who will just come in and continue writing notes on the board. [I want a] teacher who will actually sit down in the class and explain the stuff." Last, a teacher who will offer discussion as part of the learning experience was valued by all types of students. For example, Josefina, a 25-year-old second-generation Colombian student with self-reported low relational engagement, remarked that an ideal student–faculty relationship is one in which "the teacher speaks freely in front of his students, and the students reply, and they have a conversation. You know, really like a Dead Poets' Society kind of situation [in which there is] a conversation in the classroom.

IN SUM

The evidence gleaned from these interviews was in some ways surprising. We had anticipated that there would be somewhat more divergence in the stated experiences of students who reported high levels of relational engagement and those of students reporting low levels on the scaled measure when they described positive and negative encounters. We were curious to find out whether there would be any differences in their idealized hopes or aspirations for what they thought a relationship with an instructor should be like.

We learned that when it came to positive student–instructor relationships, both groups of students especially appreciated instruction that was engaging. They also looked for helpful instructors who both were available to them and demonstrated flexibility. Although participants who had reported low relational engagement were specifically likely to mention their appreciation for tangible and regular feedback from instructors on their progress in a course, highly engaged participants, on the other hand, spoke about and noted the importance of caring instructors and mentorship.

When it came to reflecting on negative experiences with faculty, there was quite a lot of overlap in concerns articulated by both the groups. Both students who had scored highly on relational engagement and those with low scores criticized faculty who were unprepared and unwilling to invest more than the minimum effort in their students and teaching. A theme of simply wanting instructors to "be there!" emerged from the responses of both groups. Being there included a variety of notions of at least an instructor's minimal presence and engagement—ranging from coming to class well prepared and going beyond material in the textbook, to making themselves available for office hours to further explain material, to demonstrating interest in their students.

The last set of questions revolved around what immigrant-origin students desired in their relationships with faculty. Again, there was remarkable overlap in responses from both groups—those with high and those with low relational engagement. Students wanted faculty who would be interested in them and would take the time to get to know them. They wanted faculty who would demonstrate their interest in them in small ways like learning their names but who also would keep office hours. They asked for faculty who would be interesting and engaging, prepared for class, and willing to engage in conversations with students in class.

Despite the similarities, some important distinctions emerged between the responses of students with high relational engagement and those with low levels of relational engagement. In particular, students who reported low levels of relational engagement were particularly sensitive to condescension. These students may have had a history of such incidences in high school that may have made them particularly sensitive to subsequent occurrences (Solorozano, Ceja, & Yosso, 2000) (see also Chapters 6 and 10). Repeated exposures to condescending interactions with teachers, we further speculate, may lead students with low levels of relational engagement to a kind of relational helplessness. On the other hand, the highly engaged students were more likely to call out unfair treatment of others. Furthermore, these students also came to develop strategies to "get to know" their teachers and to reach out to other instructors in hopes of getting assistance. In short, they appeared to have developed strategies of relational agency that empowered them to navigate any less than optimal instructional encounters.

When one reviews the reflections of study participants, it is apparent that in many ways their interactions with faculty were far from optimal and, in fact, often frustrating. Quality connections with thoughtful, well-prepared, invested faculty seem to have been the exception rather than the rule. Classes were often not as engaging as they should be, and students were left feeling incompetent or minimized (see Chapter 6). Although certainly there were examples of excellent instructors and dedicated professors mentioned, students had to seek them out.

This situation is worrisome for all students but all the more so for immigrant-origin students, who may be relatively new to the educational context within the United States or who may enter these settings with specialized needs and may require institutional agents who are attuned to them (Deil-Amen & Rosenbaum, 2003). This research provides insights into immigrant-origin students' perspectives on their relationships with faculty. Clearly, from their vantage point, there is much progress to be made.

The implications for intervention are daunting. Although small private 4-year colleges recognize the significance of student–faculty relationships, carefully select professors for their attention to pedagogy, and create small seminar classes, community colleges have much less in the way of resources and depend on rotating adjunct faculty who commute to campus, as do their students. Nevertheless, the data in this chapter point to some of the commonalities of experiences that all students seem to be facing and that faculty could address—being prepared for class, exhibiting basic respect for students, and not being condescending toward them, for example. These are basic expectations that should be made clear to faculty and enforced through meaningful evaluations (see Chapter 5). Furthermore, the data provide specific ways in which students who are particularly relationally disempowered could be provided supports and training to counteract the "college fear factor" (Cox, 2010) by learning successful strategies for approaching faculty in order to be better able to meet their learning needs (see Chapter 14).

NOTE

1. All names used in this chapter are pseudonyms.

REFERENCES

Alicea, S., Suárez-Orozco, C., Singh, S., Darbes, T., & Abrica, E. J. (2016). Observing class-room engagement in community college: A systematic approach. *Educational Evaluation and Policy Analysis, 38*(4), 757–782.

Astin, A. W. (1993). *What matters in college? Four critical years revisited* (Vol. 1). San Francisco, CA: Jossey-Bass.

Babbie, E. (2004). *The practice of social research* (10th ed.). Belmont, CA: Wadsworth.

Bailey, T. R., Jaggars, S. S., & Jenkins, D. (2015). *Redesigning America's community colleges.* Cambridge, MA: Harvard University Press.

Barbatis, P. (2010). Underprepared, ethnically diverse community college students: Factors contributing to persistence. *Journal of Developmental Education, 33*(3), 14.

Barnett, E. A. (2011). Validation experiences and persistence among community college students. *The Review of Higher Education, 34*(2), 193–230.

Berardi, L. (2012). The first year college experience: Predictors of natural mentoring relationships & students' academic outcomes. *College of Science and Health Theses and Dissertations, 13.* Retrieved from via.library.depaul.edu/csh_etd/13

Chang, J. C. (2005). Faculty student interaction at the community college: A focus on students of color. *Research in Higher Education, 46*(7), 769–802.

Collier, P. J., & Morgan, D. L. (2008). "Is that paper really due today?": Differences in first-generation and traditional college students' understandings of faculty expectations. *Higher Education, 55*(4), 425–446.

Cox, R. D. (2010). *The college fear factor.* Cambridge, MA: Harvard University Press.

Deil-Amen, R. (2011). Socio-academic integrative moments: Rethinking academic and social integration among two-year college students in career-related programs. *The Journal of Higher Education, 82*(1), 54–91.

Deil-Amen, R., & Rosenbaum, J. E. (2003). The social prerequisites of success: Can college structure reduce the need for social know-how? *The Annals of the American Academy of Political and Social Science, 586*(1), 120–143.

Dowd, A. C., Pak, J. H., & Bensimon, E. M. (2013). The role of institutional agents in promoting transfer access. *Education Policy Analysis Archives/Archivos Analíticos de Políticas Educativas, 21*(15), 1–44.

Fereday, J., & Muir-Cochrane, E. (2006). Demonstrating rigor using thematic analysis: A hybrid approach of inductive and deductive coding and theme development. *International Journal of Qualitative Methods, 5*(1), 80–92.

Hagedorn, L. S., Maxwell, W., Rodriguez, P., Hocevar, D., & Fillpot, J. (2000). Peer and student-faculty relations in community colleges. *Community College Journal of Research & Practice, 24*(7), 587–598.

Hurtado, S., & Carter, D. F. (1997). Effects of college transition and perceptions of the campus racial climate on Latino college students' sense of belonging. *Sociology of Education, 70*(4), 324–345.

Hurtado, S., & Ponjuan, L. (2005). Latino educational outcomes and the campus climate. *Journal of Hispanic Higher Education, 4*(3), 235–251.

Karabenick, S. A. (2004). Perceived achievement goal structure and college student help seeking. *Journal of Educational Psychology, 96*(3), 569.

Lareau, A., & Cox, A. (2011). Social class and the transition to adulthood. In M. J. Carlson & P. England (Eds.), *Social class and changing families in an unequal America* (pp. 134–164). Palo Alto, CA; Stanford University Press.

Lawson, M. A., & Lawson, H. A. (2013). New conceptual frameworks for student engagement research, policy, and practice. *Review of Educational Research, 83*(3), 432–479.

Lieber, E. (2009). Mixing qualitative and quantitative methods: Insights into design and analysis issues. *Journal of Ethnographic & Qualitative Research, 3*(4), 218–227.

Martinez, G. F., & Deil-Amen, R. (2015). College for all Latinos? The role of high school messages in facing college challenges. *Teachers College Record, 117*(3).

Museus, S. D., & Ravello, J. N. (2010). Characteristics of academic advising that contribute to racial and ethnic minority student success at predominantly White institutions. *NACADA Journal, 30*(1), 47–58.

Rios-Aguilar, C., & Deil-Amen, R. (2012). Beyond getting in and fitting in: An examination of social networks and professionally relevant social capital among Latina/o university students. *Journal of Hispanic Higher Education, 11*(2), 179–196.

Saldaña, J. (2015). *The coding manual for qualitative researchers.* Thousand Oaks, CA: Sage.

Solorozano, D., Ceja, M., & Yosso, T. (2000). Critical race theory, racial microaggressions, and campus racial climate: The experiences of African American college students. *The Journal of Negro Education, 69*(1), 60–73.

Stanton-Salazar, R. D. (2011). A social capital framework for the study of institutional agents and their role in the empowerment of low-status students and youth. *Youth & Society, 43*, 1066–1109.

Tinto, V. (1993). *Leaving college: Rethinking the causes and cures of student attrition* (2nd ed.). Chicago, IL: University of Chicago Press.

Tinto, V. (1997). Classrooms as communities: Exploring the educational character of student persistence. *The Journal of Higher Education, 68*(6), 599–623.

Tinto, V. (2006). Research and practice of student retention: What next? *Journal of College Student Retention: Research, Theory & Practice, 8*(1), 1–19.

Umbach, P. D., & Wawrzynski, M. R. (2005). Faculty do matter: The role of college faculty in student learning and engagement. *Research in Higher Education, 46*(2), 153–184.

Wirt, L. G., & Jaeger, A. J. (2014). Seeking to understand faculty-student interaction at community colleges. *Community College Journal of Research and Practice, 38*(11), 980–994.

Wyles, B. A. (1998). Adjunct faculty in the community college: Realities and challenges. *New Directions for Higher Education, 1998*(104), 89–93.

CHAPTER 10

Through a Lens of Deficit

Faculty and Administrator Perceptions of Immigrant-Origin Students

Heather Herrera, Margary Martin, & Natacha M. Cesar-Davis

The academic success of immigrant-origin students in higher education is often compromised by several risk factors: lack of college pathway knowledge, limited parental education, insufficient college readiness, competing familial obligations, English-language acquisition, remedial course work, and inadequate financial support (Cerna et al., 2009; Teranishi et al., 2011). Beyond the personal and structural challenges that immigrant-origin students face, research shows that academic outcomes are further shaped by high-stakes policies and practices such as admissions, placement testing, remediation, advisement, and financial aid (Leinbach & Bailey, 2006). This chapter presents findings on faculty and administrators' perceptions of immigrant-origin students at three community colleges and offers insights on how inert policy is enacted in practice, thus shaping the opportunities for and impediments to the success of immigrant-origin students (Conway, 2009).

POLICIES AND PRACTICES

Higher education is premised on policies and practices designed to serve student academic success. However, for many immigrant students, the path to college completion can be a maze of dead ends and backtracking due to arbitrary policies and ineffective practices (Zarkesh & Carducci, 2004). In many instances the educational trajectories of immigrant-origin students are thwarted by admissions policies that funnel students into community colleges with placement exams that assign them to noncredit remedial courses (Pascarella et al., 1998).

From a policy standpoint, remedial education requires that colleges and universities confront questions about access and academic standards (Soliday, 2002). Remediated courses include developmental math, English composition, reading, and English as a Second Language (ESL) and are routinely noncredit-bearing. Perceptions of remedial education may be interpreted through the lens of public opinion, which often takes a polemic stance: *Is education an expense or an invest-ment? Is it a personal privilege or a public good?* For some policymakers and educa-tors, remediation is an extension of the egalitarian promise of education (Soliday, 2002). For others, it is a drain on resources for a mythologized "always new un-deserving student" (Stanley, 2010). These perceptions have consequences for the academic pathways available to immigrant-origin community college students.

THE ROLE OF PERCEPTIONS

Research has examined stakeholder perceptions from many vantage points. For example, as a means of studying the retention and graduation rates of commu-nity college students, Moss and Young (1995) investigated how the perception of students' academic integration into an institution varies according to the roles of institutional agents such as administrators, faculty, and counselors. The study found that administrators shared the most negative views of remedial students and maintained that these students were the least prepared to be in college and were less likely than others to integrate socially. Counselors exhibited slightly fewer negative perceptions. Faculty were the most likely to believe in remedial students' abilities to succeed socially and academically.

Valadez (1993) examined the perceptions held by faculty and administrators about underrepresented students and explored how attitudes held by the institu-tional stakeholders shaped the academic achievement of students. His research found that faculty and administrators often projected expectations rooted in their own backgrounds and in the values of "traditional students" (students not of immigrant origin who enroll in college immediately after high school) onto "nontraditional" students (adults who enter in their mid-20s or when older). The expectations about what a student should be expected to do contradicted what faculty and administrators acknowledged was reasonable to expect for nontradi-tional students who faced a variety of obstacles. The faculty and administrators in Valadez's study resolved the tension in their contradicting perceptions (what they believe and what was realistic) by concluding that nontraditional students were un-suited to the demands of college. These findings highlight the detriment caused by projecting one's cultural norms onto marginalized students. In Valadez's study, he discovered faculty and administrators practicing *deficit thinking* as they perceived nontraditional students as inherently inadequate, and they ignored or discounted the role of structural issues that interfere with academic achievement (Smit, 2012).

CHAPTER AIMS

With limited research available on institutional perceptions of immigrant-origin community college students, we sought to answer the following founda-tional questions: *(1) What perceptions do faculty and administrators hold about their immigrant-origin students, and (2) how do these perceptions shape their per-spectives of how their institutions should address the needs of immigrant-origin students?*

To examine these questions, we applied an analytical approach grounded in the concept of *mental models* that emanates from Senge's (1994) theory of systems thinking. Senge (1994) defines mental models as deeply held subconscious navigational tools that individuals use to maneuver and operate in daily life; hence, they are instructive for understanding policy and pedagogical decision-making. Another concept of mental models is the idea that problems arise when mental models are tacit and located at the subconscious level. If we remain unaware of our mental models, systems thinking contends, our pervasive assumptions limit our ability to imagine alternative possibilities; therefore, behaviors, ideas, practices, and relationships become inert and stagnate (Duffy, 2006).

Twenty-three faculty members and administrators across three participating community colleges were interviewed in the Research on Immigrants in Community College Study using a semistructured protocol (see online appendix for details). Nine administrators were interviewed; they included two provosts and a vice president as well as three deans and three counseling program administrators evenly distributed across the three campuses. Fourteen faculty interviews from the larger study were drawn randomly by campus; these were with five instructors of either remedial math or remedial English, three ESL instructors, and six instructors of general education courses.

To analyze the interviews, we used both deductive and inductive coding strategies. Using Senge's (1994) model, we used deductive coding to identify categories of mental models. Within each category, inductive coding (Glaser & Strauss, 1967) allowed for key themes to emerge within and across the individual interviews (see Table 10.1 in online appendix to view code definitions and examples). Finally, we examined these mental models together to see how they related to and contradicted each other.

ADMINISTRATOR AND FACULTY PERCEPTIONS
OF IMMIGRANT-ORIGIN STUDENTS

Administrators and faculty members were asked to reflect on how their immigrant-origin students were similar to and distinct from their nonimmigrant-origin students. Our analysis of faculty members' and administrators' interviews reveal a typology of perceptions about immigrant-origin students that primarily consists of mental models of students as academically deficient, academically unsocialized, yet persistent. Similarly, administrators and faculty recognized the personal demands such as work placed on students that competed with their study time, but they simultaneously assigned blame to students for their academic underperformance and poor rates of completion, views that exposed contradictions and cognitive dissonance.

Academic Deficiencies

Faculty and administrators exhibited a prevalent mental model that immigrant-origin students generally lacked academic and socioemotional readiness for college-level work. In some cases, faculty specifically noted that their students were unprepared for college. In one interview, a math instructor expressed a common perception:

> I go into precalculus with a certain expectation that they have already taken and passed college algebra with trig, . . . that they remember, retain some of the stuff, and a lot of time I would find, especially in precalc and also in business precalc, . . . that's not the case. So I have to spend time reviewing or spend time to go over things that I expect them to already remember, know from the past, and they don't. So that tends to be difficult for me.

Similarly, administrators remarked that students were not ready for college-level work and attributed the "deficiencies" to their immigrant status. One administrator said, "I think that immigrant-origin students who may be first generation here may have deficiencies in English as English skill sets." Another administrator explained, "I get a lot of students who are not ready because they are recent immigrants. So a lot of them don't have the English that they need to continue [in] a lot of the upper-level courses."

Other administrators spoke of their immigrant-origin students as academically unprepared regardless of generational status:

> The irony is [that] when you talk about the immigrant that actually came [to the U.S.] at an early age or [who is] American born, excuse me, American educated, or second generation, it seems a lot of them have the same unpreparedness as everybody else. . . . I've seen students who were completely unprepared. They shouldn't really be here, and either they're immigrants and they're not literate in their own languages, . . . [or they are] students who are second generation and [were] educated here who for whatever reason did not get the education they needed.

Administrators and faculty alike perceived the lack of preparedness as adversely interfering with students' abilities to earn their degrees on time and transfer to 4-year universities. Despite some immigrant-origin students' entering community college underprepared, when asked, six out of seven faculty members optimistically asserted that these students' graduating in 2 years was nonetheless "doable." A faculty member shared,

> If a student's coming in prepared enough and is ready enough, [she or he] certainly can complete the associate degree in two years and then transfer. The problem we encounter is [that] a lot of students come in and they're not

prepared; they're underprepared. They either have to [take] development courses, which most of the time it's not just one [course;] it's a few; it's English and math. . . . Having to repeat courses set[s] them back, failing and just not completing, you know, so a lot of time because of those reasons, it's a lot longer than two years. But certainly, it's doable.

Others were more pessimistic. In response to our question about what could be done to shorten these students' time to graduation, an administrator responded, "How does that happen? If they get to us and they're not prepared, it's too late." Another administrator, recognizing the multiplicity of issues contributing to the challenge of graduating on time, explained, "I think that most of our immigrant students have some level of underpreparedness that will extend that time. I think that most of our immigrant students have other equal priorities that make it unlikely for them to [attend] continuously for two years."

Academic Socialization

Faculty often lamented immigrant-origin students' social behaviors and dispositions, such as their work ethic, time management, motivation, self-regulation, maturity, and persistence. When asked to describe the academic abilities of their students, faculty instead frequently described students' social behaviors. For example, a remedial English instructor responded, "They don't do homework, they don't buy the book, [and] they don't have pencils. They don't understand what they're doing, they don't have study habits, [and] they don't know how to develop a plan and work toward it. They need to learn all about that. Which is fine, but they do need to learn it."

The faculty particularly focused on classroom behaviors that they attributed to students' lack of acclimation to higher education—sometimes termed *academic socialization* (Weidman & Stein, 2003). Faculty attributed student behaviors to a lack of "training" to attain academic social skills. One instructor asserted the need for a "survival orientation" course for incoming students: "Sometimes [students'] lack of paying attention and . . . lack of training [about] how to survive in college [are problems]. . . . It's not because they are bad students; they are good students, but [there is a] lack of training for how [to] survive [in college]." Another instructor observed:

Well, usually the students have to take notes when [they] learn something new, and students have to come here, come to [the] classroom. One thing they can't [do is to] come to school, take notes, and [also be] doing homework and doing exercise[s] in class; that's very basic, right? But the people, the students who don't have those kinds of skills, they look very lazy. So I'm saying it's called lack of training.

Similar to their proffering explanations of students' lack of academic readiness due to their immigrant status, some administrators attributed being an immigrant-origin student as the reason for students' lack of academic socialization. As one explained, "There's a sense that our first-generation immigrants specifically might need additional support, might need more time to become acclimated to an academic environment or an academic culture." In this example, the first-generation immigrant is understood to also be a "first-generation college student" and as such is assumed to not have received the cultural tools from his or her family to know how to "acclimate" to college.

Other faculty attributed the students' lack of academic socialization to their continuance of "high school" behaviors or general immaturity. For example, a general education instructor related, "So now you have to get them acclimated to [being] a college student where, okay, what happened in high school doesn't work here. So . . . you have to get them used to that as well. So . . . I think *getting them prepared* is probably a better term than *training*." An ESL instructor concurred: "Oh, not doing homework, [being on] Facebook in class, not showing up to class, talking in class, those sorts of things. High school behavior is what it is. I mean I don't, as a rule, expect college students to act like that."

A math instructor described how the lack of maturity impacted students' understanding of what it takes to be successful in community college: "I think it is somewhat of an academic maturity level that they're not [at]. They don't understand [that] in order to be a success in class, you need to actually spend [a] certain amount of time outside of the classroom to prepare for the class, and they're not doing it." A business instructor applied a developmental lens to rationalize a lack of academic socialization:

> I tend to look at it . . . generally [as] a sense of what we would call maturity, right, which is a bundle of stuff. It's a level of maturity, sense of self-efficacy, responsibility, you know, self-directedness. If you look at Malcolm Knowles and what he talks about and . . . [at] these elements of what makes up an adult learner, and I look at people like Kegan and Ellie Dragel Severson from Harvard University and what they say about . . . adult development levels today and [how] instrumental . . . they [are] today, what they call socializing, . . . or self-authoring, . . . or those kinds of things by paying attention to those things. So, yeah, that's how I do it, but one could argue that if, . . . no matter what . . . they are on the adult developmental low scale, they're still an adult, so I think it is a maturity thing [in its] vaguest most vague sense.

COMPETING DEMANDS

Faculty and administrators identified work as a significant competing demand that interferes with immigrant-origin students' persistence. As one faculty said, "[Immigrant students] have to go to work—like this kid yesterday wishes to support her family because her mother lost her job." Although most students work to survive, most often the faculty and administrators linked their working to paying for college. One counselor described work as a catch-22: Students work to cover tuition, but working restricts a student's ability to complete college. "A slight change in financial regulations impact[s] heavily on them," he claimed. "If a student has to pay just $500 extra . . . it means that [he or she] would have to work, and when they work, it means they don't have the time [for school], and then the cycle begins to repeat itself."

Work, several faculty members asserted, also impacts academic performance. One remedial English professor explained, "I mean, I have kids fall asleep in class all the time because they're working night shifts." Another professor maintained that working off campus prevents students from attending tutoring: "We have a learning center also on campus [where] students go for help with paper writing. . . . Fifty percent of our students work 20 hours or more, so for them to create a space to go for tutoring becomes even [more] difficult." Notably, no one suggested expanding or adjusting support service hours to meet the needs of working students, once again placing the onus of responsibility for academic achievement directly on the students.

COMPLETION AND REMEDIATION

Several administrators attributed delays in the time needed for students to complete college to the added burden of their having to take remedial courses, including ESL, listing it as a major impediment to on-time college completion. One dean described how remedial courses can be costly and challenging for even the most "persistent and resilient" student:

> I think that [a student's placement in] remedial courses impacts so many of those challenges. It certainly impacts persistence because you're adding . . . a semester [of] remediation or two semesters, math, maybe reading, maybe English, so somebody has to be incredibly persistent and resilient to continue and get up and keep trudging along when our process is adding a semester or more to the past events to earn an associate degree. Of course . . . it has financial implications as [well as] implications of time and work obligations. It impacts on all of those things, so I think one of the challenges we face as an institution is serving and really teaching remediation in a way that's very different from what we're doing now.

One associate dean explained the obstacle that remediation can be and what is required of the immigrant-origin student to overcome it:

> After [having taken] beginning development courses, [students] understand that those [remedial] courses are not credit worthy and [that] taking them is

going to prolong the completion of their degree. So . . . they persist despite issues of transportation or child care or lack of finances. They know how to reach out to make connections with support services or individuals who are here and who are going to help them succeed, so it's those kinds . . . of subjective nonacademic strengths that I think really distinguish the students who persevere from those who can't.

Interestingly, while the administrator explained that students who are required to take developmental courses initially are unaware that remedial courses are noncredit-bearing, he nonetheless places the onus on students to access institutional resources independently, overlooking the fact that a student who is unaware of the difference between credit and noncredit may also not know how to seek help.

PERSISTENCE IN THE FACE OF LONG ODDS

Despite their criticism of immigrant-origin students for demonstrating immaturity and lack of academic preparation, by and large faculty and administrators described these students as persistent. Across all interviews, faculty and administrators recognized that immigrant-origin students grapple with institutional barriers, personal obstacles, and lack of academic readiness that interfere with their educational success. The faculty and administrators unanimously credited those who do succeed and overcome serious roadblocks as being persistent and hardworking. An instructor commented that immigrant-origin students expend a great deal of energy to achieve academic success:

> They work very hard and generally they have aspirations. A lot of them come here and have dreams. Very few of them come in here and say, "I don't know what I want to do." They know what they want to do. . . . It's weird. I get students that can barely communicate with me, and I get those that can communicate really [well], but whatever they do, the amount of work they put in is incredible. So . . . there's a lot of work ethic. That's what I'm saying. It's a prism of different values, different areas, different abilities.

Another instructor asserted that success is determined by work ethic rather than by intelligence:

> I think it's much more about effort than it is about ability. . . . I think I have brilliant students who . . . don't show up and don't do well, and I have struggling students who show up and go to the writing tutorial and come to office hours and work hard, so I think it's about consistency and dedication; that's how I would describe it.

One administrator perceived persistence as being linked to the particular cultural background of the immigrant-origin student:

> The Asian immigrant tends to have a lot of those at-risk factors. Obviously, what I see is they [Asians] believe in education whole-heartedly, and they're pretty confident and optimistic that they can do anything that they undertake and, again, they're persistent. If something doesn't work out for them, they continue. For the black immigrant, a lot of them have a great sense that they can do it. A lot of our Caribbean students, a lot of the students that are West African immigrants, you know, they come in and there's an aura of confidence with them and, again, they're very persistent. . . . In my experience, Latino immigrants succeed, in great part, because of their aspirations, because of the priority that education plays for them and for their family, and because of their ability to persist despite lack of academic readiness or even if they are academic[ally] ready despite other challenges they might have to overcome.

Whether or not faculty and administrators perceived immigrant-origin students as lacking academic and/or social readiness for college or admired their persistence and work ethic, the faculty and administrators in our study displayed perceptions whereby deficiencies and strengths were seen as being embodied within individuals.

CULTURAL DEFICIT MENTAL MODELS

Critics and scholars have noted that a significant amount of research about urban immigrant-origin low-income students has concentrated on their underperformance via the prism of a cultural deficit model (Boykin & Noguera, 2011). Deficit thinking can be seen at the center of our findings in the ways in which faculty and administrators discussed the academic readiness, socialization, and persistence of their immigrant-origin students.

"They Don't Have the Skill"

For this analysis, *academic readiness for college* refers to the student's "academic resources" and is a composite measure of the academic content and performance that students bring from secondary school into higher education (McBeth, 2006). Academic readiness includes cognitive and skill-based areas such as reading, writing, testing, computation skills, and critical thinking. In the majority of references to academic readiness, faculty conflate academic aptitude with behaviors and, in turn, pathologize students as lacking motivation and engagement without recognizing or considering the intellectual ability of students.

"The Way They Behave"

For the purpose of this analysis, the theme of academic socialization is present when faculty target socioemotional and nonacademic traits, behaviors, and dispositions such as student work ethic, time management, motivation, self-regulation, maturity, and persistence as signs that students are ill-equipped for college. For example, faculty may label students as apathetic for neglecting to bring a book to class when in some cases students may be attending class without books because of a delay in their financial aid disbursement (see Chapter 6 for an example).

The default perception that students are lazy and indifferent misdirects attention from problem solving to blaming, with negative repercussions for students. For example, faculty and administrators agreed that students attribute their poor performance to internal forces and feel "frustrated [and] embarrassed and blame themselves" (Schutz, 2007). This perception is powerful. In the case of immigrant-origin college students, perceptions held by faculty and administrators may convey to students that they are incapable of achieving academic success. By referencing academic readiness to describe "undesirable" student behavior, Valenzuela (1999) argues, the academy is reproducing a system based on the immigrant-origin students' assimilation status—a perception that "defines them as [being] in need of continuing socialization" (p. 108).

Furthermore, the danger in justifying a lack of engagement or disruptive behavior as a sign of poor college readiness may obfuscate the dynamic between the student and the course and between the student and the professor. The perception held by faculty that resistance or oppositional behaviors reflect a lack of engagement on the part of students overlooks other possible explanations such as students finding a course and the instructor unengaging or the course work not challenging (Suárez-Orozco, Pimentel, & Martin, 2009).

The perceptions that faculty have about students' academic performance that are based on their behaviors may conceal what actually transpires in the classroom, as seen in Chapter 5. Research has shown that student engagement predicated on student-centered modes of delivery such as those that involve learning communities, group work, and project-based collaborative learning have greater rates of engagement and retention among underprepared students (Suárez-Orozco et al., 2009).

THE GUISE OF GRIT

Though we found prevalent examples of deficit thinking, the faculty and administrators also praised students as "persistent," "resilient," and "remarkable." These perceptions of persistence may appear to be positive reflections of immigrant-origin students, but in focusing on the tenacity of these students, the faculty and administrators deflect attention from the institutional policies and practices as well as from the structural barriers that can hinder academic achievement (Kundu &

Noguera, 2014). When faculty and administrators look past ineffective policies and practices and the social inequities that immigrant-origin students face and maintain that students demonstrate their agency through hard work and persistence, they reference a "bootstraps mentality" that reinforces social inequality (Giroux et al., 1996). As such, by unconsciously relegating a student's academic success to grit, faculty and administrators fail to rethink institutional policies and practices and overlook the opportunity to develop alternative models to support the academic achievement of immigrant-origin students (Almeida, 2016).

COGNITIVE DISSONANCE

The final theme present in the data is cognitive dissonance. Cognitive dissonance theory is concerned with how perception and cognition influence and are influenced by motivation and emotion. Festinger (2007) argues that when faced with contradictory realities, such a phenomenon results in a mental state of discomfort because individuals strive for mental and emotional consistency. Therefore, when faced with contradictory realities, individuals seek ways to reduce or eliminate the discomfort of holding two opposing ideas (Festinger, 2007).

Our findings indicate that while administrators and faculty are cognizant of the shortcomings of their institution and its inability to correct the policies and practices to ameliorate the obstacles that students face, they maintain cultural deficit mental models of their students' abilities and dispositions. Despite recognizing the institutional, socioeconomic, and political barriers beyond academic readiness that immigrant-origin students face, faculty and administrators often fault students for failing to take responsibility for their academic achievement. Thus, the perception that the key to academic success rests with the students and their determination and resiliency coexists with the acknowledgment of external obstacles that interfere with academic success.

When faculty and administrators recognize the external structural causes and personal issues that interfere with student persistence but also fault students for being irresponsible and immature, they ironically overlook the adult responsibilities imposed on many immigrant-origin students (e.g., balancing work and school) that routinely interfere with their success as students. By labeling students as irresponsible and distracted, the faculty blur the line between their own discomfort with the policies and practices of the institution and their role in perpetuating them. Ultimately, these perceptions of students' irresponsibility mean that immigrant-origin students are left to sink or swim according to their own "merit."

IN SUM

Although we were able to uncover rich themes from our analysis of interviews with faculty and administrators across the three campuses, our research had some limitations. First, our findings represent a small number of faculty and administrators from three specific campuses and cannot be generalized to all community colleges. Second, our findings are derived from single interviews with each participant. That said, when triangulated across chapters, our findings complement the themes that emerge from the student interviews and classroom observations described in other chapters in this volume. Some of our findings are unique to immigrant-origin students, but many are also consistent with the challenges faced by students of color attending community colleges.

Our hope with this chapter is that by uncovering beliefs held by those who shape policy and those who implement it, we might stimulate dialogue and develop approaches for moving beyond inert policies and ineffective practices that impinge on the academic achievement of immigrant-origin students. By making the imperceptible perceptible, as a community of postsecondary stakeholders, we may create the meaningful change necessary to improve the academic outcomes for immigrant-origin students.

REFERENCES

Almeida, Daniel. (2016). Understanding grit in the context of higher education. In M. Paulsen (Ed.), *Higher education: Handbook of theory and research* (pp. 559–609). Switzerland: Springer International Publishing.

Boykin, A. W., & Noguera, P. (2011). *Creating the opportunity to learn: Moving from research to practice to close the achievement gap*. Alexandria, VA: Association for Supervision & Curriculum Development (ASCD).

Cerna, O. S., Perez, P. A., & Saenz, V. (2009). Examining the precollege attributes and values of Latina/o bachelor's degree attainers. *Journal of Hispanic Higher Education, 8*(2), 130–157.

Conway, K. (2009). Exploring persistence of immigrant and native students in an urban community college. *The Review of Higher Education, 32*(3), 321–352.

Duffy, F. M. (2006). Step-up-to-excellence: A protocol for navigating whole-system change in school districts. *Techtrends, 50*(2), 41.

Festinger, L. (2007). Does cognitive dissonance explain why behavior can change attitudes? In J. Nier (Ed.), *Taking sides: Clashing views in social psychology* (pp. 74–91). New York, NY: McGraw-Hill/Dushkin.

Giroux, H., Lankshear, C., McLaren, P., & Peters, M. (1996). *Counternarratives: Cultural studies and critical pedagogies in postmodern spaces*. New York, NY: Routledge.

Glaser, B. G., & Strauss, A. L. (1967). *The discovery of grounded theory: Strategies for qualitative research*. Chicago, IL: Aldine.

Kundu, A., & Noguera, P. (2014). Why America's infatuation with "grit" can't solve our educational dilemmas. *Virginia Policy Review, 11*(Summer), 49–53.

Leinbach, T. D., & Bailey, T. R. (2006). Access and achievement of Hispanics and Hispanic immigrants in the City University of New York. *New Directions for Community Colleges, 2006*(133), 27–40.

McBeth, M. (2006). Arrested development: Revising remediation at John Jay College of Criminal Justice. *Journal of Basic Writing, 25*(2), 76.

Moss, R. L., & Young, R. B. (1995). Perceptions about the academic and social integration of underprepared students in an urban community college. *Community College Review, 22*(4), 47–61. doi:10.1177/009155219502200407

Pascarella, E. T., Edison, M., & Nora, A. (1998). Does community college versus four-year college attendance influence students' educational plans? *Journal of College Student Development, 39*(2), 179.

Schutz, P. A. (2007). *Examining emotional diversity in the classroom: An attribution theorist considers the moral emotions* (p. 75). San Diego, CA: Elsevier Academic Press.

Senge, P. M. (1994). *The fifth discipline: The art and practice of the learning organization.* New York, NY: Currency Doubleday.

Smit, R. (2012). Towards a clearer understanding of student disadvantage in higher education: Problematising deficit thinking. *Higher Education Research & Development, 31*(3), 369–380.

Soliday, M. (2002). *The politics of remediation: Institutional and student need in higher education.* Pittsburgh, PA: University of Pittsburgh Press.

Stanley, J. (2010). *The rhetoric of remediation: Negotiating entitlement and access to higher education.* Pittsburgh, PA: University of Pittsburgh Press.

Suárez-Orozco, C., Pimentel, A., & Martin, M. (2009). The significance of relationships: Academic engagement and achievement among newcomer immigrant youth. *Teachers College Record, 111*(3), 712–749.

Teranishi, R. T., Suárez-Orozco, C., & Suárez-Orozco, M. (2011). Immigrants in community colleges. *The Future of Children/Center for the Future of Children, the David and Lucile Packard Foundation, 21*(1), 153–169.

Valadez, J. (1993). Cultural capital and its impact on the aspirations of nontraditional community college students. *Community College Review, 21*(3), 30–43. doi:10.1177/009155219302100304

Valenzuela, A. (1999). *Subtractive schooling: U.S.-Mexican youth and the politics of caring.* Albany: State University of New York Press.

Weidman, J. C., & Stein, E. L. (2003). Socialization of doctoral students to academic norms. *Research in Higher Education, 44*(6), 641–656.

Zarkesh, M., & Carducci, R. (2004). Increasing success for Latinos/as in community colleges. *Community College Journal of Research and Practice, 28*(8), 705–709.

CHAPTER 11

The Significance of Networks of Relationships for Immigrant-Origin Students

Stacey Alicea

Despite evidence that institutional and peer supports matter for community college student outcomes (Booker, 2007; Calcagno, Bailey, Jenkins, Kienzl, & Leinbach, 2008), we know very little about the social processes that support the achievement of students' postsecondary goals. *Social networks*—social structures containing relational ties between individuals—can play an important role in unpacking social processes in community colleges. The various types of resources (e.g., information, material goods) and supports (e.g., practical, emotional) that flow between relational ties within and across social networks are, in essence, social capital (Burt, 2000, 2005).

Community colleges are uniquely situated as one of the few post–high school avenues through which emergent adults from resource-poor contexts can gain access to social networks containing social capital that can be used to achieve educational and employment goals (Bailey & Morest, 2006; Karp, 2011). To better understand how social capital develops and is linked to student outcomes in community colleges, it is necessary to examine the structure and composition of youths' social networks in these settings. Identifying and describing existing social networks in these settings and linking them to important markers of young adult success can provide community colleges with critical information that can aid them in better serving their target population. This approach is particularly relevant given current economic challenges in which material resources are scarce and innovative low-cost alternatives for increasing student resources and supports are sorely needed.

THEORETICAL FRAMEWORK

Burt's (2005) social network theory (SNT) distinguishes two types of social capital based on the work of Coleman (1988) and Granovetter (1973): close ties, herein referred to as *bonding capital,* and weak ties, herein referred to as *bridging capital.* *Bonding capital* is defined as "a strong relationship in a closed network" (Burt, 2005,

p. 25) and is characterized by close-knit relationships embodied by trust between dyads who share similar attributes (e.g., ethnicity, immigrant status). High levels of bonding capital have been shown to increase information flow, social support, and social control among close-knit relational ties (Burt, 2005; Coleman, 1988). *Bridging capital* is defined as weak relational ties among clusters of diverse individuals. The absence of ties in a social network—*structural holes*—creates opportunities for development of bridging capital. Individuals who recognize and bridge structural holes have higher social capital than those who cannot identify structural holes. High bridging capital is associated with (1) earlier access to information, (2) control over the information obtained, and (3) fewer instances of obtaining redundant information when it comes from someone outside of a close-knit network (Burt, 2005; Granovetter, 1973). Bonding capital and bridging capital are conceptualized as complementary ingredients in social capital accrual; the combination of both forms of capital produces the highest levels of individual social capital (Burt, 2005).

Within this framework, social capital can be conceptualized as being instrumental in nature, meaning that resources and support accrued from social relations can be used to achieve goals (Burt, 2005; Lin, 2001; Stanton-Salazar & Spina, 2000). Figure 11.1 provides a conceptual model for how social capital may

Figure 11.1. Community College Social Network Opportunities Across Formal and Informal Campus Spaces

Network structure: Size, density (i.e., interconnectedness), structural holes.

Network composition: Homophily/heterophily (e.g., ethnicity, immigrant origin, gender), resources (e.g., information, advice, support), relationship types (e.g., professor, adviser, friend), frequency of contact between ties.

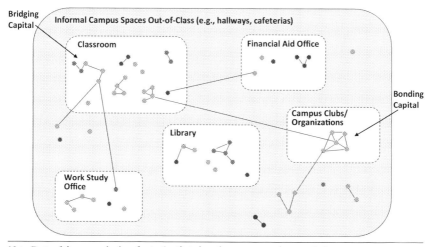

Note: Dots of the same shade refer to ties that share homogenous characteristics.

be accrued via social networks in community colleges. The model pays particular attention to social networking opportunities available in *classroom* settings and *out-of-class* campus settings, depicting these settings as structured/formal and unstructured/informal spaces. Structured spaces include classrooms and out-of-class settings structured by the college (e.g., the financial aid office, work-study areas, and campus clubs). These spaces are represented by boxes with dashed lines, indicating their bounded nature while acknowledging that students and institutional agents are able to move between such spaces. Unstructured spaces include settings that are not intentionally structured by the college (e.g., hallways, cafeterias). These spaces are represented by the gray area in the figure, indicating their unbounded nature and transient state—students and institutional agents move through these spaces as they make their way to bounded spaces in the larger setting. Individuals on campus are represented by dots. Dots of the same color refer to ties that share homogenous characteristics (e.g., immigrant origin, department). Solid lines represent ties between individuals within and across settings. As an example, the figure depicts a closed, tight-knit network of homogenous students in the campus clubs' box. Two of the students in this network also have ties with individuals in other settings within the college, suggesting they may have access to other forms of information or support that further increase their social capital.

CONTEXT MATTERS: EDUCATIONAL CONSIDERATIONS

Research on community colleges indicates students must contend with many institutional barriers to academic success and degree completion, including limited institutional resources, socially integrated activities, and peer academic support and low instructor expectations (Dougherty, 1994) in addition to mediocre instruction, inadequate student services, and unsupportive setting climates (Bailey & Weininger, 2002; Bensimon, 2007). These barriers have led to overall weak social integration and limited academic support for students and have been linked to high rates of students dropping out and not completing degree programs (Brint, 2003). Although enrollments are increasing, completion rates are decreasing (Bailey, Jenkins, & Leinbach, 2005; Soares & Mazzeo, 2008). Scholars have argued that both academic preparedness and student retention must be addressed in order to bolster student success in these settings (Bliss & Sandiford, 2004; Burgess & Samuels, 1999; Engle, 2007; Tinto, 1998). Studies have linked these outcomes to institutional and peer supports within community colleges (Booker, 2007; Calcagno, Bailey, Jenkins, Kienzl, & Leinbach, 2008). For instance, peer relationships have been associated with improved learning (Booker, 2007). Conversely, increases in the proportion of part-time faculty have been negatively associated with students' 2-year degree completion and transfer rates (Calcagno et al., 2008). In order to address the aforementioned barriers, we must consider community colleges as more than academic and vocational institutions—they are also organizations that have inherent social processes that can impact youths' opportunities for success across multiple life domains (Tseng & Seidman, 2007).

Few empirical studies undertaken to understand and enhance social capital in these settings have done so using theory that links social networks—the very structures through which students accrue social capital—to student outcomes. The most well-known example is the use of learning communities (LCs) (Tinto & Russo, 1994). LCs generally involve the coenrollment of students in two or more courses and/or advisement groups outside of classes. Such interventions are implicitly trying to broaden and enrich student networks in order to enhance social capital. Participation in LCs has resulted in student reports of intellectual gains, a greater sense of belonging, and academic and social adjustment (Tinto & Russo, 1994; Zhao & Kuh, 2004), particularly for racial/ethnic minority students (Cabrera et al., 2002; Meeuwisse, Severiens, & Born, 2010). A 7-year randomized impact study of more than 1,500 students at a large urban community college in New York City found that LCs that coenrolled students in multiple courses in addition to providing tutors and case managers had positive effects on credit accumulation (Weiss, Mayer, Cullinan, Ratledge, Sommo, & Diamond, 2014). However, despite positive findings, research also indicates that Black, Latino, and first-generation college students—the very students who may receive the greatest benefits from such an intervention—are the least likely to participate in LCs (Mercado, 2012). This finding suggests that social processes underlying programs that connect students to institutional supports may be perceived and experienced differently based on student characteristics.

Qualitative methods have more explicitly employed social network frameworks to study social outcomes. These studies have focused on strong ties within networks. Among a sample of 44 students at two Northeastern urban community colleges, those reporting strong relationships with network ties were more likely to report being socially integrated into their college environments and making headway toward degree attainment (Karp, Hughes, & O'Gara, 2010). Nontraditional community college students (i.e., the first generation to attend college, ethnic minorities, and immigrants) with connections to strong, positive relationships with external and informal institutional agents (i.e., parents, siblings, and peers and faculty outside of their classrooms) who engage in extracurricular student clubs and organizations have also reported being highly involved and successful in their first year of college (Rendon, 1994).

Discussions of weak ties and disconnected ties (i.e., structural holes) are not represented in this literature. Theories of student persistence posit nonacademic support found in out-of-class spaces, where weak ties are likely to be cultivated, is critical to cultivating social relationships that support the development of aspirations, commitment, and college "know-how" that may improve student outcomes (Karp, 2011; Tinto, 1993). Sadly, the field still lacks explicit examination of out-of-class social networks in community colleges.

CHAPTER AIMS

Students' social networks may constitute untapped school-based social capital that can be leveraged to bolster both retention and completion rates. It is critical that we better understand where, within community college campuses, students are cultivating network ties. If students are cultivating all of their ties in classrooms or structured programs, as existing literature suggests (Bailey & Morest, 2006; Karp, 2011), then this is where change efforts should be focused. However, if ties are also being forged across a variety of campus spaces, we should aim to better understand which spaces cultivate different types of relational ties and what resources are embedded in those ties. Using data from the Research on Immigrants in Community College (RICC) Study, this chapter:

1. Describes *where* social network ties are originating in community college campus settings.
2. Explores both *structural* (e.g., size, density) and *compositional* (e.g., types of relationships and resources) characteristics of students' existing social networks in community colleges.
3. Examines to what extent the origin of network ties and the structure and composition of student social networks differ by student characteristics (i.e., gender, ethnicity, immigrant-origin status) and setting (i.e., classrooms, outside of classrooms, school).

RICC STUDY SOCIAL NETWORK FINDINGS

Of the 644 students who participated in the RICC Study, 195 completed an Ego Network Survey.[1] Social network analysis was conducted using ENET (Borgatti, 2006) to calculate all social network variables, and SPSS 22.0 (IBM, 2010) was used to run descriptive analyses (see online appendix at www.tcpress.com for full statistics referenced throughout the remainder of this chapter).[2]

Network Tie Origin

Based on existing literature and theory, four types of community college settings were examined: (1) *classrooms,* defined as formal spaces designed to structure learning in ways that promote knowledge acquisition; (2) spaces outside of classrooms that are intentionally structured by community colleges and are involuntary in nature, meaning that students must interact with individuals in these spaces as part of their enrollment (OCS-IV; e.g., registrar's and bursar's offices); (3) out-of-class spaces that are intentionally structured by community colleges or students and are voluntary (OCS-V; e.g., student clubs, sports); and (4) out-of-class spaces that are not intentionally structured by community colleges or students (OCUS).[3] On average, 41.2% of student network ties originated in class, 24.6% originated in OCS-IV spaces, 7.7% originated in OCS-V spaces, and 22.9% originated in OCUS spaces.

Structure of Networks: Size and Density

The average *network*[4] *size* included 6.48 individuals; however, there was substantial variation in network size across students (*Standard deviation (SD)* = 4.38). The most common network size reported included three ties. Additionally, 12.8% of students reported having 15 ties (i.e., maximum ties) while 7.2% of students reported having only one or no school-based ties. To assess how interconnected ties were within youths' existing social networks, *network density* was calculated. *Density* refers to the number of connections among members in a network. On average, density appeared to be relatively low, suggesting that the majority of a student's ties were not connected to each other (*Mean (M)* = .18). Twenty-six students (14.4%) reported no interconnections among their network ties, and 13 students (7.2%) reported saturation of connections.

Composition of Networks: Roles, Relationships, and Resources

Four types of school-based *roles* were considered, based on community college settings: student, instructor, adviser/counselor, and other staff. On average, students reported their networks consisted primarily of students ($M = 51.8$), followed by instructors ($M = 18.2$), advisers ($M = 13.2$), and other school staff ($M = 9.6$). Students were also asked to report the type of *relationship* they had with each member in order to ascertain which ties were strong (e.g., close friends, mentors) and which were weak (e.g., strangers, acquaintances). On average, students reported that their networks consisted primarily of close friends ($M = 38.2$), followed by acquaintances ($M = 28.8$), mentors ($M = 14.8$), and strangers ($M = 13.1$). Finally, three types of *resources* were explored: academic, professional, and socioemotional. On average, 31.8% of ties provided academic resources, 18.5% of ties provided professional resources, and 45.2% of ties provided socioemotional resources.

DEMOGRAPHIC AND SETTING-LEVEL DIFFERENCES ACROSS NETWORK CHARACTERISTICS

Demographic and setting-level differences in network tie origin as well as structural and compositional network characteristics across three variables were explored: immigrant-origin status, ethnicity, and school. First-generation immigrant-origin students ($M = 51.8$) reported significantly higher percentages of in-class ties in comparison with both second- ($M = 37.5$) and third-generation students ($M = 33.3$) and reported lower percentages of OCUS ties ($M = 12.7$) than both second- ($M = 27.9$) and third-generation students ($M = 28.1$). White students ($M = 35.4$) reported significantly higher percentages of instructors in their networks in comparison with Black ($M = 14.9$), Latino ($M = 14.4$), and mixed students ($M = 16.7$). Students at Taino had higher percentages of other school staff ties ($M = 16.7$) in their networks than students at both Domino ($M = 6.1$) and Oakmont ($M = 8.5$) did.

NETWORK SIZE AND DENSITY

The majority of student networks were relatively small. Each student, on average, reported connections to seven individuals. Scholars have long argued that community college students are often commuters who attend intermittently or part-time, enroll in evening courses, and work full-time jobs (Bailey & Morest, 2006). Such challenges make it difficult for them to spend the necessary time on campus needed to cultivate relationships. Across all three participating community colleges, student enrollment ranges from 6,400 to 13,000 students, and the faculty-to-student ratio is at least 16:1 (Taino is 19:1) (AACC, 2014). Given the size of these institutions, even when students are faced with significant challenges to spending time on campus, student networks should and could be larger. Larger networks are more likely to contain a greater diversity of resources and supports. Indeed, in this study larger networks were significantly correlated with more resource diversity as well as with ties that originated across a variety of campus settings.

Networks were also low in density—a marker of structural holes—indicating that they were not highly interconnected. This finding suggests that available resources and supports may not be shared among ties. The presence of structural holes, however, also means that there are opportunities to bridge ties and increase resource flow within student networks. Community colleges, then, have a unique opportunity to help students create bridges that increase resource flow between ties. Networks with disconnected ties that have a diversity of resources (e.g., socio-emotional, academic, professional), as was the case in this study, can benefit most from bridging structural holes.

ORIGIN AND COMPOSITION OF NETWORK TIES

It was expected that a large percentage of ties would originate in classrooms based on current literature that suggests students do not spend meaningful amounts of time on campus outside of class (Bailey & Morest, 2006). Interestingly, however, close to two-thirds of ties originated in out-of-class spaces. Of these ties, roughly one-third were cultivated in OCS-IV (e.g., registrar's office, advisers) or OCUS spaces (e.g., hallways, cafeteria).

Students who reported having a greater percentage of ties originating from OCS-IV spaces reported greater numbers of ties among advisers and other school staff. This finding suggests that students may be garnering resources from ties within these spaces. Research supports the notion that involuntary spaces are indeed important for student success but are often heavily flawed. For example, community colleges have increasingly replaced counseling staff and full-time faculty with administrative staff and adjunct faculty (Bailey & Morest, 2006). In a large-scale survey of 4,300 community college students, 45% of students reported having taken courses that they later discovered did not count toward their degree. This problem was attributed to high student-to-counselor ratios and limited student advisement (Deil-Amen & Rosenbaum, 2003). Given that the findings suggest that a substantial number of ties originated in spaces that contained student support services, a better understanding of standing patterns of behavior that support tie development and a deeper evaluation of the quality of available resources held by institutional agents in these settings are needed.

OCUS spaces are also of interest given that students report cultivating close to one quarter of their ties there. This finding seems particularly relevant in light of theoretical and empirical literature that argues that student integration and belonging are key to persistence (Tinto, 1993, 1998; Tinto & Russo, 1994). OCUS ties were the only ties correlated with perceived socioemotional support. However, students who reported greater percentages of OCUS ties in their networks also reported less diversity in their relational ties. Said another way, students lacked ties to instructors, advisers, and other staff more likely to provide the academic and professional resources needed to improve persistence and degree attainment. Students who have high percentages of OCUS ties may benefit from more involvement in OCS-IV spaces that increase access to information from weak ties. It could also be possible that strategies to cultivate classroom engagement may help students with disproportionate numbers of OCUS ties increase their in-class ties, which in turn could provide greater access to academic resources. The community college literature is largely silent when it comes to OCUS spaces; however, in the 4-year literature such spaces have been associated with a plethora of positive outcomes for students (e.g., self-awareness, self-confidence, altruism, autonomy, time management, academic and social development, persistence) (Bensimon, 2007; Kuh, 1995; Pascarella & Terenzini, 2005; Tinto, 1998). Scholars should aim to gain a deeper understanding of these spaces and their standing patterns of behavior and resource exchange.

Turning to composition, I explored three characteristics of network ties: school roles, relationships, and resources. Students represented half of the ties in networks, with instructors, advisers, and other school staff representing the remainder of ties. In line with these findings, networks consisted primarily of close friends, followed by acquaintances and very few mentor and stranger ties. This finding suggests students are receiving roughly half of their resources from close friends in the form of socioemotional support. Moreover, students reported that only one-third of their ties provided academic resources, and fewer than one-fifth provided professional resources. The highest levels of social capital come from having both strong and weak ties. Perhaps students in community colleges are lacking weak ties that provide the very resources most likely to impact their educational goals.

Across all compositional characteristics of networks, students with more diverse sets of ties across campus spaces reported greater diversity of relational ties and resources embedded across ties (see Table 11.3 in the online appendix). These diverse relationships can bring with them the diverse sets of resources needed to achieve educational goals. Still, only a third of students reported having more than one type of resource available within their networks, and few students were accessing the academic and professional resources needed to successfully navigate an educational setting. Furthermore, the quality of these relationships and the resources embedded in ties and across different community college spaces remain largely unknown, and more research is needed to better understand how useful existing resources are to students in meeting their goals.

VARIATION IN NETWORK TIE ORIGIN AND COMPOSITION

Demographic and school differences across compositional characteristics of student networks emerged. First, White students had higher percentages of instructors in their networks in comparison with all other ethnic groups except Asian students. There is general consensus in the community college literature that students of color often perceive the majority White faculty at their institutions as being socially, economically, and culturally different from themselves (Chang, 2005; Santos & Reigadas, 2002). Studies at 4-year colleges have linked such feelings to experiences of prejudice (Eimers, 2000). There is some evidence that student–faculty interactions for students of color at community colleges, in particular Latino and Asian American/Pacific Islander students, are lower than those for their White counterparts (Chang, 2005). This finding is important given calls for increasing meaningful interactions between ethnic minority students and faculty as a means toward increasing students' persistence and integration (Terenzini et al., 1994) and diversifying students' social networks (Santos & Reigadas, 2002).

Second, tie origin differed by immigrant origin. First-generation students reported having more ties that originated in class in comparison with second- and third-generation students and fewer OCUS ties in comparison with these groups as well. Immigrant students often arrive at community colleges with varying degrees of academic preparedness, have a large range of language-related needs, and are typically placed in remedial and ESL education courses (Teranishi, Suárez-Orozco, & Suárez-Orozco, 2011). ESL courses allow students to communicate with their peers and instructors in their native language. This situation results in increased in-class time spent with similar peers and informal counseling from ESL instructors (Suárez-Orozco, Suárez-Orozco, & Todorova, 2009). First-generation immigrant-origin students may indeed find it easier to cultivate relationships in ESL classrooms due to the challenges that come with pursuing postsecondary degrees. Immigrant students are more likely to have increased familial obligations in comparison with those of their native-born counterparts, including caring for family members, providing translation services, and contributing to household income (Teranishi, Suárez-Orozco, & Suárez-Orozco, 2011). Often, they also have dependents and work either part- or full-time jobs (Horn, Nevill, & Griffith, 2006). Competing demands such as these may prevent them from spending time on campus in out-of-class spaces. This finding speaks to the importance of further exploring which types of relationships and resources may benefit immigrant students across school settings in promoting positive student outcomes. Additionally, although the sample size did not allow for the exploration of intersectionality of immigrant status and ethnic minority identity, this is a critical topic that should be studied.

Finally, school roles differed by campus. Taino students reported having higher percentages of other school staff (e.g., financial aid officers, bursar personnel) ties in their networks when compared with both Domino and Oakmont students. This result is interesting given that Taino was founded by community activists and has a long history of working with students who need intensive remediation and access to institutional resources. The literature on community college institutional characteristics has focused largely on institution size, proportion of part-time/adjunct faculty, and expenditures related to instruction, administration, and student services as predictors of student success. Student services are often operationalized as money spent on services rather than as the processes and content of these services (Calcagno et al., 2008), thus it is hard to draw additional conclusions about this finding based on available literature. It is possible that Taino has found ways to enhance student services and supports. These may include increasing the number of nonadvising support staff or structures that allow for easier access to such staff, thereby increasing opportunities for tie formation between students and school staff outside of the classroom and advisory settings (Calcagno et al., 2008). Future research must better understand the ways in which institutional structures support greater opportunities for tie formation with support staff who hold crucial college "know-how" information (Deil-Amen & Rosenbaum, 2003).

IN SUM

Over the past decade, community colleges have received increasing attention in political and educational spheres. New federal initiatives to provide tuition-free enrollment for millions of public community college students have been implemented (Davis & Lewin, 2015), assuming that the primary problem to obtaining a postsecondary degree is income based. Equally important are poor institutional and peer supports and unsupportive climates in community colleges, which remain key barriers to student success. For tuition-free programs to be successful in helping students reach educational goals, they must be coupled with thoughtful and responsive policies and practices that address these issues. Cultivating and leveraging student social networks represent one avenue that may be worth exploring.

NOTES

1. *Ego networks* are reports from a person about people to whom they are connected. Examining these is theorized to be the optimal way to estimate an individual's social capital (Burt, 2005).

2. See Alicea (2015) for a full description of study methods and additional results; see online appendix for RICC study methods.

3. Categories were developed using concepts from behavior settings theory (Barker, 1978), which posits that behavior is not just a physical place; it also includes a standing and distinct pattern of behavior.

4. All network structural analyses use the 181 students who reported at least two ties, which by definition constitute a network (Burt, 2005).

REFERENCES

Alicea, S. (2015). *Social networks in CCs: Influences on social capital, academic achievement, employment skills and psychosocial wellbeing.* Doctoral dissertation. Retrieved from Proquest LLC (UMI No. 3705207).

Bailey, T., Jenkins, D., & Leinbach, T. (2005). *What we know about CC low-income and minority student outcomes: Descriptive statistics from national surveys.* New York, NY: Teachers College, Columbia University.

Bailey, T., & Morest, V. S. (Eds.). (2006). *Defending the CC equity agenda.* Baltimore, MD: Johns Hopkins University Press.

Bailey, T., & Weininger, E. B. (2002). Performance, graduation, and transfer of immigrants and natives in City University of New York Community colleges. *Educational Evaluation and Policy Analysis, 24*(4), 359–377.

Barker, R. G. (1978). *Theory of behavior settings: Habitats, environments and human behavior.* San Francisco, CA: Jossey-Bass.

Bensimon, E. M. (2007). The underestimated significance of practitioner knowledge in the scholarship of student success. *The Review of Higher Education, 30*(4), 441–469.

Bliss, L. B., & Sandiford, J. R. (2004). Linking study behaviors and student culture to academic success among Hispanic students. *CC Journal of Research & Practice, 28*(3), 281–295.

Booker, K. C. (2007). Perceptions of classroom belongingness among African American college students. *College Student Journal, 41*, 178–186.

Borgatti, S. P. (2006). *E-NET software for the analysis of ego network data.* Needham, MA: Analytical Technologies.

Brint, S. (2003). Few remaining dreams: CCs since 1985. *The Annals of the American Academy of Political and Social Science, 586*(1), 16–37.

Burgess, L. A., & Samuels, C. (1999). Impact of full-time versus part-time instructor status on college student retention and academic performance in sequential courses. *CC Journal of Research and Practice, 23*, 487–498.

Burt, R. S. (2000). The network structure of social capital. *Research in Organizational Behavior, 22*, 345–423.

Burt, R. S. (2005). *Brokerage and closure: An introduction to social capital.* Oxford, UK: Oxford University Press.

Cabrera, A. F., Crissman, J. L., Bernal, E. M., Nora, A., Terenzini, P. T., & Pascarella, E. T. (2002). Collaborative learning: Its impact on college students' development and diversity. *Journal of College Student Development, 43*(1), 20–34.

Calcagno, J. C., Bailey, T., Jenkins, D., Kienzl, G., & Leinbach, T. (2008). CC student success: What institutional characteristics make a difference? *Economics of Education Review, 27*(6), 632–645.

Chang, J. C. (2005). Faculty student interaction at the CC: A focus on students of color. *Research in Higher Education, 46*(7), 769–802.

Coleman, J. S. (1988). Social capital in the creation of human capital. *American Journal of Sociology, 94*, S95–S120.

Davis, J. H., & Lewin, T. (2015, January 8). Obama plan would help many go to community college free. *New York Times*, p. 8.

Deil-Amen, R., & Rosenbaum, J. E. (2003). The social prerequisites of success: Can college structure reduce the need for social know-how? *The Annals of the American Academy of Political and Social Science, 586*(1), 120–143.

Dougherty, K. J. (1994). *The contradictory college: The conflicting origins, impacts, and futures of the community college.* Albany, NY: SUNY Press.

Eimers, M. T. (2000, May 21–24). *The impact of student experience on progress in college: An examination of minority and non-minority differences.* Paper presented at the annual forum of the Association for Institutional Research, Cincinnati, OH.

Engle, J. (2007). Postsecondary access and success for first-generation college students. *American Academic, 3*(1), 25.

Granovetter, M. S. (1973). The strength of weak ties. *American Journal of Sociology, 6*, 1360–1380.

Horn, L., Nevill, S., & Griffith, J. (2006). Profile of undergraduates in U.S. postsecondary education institutions: 2003–04 with a special analysis of CC students (NCES 2006-184). U.S. Department of Education. Washington, DC: National Center for Educational Statistics.

IBM Corp. Released 2010. IBM SPSS Statistics for Windows, Version 19.0. Armonk, NY: IBM Corp.

Karp, M. M. (2011). *Toward a new understanding of non-academic student support: Four mechanisms encouraging positive student outcomes in the CC* (CCRC Working Paper, Assessment of Evidence Series). New York, NY: Columbia University, Teachers College, CC Research Center.

Karp, M. M., Hughes, K. L., & O'Gara, L. (2010). An exploration of Tinto's integration framework for CC students. *Journal of College Student Retention: Research, Theory and Practice, 12*(1), 69–86.

Kuh, G. D. (1995). The other curriculum: Out-of-class experiences associated with student learning and personal development. *The Journal of Higher Education, 66*(2), 123–155.

Lin, N. (2001). *Social capital: A theory of social structure and action.* New York, NY: Cambridge University Press.

Meeuwisse, M., Severiens, S. E., & Born, M. P. (2010). Learning environment, interaction, sense of belonging and study success in ethnically diverse student groups. *Research in Higher Education, 51*(6), 528–545.

Mercado, M. (2012). *Examining the effects of contextual factors on students' educational outcomes: A special focus on CCs.* Doctoral dissertation. Retrieved from Proquest LLC (UMI 3512663).

Pascarella, E. T., & Terenzini, P. T. (2005). *How college affects students: A third decade of research.* San Francisco, CA: Jossey-Bass.

Rendon, L. I. (1994). Validating culturally diverse students: Toward a new model of learning and student development. *Innovative Higher Education, 19*(1), 33–51.

Santos, S. J., & Reigadas, E. T. (2002). Latinos in higher education: An evaluation of a university faculty mentoring program. *Journal of Hispanic Higher Education, 1*(1), 40–50.

Soares, L., & Mazzeo, C. (2008). *College-ready students, student-ready colleges: An agenda for improving degree completion in postsecondary education.* Washington, DC: Center for American Progress.

Stanton-Salazar, R. D., & Spina, S. U. (2000). The network orientations of highly resilient urban minority youth. *Urban Review: Issues and Ideas in Public Education, 32*, 227–261.

Suárez-Orozco, C., Suárez-Orozco, M. M., & Todorova, I. (2009). *Learning a new land: Immigrant students in American society.* Cambridge, MA: Harvard University Press.

Teranishi, R. T., Suárez-Orozco, C., & Suárez-Orozco, M. M. (2011). Immigrants in CCs. *The Future of Children, 21*(1), 153–169.

Terenzini, P. T., Rendon, L. I., Upcraft, M. L., Millar, S. B., Allison, K. W., Gregg, P. L., & Jalomo, R. (1994). The transition to college: Diverse students, diverse stories. *Research in Higher Education, 35*(1), 57–73.

Tinto, V. (1993). *Leaving college: Rethinking the causes and cures of student attrition* (2nd ed.). Chicago, IL: University of Chicago Press.

Tinto, V. (1998). Colleges as communities: Taking research on student persistence seriously. *The Review of Higher Education, 21*(2), 167–177.

Tinto, V., & Russo, P. (1994). Coordinated studies programs: Their effect on student involvement at CC. *CC Review, 22*(2), 16–25.

Tseng, V., & Seidman, E. (2007). A systems framework for understanding social settings. *American Journal of Community Psychology, 39*(3–4), 217–228.

Weiss, M. J., Mayer, A., Cullinan, D., Ratledge, A., Sommo, C., & Diamond, J. (2014). *A random assignment evaluation of learning communities at Kingsborough CC: Seven years later.* New York, NY: MDRC.

Zhao, C., & Kuh, G. D. (2004). Adding value: Learning communities and student engagement. *Research in Higher Education, 45*(2), 115–138.

CHAPTER 12

The Role of Instructor Relationships in Predicting Academic Outcomes Among Immigrant-Origin Community College Students

McKenna Parnes, Sarah Schwartz,
Carola Suárez-Orozco, & Olivia Osei-Twumasi

The key role that relationships play in learning has long been recognized in primary and secondary education (Hamre & Pianta, 2001). As Lev Vygotsky (1986) famously wrote, "The true direction of the development of thinking is not from the individual to the social, but from the social to the individual" (p. 36). Yet too often in postsecondary education, a hyperfocus on academic preparation and individual student characteristics has resulted in limited attention being given to the relational context. In a recent review of meta-analyses examining instruction variables connected to student achievement in postsecondary education, however, factors related to social interaction and relationships with students were most frequently associated with positive effect sizes when compared with other categories such as stimulating meaningful learning, assessment, presentation, and use of technology (Schneider & Preckel, 2017). Within this context, relationships with instructors play a particularly important role.

Research has demonstrated that relationships with instructors provide a number of benefits, both direct and indirect, for students. Those who have positive relationships with their instructors can receive more specific feedback and instruction and can more effectively address potential conflicts and problems (Jacobson, 2000). Close relationships with instructors can also increase students' sense of belonging and identity development. Such relationships represent a valuable form of social capital that can facilitate important access to information and guidance on how to navigate the college experience (Stanton-Salazar, 2011) as well as to services, resources, and opportunities such as providing connections to internships and jobs (Hurtado & Carter, 1997). Indeed, about a third of recent college graduates report obtaining an internship or job related to their major through a professor (Gallup Inc., 2016). Finally, research suggests that relationships with instructors both inside and outside the classroom contribute to academic engagement, academic achievement, student retention, and student well-being (Baker, 2013; Barbatis, 2010; Deil-Amen, 2011; Garriott, Hudyma, Keene, & Santiago, 2015; Ishitani, 2016; Umbach & Wawrzynski, 2005). In fact, some scholars have pointed to supportive interactions with caring faculty and staff in college as the "single most potent retention agent on campus" (Crockett, 1985, p. 245). A more recent Gallup Poll that utilized a range of measures to determine well-being after graduation found that one of the most significant predictors of students' thriving was having professors who "cared about me as a person" (Gallup Inc., 2014, p. 10). Notably, however, only 27% of undergraduates strongly agreed with this statement (Gallup Inc., 2014).

The lack of close relationships between students and faculty may be even more pronounced at community colleges, which serve high-need populations and have fewer available resources than 4-year colleges do (Bailey, Jaggers, & Jenkins, 2015). In one of a very small number of studies that have examined this issue specifically at community colleges, Hagedorn, Maxwell, Rodriguez, Hocevar, and Fillpot (2000) report low rates of contact between students and faculty outside the classroom at a middle-class, predominantly blue-collar suburban community college. Chang (2005) also uncovered low levels of student–faculty interaction in a study examining the Los Angeles Community College District. Community colleges may present limited opportunities for building strong relationships between students and instructors for a multiplicity of reasons, including these colleges' dependence on adjunct faculty (Wyles, 1998), who spend less time on campus and the particular tightrope feat of balancing home, work, and academic demands faced by many marginalized students, especially immigrant-origin students (Katsiaficas, Suárez-Orozco, & Dias, 2015).

Although research conducted on student–faculty relationships at community colleges has been extremely sparse, there are indications that these relationships, when they exist, can benefit students along multiple dimensions. Thompson (2001) found that community college students who had higher perceived levels of informal interaction with faculty members had greater perceived gains in science and math education. In part, this result may be due to informal student–faculty relationships' promotion of higher levels of in-class effort. Furthermore, a qualitative study conducted among ethnically diverse community college students emphasized the importance of connections with faculty and instructors in contributing to the persistence of diverse community college students (Barbatis, 2010). In a similar vein, Barnett (2011) used quantitative methods to show that students receiving validation from faculty were more likely to feel academically integrated and to express their intent to continue their education. In this chapter, we identified several subconstructs of validation as a specific form of student–faculty interaction, including students' feeling that they were known and valued, caring instruction, appreciation for diversity, and mentoring. All four of these subconstructs were associated with increased academic integration and a stronger intention to persist. Taken together, this research suggests that investing in student–instructor relationships may represent an underutilized but potentially efficacious approach to supporting community college students.

The importance of student–instructor relationships to academic success suggests that this area may represent an important pathway through which other student characteristics may exert their influence. However, few studies have moved beyond exploring student–instructor relationships as predictors of student outcomes to exploring factors contributing to the development of such relationships, especially in the context of community colleges. Chang (2005) found that older students and students with more highly educated parents were more likely to develop relationships with instructors but that Asian American/Pacific Islander (AAPI) and Latinx students were likely to report particularly low levels of student–faculty interaction. More broadly, a number of studies at 4-year schools suggest that marginalized students are less likely to form close relationships with instructors (Berardi, 2012; Museus, 2010; Rios-Aguilar & Deil-Amen, 2012; Tinto, 1993).

Relatedly, although limited research has looked at how racial and ethnic minority status and first-generation college student status may influence how likely students are to form relationships with instructors, little research has focused on student–instructor relationships among immigrant-origin college students, particularly at community colleges. Research on student–teacher relationships in primary and secondary education suggests that teacher relationships play an important role in immigrant-origin students' academic experiences and that first-generation immigrant students tend to have more positive relationships with teachers than second-generation immigrant students do (Peguero & Bondy, 2011; Peguero, Shekarkhar, Popp, & Koo, 2015; Suárez-Orozco, Pimentel, & Martin, 2009), but it is unclear whether a similar pattern occurs in postsecondary education.

Beyond students' demographic characteristics, their relational characteristics could also contribute to whether student–faculty relationships develop. Students bring with them different relational experiences, especially those associated with receiving support, and differ in terms of their comfort levels when engaging with and seeking support from instructors (Karabenick, 2004). Some research suggests these differences are connected to cultural and class differences in norms and expectations (Collier & Morgan, 2008; Lareau & Cox, 2011). However, the role of students' relational characteristics in influencing their relationships with instructors has yet to be explored in the community college setting.

CHAPTER AIMS

In this chapter, we aim to understand the role that relationships with instructors play in the lives of immigrant-origin and nonimmigrant-origin community college students. Specifically, drawing on the full sample of students from the RICC survey (see online appendix for more information about the sample), we hypothesized that the relationships students were (or were not) able to form with instructors would significantly predict their academic engagement and academic achievement. We also sought to understand student characteristics that may have contributed to whether or not they developed close relationships with instructors. Finally, we investigated whether student–instructor relationships may have mediated the association between student characteristics and academic outcomes. Put another way, we expected that specific student characteristics would be associated with better relationships with instructors, which in turn would be associated with higher academic engagement and higher grade point average (GPA). In particular, we hypothesized that immigrant generational status, part-time student status, and student relational factors would be associated with academic engagement and achievement through their influence on students' relationships with instructors.

Modeling Engagement

Drawing on student survey data and academic records, we used advanced statistical modeling (structural equation modeling) to understand how these factors may be related to each other (see online appendix for details).

Demographic variables. First, we included a range of potential student factors that may have influenced the relationships that students formed with instructors, including gender, age, race, immigrant generational status, first-generation college student status, part-time or full-time student status, and semester in college, and which of the three campuses students were attending.

Predictors. We also included some individual relational factors that we thought might have played an important role in the development of students' relationships with instructors. These included (1) a single-item question asking students if they had a *mentor* and (2) a four-item scale examining *help-seeking* by having students rate how likely they were to try to handle various problems on their own as opposed to seeking help or support from someone else.

Mediator. We examined how all of these factors predicted *instructor relationships* as measured by a nine-item self-reported scale focusing on students' perceptions of having instructors who could provide them with support and advice and who cared about and respected them. Then, we looked at how instructor relationships predicted outcomes, including academic engagement and GPA.

Outcomes. Academic engagement included both self-reported behavioral and cognitive aspects of students' academic engagement using a five-point Likert scale, with student ratings ranging from 1 = *strongly disagree* to 5 = *strongly agree*. *Cognitive engagement* was measured using a six-item measure adapted from Martin's (2012) nine-item measure, focusing on the extent to which students were interested and intellectually engaged in their learning. Sample items included, "I feel good when I learn something new even if it is hard" (α_1 = .80). *Behavioral engagement* was measured using a six-item measure adapted from scale used by Suárez-Orozco, Pimentel, & Martin (2009), focusing on the extent to which students engaged in effortful behaviors for the class. Sample items included, "I turned in my assignments on time" (α_1 = .80).

What Matters in Engagement

Prior to testing our model, we looked at students' ratings of their relationships with instructors. There was substantial variation in responses, with scores ranging from 1, the lowest possible score, to 5, the highest possible score. The average score was 3.86 (with a standard deviation of 0.76), indicating that in general students were more positive than negative when rating their instructor relationships but that there was also room for improvement in most of the students' self-reported relationships.

Our analyses also showed that some student demographic and situational factors were related to whether students formed supportive relationships with instructors. Specifically, older students reported having better relationships with instructors than younger students did (within the context of a sample that included students ages 18 through 25), and full-time students reported having better relationships than part-time students did. The campus that students attended also was a factor in whether students formed supportive relationships with instructors, with students who attended the Taino campus reporting better relationships with instructors than students who attended the Domino campus did. Surprisingly, within our sample, student–instructor relationships did not differ based on gender, race, semester in college, immigrant generational status, or first-generation college student status. However, relational characteristics played an important role in predicting better student–instructor relationships: students with higher support-seeking attitudes and students with a mentor reported having closer relationships with instructors.

We then turned to exploring the effect of these relationships with instructors on students' academic success. Results showed that, overall, our hypothesized model was a good fit for the data (see Figure 12.1). Student–instructor relationships were significantly associated with behavioral engagement as well as cognitive engagement. In turn, these relationships were also significantly associated with college GPA.

Additionally, we observed important indirect effects on academic outcomes via student–instructor relationships. Specifically, such relationships significantly mediated both the association between support-seeking attitudes and academic engagement and the association between having a mentor and academic engagement. Student–instructor relationships also significantly mediated the association between students' support-seeking attitudes and GPA and the association between their having a mentor and GPA. In other words, students who reported having a mentor and those who reported increased help-seeking were more likely

Figure 12.1. Standardized Parameter Estimates of Structural Equation Model

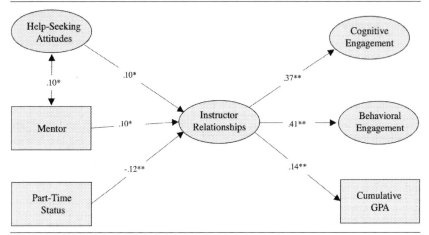

Notes: Covariates are not shown. *$p < .05$. **$p < .01$.

to have supportive relationships with instructors, which in turn predicted higher academic engagement and GPA. Finally, student–instructor relationships significantly partially mediated the relationship between part-time student status and academic outcomes, with part-time students reporting having less supportive relationships with instructors than full-time students did, a result that in turn was associated with lower academic engagement and lower GPA. These findings suggest that part-time student status, attitudes about support-seeking, and having a mentor may indirectly influence students' academic success through their relationships with instructors.

IN SUM

This chapter calls attention to the key role that student–instructor relationships can play in the academic success of community college students, including both immigrant-origin and nonimmigrant-origin (defined as third-generation or more immigrant) students. We found that student–instructor relationships were significantly associated with all of the outcomes we examined, including both behavioral and cognitive aspects of academic engagement and students' GPAs. Although causality cannot be concluded from the current analyses alone, in the context of theory and research from 4-year college settings indicating the importance of student–instructor relationships (Baker, 2013; Garriott, Hudyma, Keene, & Santiago, 2015; Ishitani, 2016; Stanton-Salazar, 2011; Umbach & Wawrzynski, 2005), along with qualitative data from community college settings (Barbatis, 2010; Deil-Amen,

2011), these results build the case for the role of student–instructor relationships in the academic success of marginalized students in community college settings.

In the context of increasing research that points to the significant role such relationships play, it is also important to understand the factors that influence whether such relationships develop. Surprisingly, we did not observe significant differences in student–instructor relationships based on immigrant generational status. This finding contrasts with those of research conducted in secondary school settings that indicate that first-generation immigrant students have more positive relationships with teachers than second-generation immigrant students do (Peguero & Bondy, 2011; Peguero et al., 2015; Suárez-Orozco, Pimentel, & Martin, 2009). In part, this result may be due both to the limited opportunities within the community college context for immigrant students of either generation to engage in such relationships given their heavy work/home commitments outside of campus life (Katsiaficas, Suárez-Orozco, & Dias, 2015) and to the teaching schedules of most adjunct faculty that allow only limited time on campus to invest in students (Wyles, 1998).

Additionally, first-generation college students (those who were the first in their families to go to college) did not significantly differ from continuing-generation college students in their relationships with instructors. Again, this finding contrasts with previous research that has observed that first-generation college students tend to have less supportive relationships with instructors (Collier & Morgan, 2008; Engle & Tinto, 2008). However, most of this prior research was conducted at 4-year colleges and universities, suggesting differences from conditions in the community college context. At the same time, it also may be that first-generation college student status is less beneficial for immigrant students coming from countries with distinct educational systems in which navigating college and student–instructor relationships may look very different.

In fact, the only student demographic characteristic that emerged as significantly associated with student–instructor relationships was age, with older students reporting having more supportive relationships with faculty. Older students may be more skilled at connecting with instructors, in part because they are more similar in age. They also may enter college with a clearer sense of what they want to get out of college and feel more comfortable reaching out to instructors and asking for support.

Part-time students also reported having less supportive relationships with instructors than full-time students did, and this situation indirectly contributed to part-time students' lower academic engagement and GPA. Although there are a number of reasons why part-time students may demonstrate lower academic engagement and achievement than full-time students do, including having other responsibilities that may interfere with their ability to fully engage in college, it is notable that part-time students' lower academic outcomes were in part explained by their weaker relationships with instructors. This finding suggests that interventions designed to strengthen part-time students' connections with instructors may be a particularly effective approach to supporting their academic engagement and success.

Finally, this chapter also explored how students' prior relationship experiences and relational orientation may influence the extent to which they form supportive relationships with instructors. Specifically, our results suggest that students' willingness to seek help and their prior experiences with supportive adults or mentors may indirectly influence their academic success by impacting their relationships with instructors. This finding is in line with previous research and theory indicating a great deal of consistency across an individual's relationships, particularly among *vertical relationships,* that is, relationships with others who have more knowledge and power. Relationships with peers are *horizontal relationships,* that is, relationships between equals (Hartup, 1989). This result means that students who have previously had positive experiences with mentors may be more likely to develop mentoring relationships with instructors. This finding is also supported by research on formal mentoring programs, suggesting that students' high-quality relationships with mentors may translate into improved relationships with teachers and others (Chan et al., 2013; Herrera, Grossman, Kauh, & McMaken, 2011).

Additionally, this research suggests that when students try to solve their problems on their own rather than reach out to others for support, their actions may indirectly have a detrimental effect on their academic success since they may be less likely to form supportive relationships with instructors. This finding may be particularly relevant for immigrant-origin students, who may have learned to be self-reliant as a survival strategy, particularly in the context of systemic discrimination (Doucet & Suárez-Orozco, 2006). Moreover, as discussed in Chapter 4, students who are undocumented or who are supporting undocumented family members may seek to avoid calling attention to themselves or sharing details about the challenges they face due to potential risks to themselves or their families. Similarly, different expectations and comfort levels concerning self-advocacy and particularly reaching out to instructors and others deemed as figures of authority may influence students' capacity to connect with instructors (Collier & Morgan, 2008; Jack, 2016; Stephens, Brannon, Markus, & Nelson, 2015). At the same time, this research also suggests that targeting students' willingness to seek help may be one way to influence students' relationships with instructors as well as their academic success.

It is important to note that although this chapter focused primarily on student factors, campus and instructor factors also play a critical role in affecting whether supportive relationships between students and instructors develop. As noted earlier, there were some significant differences in students' reports of relationships with instructors based on the campus they attended. There are likely structural differences across campuses, including factors such as class size, reliance on adjunct rather than full-time instructors, and even scheduling and campus layout, along with differences in campus culture, that may contribute to differences in student–instructor relationships. It will be important for future studies to examine the role of such factors. Additionally, further research is needed on instructors' attitudes and characteristics, including the ways in which these interact with student characteristics. For example, as examined in Chapter 6, instructor microaggressions were observed to be prevalent on campus, signaling to students a lack of safety in their relationships with instructors and deterring them from reaching out to instructors for support. Other research has documented differing responses from professors and employers to students' attempts to reach out based on their perceptions of students' demographic characteristics (Milkman, Akinola, & Chugh, 2014; Rivera & Tilcsik, 2016). In one study in which identical emails were sent to professors at colleges and universities across the country, when a student's name was perceived to be that of a racial or ethnic minority or a female, professors were less likely to respond (Milkman et al., 2014). This finding highlights the need to consider how faculty characteristics and responses to students influence the relationships they form with students.

IMPLICATIONS FOR FUTURE RESEARCH AND PRACTICE

As discussed in this book's Introduction (Chapter 1), immigrant-origin students in community colleges face significant barriers to their academic success. Yet when students are able to develop close and supportive relationships with instructors who can help them navigate the community college experience, they are more likely to weather the storms that inevitably arise, making them more likely to persist and achieve success.

In light of the key role that student–instructor relationships play, it is important to develop strategies to facilitate the development of such relationships for all students, particularly those who may be less likely to initiate such relationships on their own. Ideally, strategies could be implemented at the campus, instructor, and student levels. For example, strategies that provide opportunities for keeping students on campus (such as work-study jobs or welcoming study spaces), scheduled free times when instructors and students are not in class and available to meet, and smaller class size might serve to increase the likelihood that students will connect with instructors on campus.

Additionally, as there is increasing recognition of the time and effort it takes for instructors to be available to students and to develop student–faculty relationships, some universities are including mentoring and advising as part of the criteria by which faculty are evaluated, thereby providing incentives for faculty to allot time for and to invest in such relationships. At the same time, many instructors may need additional training and assistance in ways to establish these relationships, including strategies they can use both within and outside the classroom to build relationships with students, particularly those from marginalized backgrounds and those who may be less comfortable approaching instructors for support. Moreover, observation of relatively common incidences of instructor microaggressions on community college campuses indicates the need for instructors' explicit training about these matters as well as more general training on how to effectively teach diverse students. Workshops could be developed for instructors not only to highlight the importance of their relationships with students in promoting their academic success but also to sensitize instructors to the ways in which their own behaviors may either pose barriers to or facilitate the development of student–instructor relationships. Recent scholarship on the immigrant experience in secondary education suggests the need for teachers and teacher education programs to emphasize *cariño conscientizado,* or critically conscious and genuine care, in order to truly support and contribute to immigrant students' sense of belonging (DeNicolo, Yu, Crowley, & Gabel, 2017). Such models could also be extended to the postsecondary education context. Of course, such strategies face challenges, particularly at underresourced community colleges that often rely on staff who are already stretched thin, indicating the importance of greater financial investment in community colleges.

Although systemic support plays a critical role in the overall climate at and in individual relationships within community colleges, student-level interventions can also be designed to encourage students to connect with instructors. Student mentoring programs are a commonly employed strategy to help students build relationships with faculty and staff on campus. Research suggests that these approaches, particularly mentoring programs, can be effective in improving academic performance (Crisp, 2010). Unfortunately, however, mentoring programs are limited by their capacity to recruit a sufficient number of mentors, particularly when relying on staff and instructors, for the number of students they aspire to reach.

A novel intervention that is specifically designed to promote on-campus relationships among underrepresented college students is the Connected Scholars (CS) program. Connected Scholars explicitly teaches students the skills and approaches necessary to identify underrepresented students, recruit them, and help them maintain relationships on campus, with a focus on building their relationships with instructors and other key players who can support the attainment of these students' academic and career goals (Schwartz, Kanchewa, Rhodes, Cutler, & Cunningham, 2016).

In fact, our finding that younger students tend to have less supportive relationships with instructors suggests that these students may lack some of the skills and attitudes conducive to connecting with instructors that their older peers may have already developed. Preliminary research on this intervention in the context of first-generation college students at a 4-year public commuter campus suggests that CS may increase students' willingness to seek support, improve their relationships with instructors, and raise their first-year college GPAs (Schwartz et al., 2017). This approach, which appears promising, may also be adapted to address unique challenges to connecting students with instructors faced by different populations, including community college students and immigrant-origin students. Similarly, since our data indicate that part-time students are less likely to form supportive relationships with instructors than full-time students are, perhaps workshops or targeted mentoring programs could be developed specifically for part-time students.

LIMITATIONS AND FUTURE DIRECTIONS

Although our analyses in this chapter have a number of strengths, including the use of quantitative data drawn from a large sample of students generally under-represented in research studies, there are also a number of limitations that should be noted. Most importantly, since the data were drawn from a cross-sectional survey, we cannot make any causal conclusions. Longitudinal data measuring students' baseline characteristics when they first enter college and then measuring their relationships with instructors and their academic outcomes over time would allow for a deeper understanding of the associations we observed. Additionally, as noted earlier, studies would ideally include instructor and campus characteristics as well as perhaps those of the broader community and a sociohistorical context to better understand how these factors interact to influence students' experiences and success in college. Similarly, it would be beneficial to combine student-report surveys with other sources of data such as instructor reports of relationship quality. Finally, there is a need for the development of interventions designed to influence student–instructor relationships along with rigorous evaluation of whether and how such interventions may ultimately influence academic success.

Nevertheless, this research does provide an important step toward better understanding the role of student–instructor relationships in the experiences of immigrant-origin community college students. More broadly, this chapter helps us move beyond focusing solely on the academic outcomes of community college students to examine the processes that lead to such outcomes, potentially identifying key points of leverage where intervention may be possible.

REFERENCES

Bailey, T. R., Jaggars, S. S., & Jenkins, D. (2015). *Redesigning America's community colleges.* Cambridge, MA: Harvard University Press.

Baker, C. N. (2013). Social support and success in higher education: The influence of on-campus support on African American and Latino college students. *The Urban Review, 45,* 632–650.

Barbatis, P. (2010). Underprepared, ethnically diverse community college students: Factors contributing to persistence. *Journal of Developmental Education, 33*(3), 14.

Barnett, E. A. (2011). Validation experiences and persistence among community college students. *The Review of Higher Education, 34*(2), 193–230.

Berardi, L. (2012). *The first year college experience: Predictors of natural mentoring relationships and students' academic outcomes.* Unpublished doctoral dissertation. DePaul University, Chicago, IL.

Chan, C., Rhodes, J. E., Howard, W., Lowe, S., Schwartz, S. E. O., & Herrera, C. (2013). Pathways of influence in school-based mentoring: The mediated role of parent and teacher relationships. *Journal of School Psychology, 51,* 129–142. doi:10.1016/j.jsp.2012.10.001

Chang, J. C. (2005). Faculty student interaction at the community college: A focus on students of color. *Research in Higher Education, 46*(7), 769–802.

Collier, P. J., & Morgan, D. L. (2008). "Is that paper really due today?": Differences in first-generation and traditional college students' understandings of faculty expectations. *Higher Education: The International Journal of Higher Education and Educational Planning, 55*(4), 425–446. doi:10.1007/s10734-007-9065-5

Crisp, G. (2010). The impact of mentoring on community college students' intent to persist. *The Review of Higher Education, 34*(1), 39–60. doi:10.1353/rhe.2010.0003

Crockett, D. S. (1985). Academic advising. In L. Noel, R. Levitz, & D. Saluri (Eds.), *Increasing student retention: Effective programs and practices for reducing the dropout rate* (pp. 244–263). San Francisco, CA: Jossey-Bass.

Deil-Amen, R. (2011). Socio-academic integrative moments: Rethinking academic and social integration among two-year college students in career-related programs. *The Journal of Higher Education, 82*(1), 54–91. Retrieved from dx.doi.org/10.1080/00221546 .2011.11779085

DeNicolo, C. P., Yu, M., Crowley, C. B., & Gabel, S. L. (2017). Reimagining critical care and problematizing sense of school belonging as a response to inequality for immigrants and children of immigrants. *Review of Research in Education, 41,* 500–530. Retrieved from dx.doi.org/10.3102/0091732X17690498

Doucet, F., & Suárez-Orozco, C. (2006). Ethnic identity and schooling: The experiences of Haitian immigrant youth. In L. Romanucci-Ross, G. DeVos, & T. Tsuda (Eds.), *Ethnic identity: Creation, conflict, and accommodation* (4th ed., pp. 163–188). Walnut Creek, CA: Alta Mira Press.

Engle, J., & Tinto, V. (2008). Moving beyond access: College success for low-income, first-generation students. *The Pell Institute for the Study of Opportunity in Higher Education,* 1–30. Retrieved from files.eric.ed.gov/fulltext/ED504448.pdf

Gallup Inc. (2014). *Great jobs great lives: The 2014 Gallup-Purdue Index Report.* Washington, DC: Author.

Gallup Inc. (2016). *Great jobs great lives: The value of career services, inclusive experiences and mentorship for college graduates.* Washington, DC: Author.

Garriott, P. O., Hudyma, A., Keene, C., & Santiago, D. (2015). Social cognitive predictors of first- and non-first-generation college students' academic and life satisfaction. *Journal of Counseling Psychology, 62*(2), 253. Retrieved from dx.doi.org/10.1037 /cou0000066

Hagedorn, L. S., Maxwell, W., Rodriguez, P., Hocevar, D., & Fillpot, J. (2000). Peer and student-faculty relations in community colleges. *Community College Journal of Research & Practice, 24*(7), 587–598.

Hamre, B. K., & Pianta, R. C. (2001). Early teacher–child relationships and the trajectory of children's school outcomes through eighth grade. *Child Development, 72,* 625–638.

Hartup, W. W. (1989). Social relationships and their developmental significance. *American Psychologist, 44,* 120–126.

Herrera, C., Grossman, J. B., Kauh, T. J., & McMaken, J. (2011). Mentoring in schools: An impact study of Big Brothers Big Sisters school-based mentoring. *Child Development, 82,* 346–361.

Hurtado, S., & Carter, D. F. (1997). Effects of college transition and perceptions of the campus racial climate on Latino college students' sense of belonging. *Sociology of Education, 70*(4), 324–345.

Ishitani, T. T. (2016). First-generation students' persistence at four-year institutions. *College and University, 91*, 22–32.

Jack, A. A. (2016). (No) harm in asking: Class, acquired cultural capital, and academic engagement at an elite university. *Sociology of Education, 89*(1), 1–19. Retrieved from dx .doi.org/10.1177/0038040715614913

Jacobson, L. O. (2000, Summer). Valuing diversity—Student-teacher relationships that enhance achievement. *Community College Review Journal.* Retrieved from findarticles .com/p/articles/mi_m0HCZ/is_1_28/ai_65068894/pg_6

Karabenick, S. A. (2004). Perceived achievement goal structure and college student help seeking. *Journal of Educational Psychology, 96*, 569–581.

Katsiaficas, D., Suárez-Orozco, C., & Dias, S. I. (2015). "When do I feel like an adult?" Latino and Afro-Caribbean immigrant-origin community college students' conceptualizations and experiences of (emerging) adulthood. *Emerging Adulthood, 3*(2), 98–112.

Lareau, A., & Cox, C. (2011). Social class and the transition to adulthood: Differences in parents' interactions with institutions. In M. J. Carlson & P. England (Eds.), *Social class and changing families in an unequal America.* Stanford, CA: Stanford University Press.

Martin, M. (2012). *Situated academic engagement for immigrant origin males: Student centered studies of the relationship between school context, academic engagement, and academic outcomes.* Doctoral dissertation. Retrieved from ProQuest Dissertations and Theses database.

Milkman, K. L., Akinola, M., & Chugh, D. (2015). What happens before? A field experiment exploring how pay and representation differentially shape bias on the pathway into organizations. *Journal of Applied Psychology, 100*, 1678–1712. doi:10.1037/apl0000022

Museus, S. D. (2010). Delineating the ways that targeted support programs facilitate minority students' access to social networks and development of social capital in college. *Enrollment Management Journal: Student Access, Finance, and Success in Higher Education, 4*, 10–41.

Peguero, A. A., & Bondy, J. M. (2011). Immigration and students' relationship with teachers. *Education and Urban Society, 43*, 165–183.

Peguero, A. A., Shekarkhar, Z., Popp, A. M., & Koo, D. J. (2015). Punishing the children of immigrants: Race, ethnicity, generational status, student misbehavior, and school discipline. *Journal of Immigrant & Refugee Studies, 13*, 200–220.

Rios-Aguilar, C., & Deil-Amen, R. (2012). Beyond getting in and fitting in: An examination of social networks and professionally relevant social capital among Latina/o university students. *Journal of Hispanic Higher Education, 11*(2), 179–196. Retrieved from dx.doi .org/10.1177/1538192711435555

Rivera, L. A., & Tilcsik, A. (2016). Class advantage, commitment penalty: The gendered effect of social class signals in an elite labor market. *American Sociological Review, 81*, 1097–1131.

Schneider, M., & Preckel, F. (2017). Variables associated with achievement in higher education: A systematic review of meta-analyses. *Psychological Bulletin, 143*, 565–600.

Schwartz, S. E. O., Kanchewa, S. S., Rhodes, J. E., Cutler, E., & Cunningham, J. (2016). "I didn't know you could just ask": Empowering underrepresented college students to recruit academic and career mentors. *Children and Youth Services Review, 64,* 51–59. Retrieved from dx.doi.org/10.1016/j.childyouth.2016.03.0010190-7409

Schwartz, S. E. O., Kanchewa, S. S., Rhodes, J. E., Gowdy, G., Stark, S., Horn, J., . . . Spencer, R. (2017). "I'm having a little struggle with this, can you help me out?": Examining impacts and processes of a social capital intervention for first-generation college students. *American Journal of Community Psychology.* doi:10.1002/ajcp.12206

Stanton-Salazar, R. D. (2011). A social capital framework for the study of institutional agents and their role in the empowerment of low-status students and youth. *Youth & Society, 43,* 1066–1109. Retrieved from dx.doi.org/10.1177/0044118X10382877

Stephens, N. M., Brannon, T. N., Markus, H. R., & Nelson, J. E. (2015). Feeling at home in college: Fortifying school-relevant selves to reduce social class disparities in higher education. *Social Issues and Policy Review, 9,* 1–24. doi:10.1111/sipr.12008

Suárez-Orozco, C., Pimentel, A., & Martin, M. (2009). The significance of relationships: Academic engagement and achievement among newcomer immigrant youth. *Teachers College Record, 111,* 712–749.

Thompson, M. D. (2001). Informal student-faculty interaction: Its relationship to educational gains in science and mathematics among community college students. *Community College Review, 29*(1), 35 57.

Tinto, V. (1993). Building community. *Liberal Education, 79*(4), 16–21.

Umbach, P. D., & Wawrzynski, M. R. (2005). Faculty do matter: The role of college faculty in student learning and engagement. *Research in Higher Education, 46*(2), 153–184. Retrieved from dx.doi.org/10.1007/s11162-004-1598-1

Vygotsky, L. S. (1986). Piaget's theory of thought and speech. In *Thought and language* (rev. ed., pp. 12–57). Cambridge, MA: MIT Press.

Wyles, B. A. (1998). Adjunct faculty in the community college: Realities and challenges. *New Directions for Higher Education, 1998*(104), 89–93.

Part IV

AND NOW WHAT?

CHAPTER 13

Dreams Versus Realities

Graduation Rates of Immigrant-Origin Community College Students

Olivia Osei-Twumasi & Juliana Karras-Jean Gilles

Community colleges have been described as the "Ellis Island of higher education" (Connell, 2008), offering the promise of social mobility for immigrant-origin students. But a vast body of educational research demonstrates low graduation and transfer rates of community college students across the nation (e.g., see Brint, 2003). Although most community college students aim to achieve a bachelor's degree or higher, in reality, national bachelor's degree graduation rates for students starting out at community colleges are very low (Bailey, Jaggars, & Jenkins, 2015). This finding has implications for the role of community colleges in providing social mobility for marginalized groups, including immigrant-origin students—for whom research suggests educational expectations are high (Conway, 2010; Kao & Tienda, 1995).

Despite the fact that immigrant-origin students constitute nearly a quarter of students in higher education and nearly a third of students in community colleges (see Chapter 1), there is a dearth of research examining the postsecondary outcomes of immigrant-origin students generally and, more specifically, the outcomes of the more than half who first enroll at community colleges. City University of New York (CUNY) community colleges serve high rates of immigrant-origin students (CUNY Office of Institutional Research and Assessment, 2018), thus providing an excellent opportunity to analyze the graduation rates of immigrant-origin students who begin their educational journeys at a community college. In this chapter we examine students' dreams as compared to their realities by juxtaposing survey data on expectations from our Research on Immigrants in Community College (RICC) survey with administrative CUNY data on actual bachelor's degree completion rates.

THE COMMUNITY COLLEGE MANDATE
AND STUDENT EXPECTATIONS

Community colleges have a broad mandate with a variety of roles (Rosenbaum, Deil-Amen, & Person, 2007). These roles include providing technical and vocational education as well as preparing students to transfer to 4-year universities for further studies. Additionally, many community colleges offer a wide variety of not-for-credit courses, including remedial education and basic skills training; short-term vocational programs that provide high employment potential; and classes for specific groups such as parents, older adults, and persons with substantial disabilities. Some of these colleges, especially those in urban areas, offer classes that are particularly useful for immigrants, such as English as a Second Language (ESL), citizenship classes, and workforce preparation classes (Szelényi & Chang, 2002). Given the broad mandate of community colleges and the various roles they try to fulfill, it is important to understand the expectations of students who enter these institutions.

In fact, based on nationally representative data, nearly 90% of community college students express their intention to obtain a certificate or degree (Hoachlander, Sikora, & Horn, 2003), and more than 80% report that they are seeking a bachelor's degree or higher (Horn & Skomsvold, 2011). Furthermore, previous research has shown that most students start college expecting to complete their intended courses of study. For example, drawing on a large longitudinal study of students in Wisconsin, Goldrick-Rab (2016) reports that the vast majority of college students do not have even "an inkling that they could leave college without a degree" (p. 33).

Students have good reason to seek a bachelor's degree since holders of this credential enjoy a substantial wage premium and lower unemployment rates (Toutkoushian & Paulsen, 2016). Associate's degrees also lead to a wage premium, as do certificates, with wide variation, depending on the specific field of study (Jepsen, Troske, & Coomes, 2014). Unsurprisingly, students who completed their programs and received a credential report have substantially better labor market outcomes (i.e., higher wages and lower unemployment rates) than do students who did not complete their courses of studies (Hoachlander et al., 2003).

If young people on average have high educational expectations, how do the expectations of immigrant-origin community college students compare? The extant literature suggests that their expectations are even higher than the average (Kao & Tienda, 1995). In part, this hope may be fueled by a sense of obligation to repay their immigrant parents for the sacrifices they made to come to the United States and a desire to support their families through well-paying jobs in the future (Fuligni & Witkow, 2004). The majority of this work has examined the educational expectations of immigrant-origin students and their families through students' high school years (e.g., Fuligni, 2001; Perreira, Harris, & Lee, 2006), so little is known about their expectations at the college level. However, Kirui and Kao (2018) used nationally representative data to show that second-generation immigrant students in higher education have higher expectations (and higher graduation rates) than native-born students do, controlling for a host of other characteristics. Furthermore, Conway (2010) examined the educational expectations of first-year freshmen at one of the community colleges within the system studied in this chapter and found that foreign-born students anticipated attaining a bachelor's degree at a higher rate than second-generation or third-plus–generation students did, with U.S. high-schooled immigrants having the highest rate.

However, students' high expectations stand in stark contrast to the actual outcomes of community college students across the nation. Bailey and colleagues (2015) report that fewer than 4 of every 10 community college students complete any type of degree or certificate program within 6 years. Furthermore, Horn and Skomsvold (2011) show that just 12% of community college students had attained a bachelor's degree or higher within 6 years of their initial enrollment.

Despite the large and increasing representation of immigrant-origin students at community colleges (see Chapter 1), detailed information on their outcomes is extremely difficult to find. Rates of degree attainment are often reported by race/ethnicity, gender, and socioeconomic status but not by immigrant status or nativity. The majority of existing studies that focus on immigrant-origin students only go as far as college enrollment (e.g., Glick & White, 2004; Vernez & Abrahamse, 1996) or do not differentiate explicitly between the outcomes of 2-year and 4-year students (Kirui & Kao, 2018). Nonetheless, Erisman and Looney (2007) have reported detailed enrollment and attainment data for immigrant-origin students and highlighted differences by age of arrival and race/ethnicity. They have shown that although immigrant-origin undergraduates complete college at the same rate as the overall student population does, they are more likely to earn certificates or associate's degrees rather than bachelor's degrees. Furthermore, Bailey and Weininger (2002) looked specifically at the effects of immigrant generation and race on students who had enrolled in the CUNY community colleges in 1990. They found that bachelor's degree attainment was very low (only 10% of students had earned a bachelor's degree within 8 years of their initial enrollment) when contrasted with students' initial high expectations (more than 70% had stated that they aspired to complete at least a bachelor's degree). However, the researchers did find that immigrant students earned more credits and were more likely to complete an associate's degree than native students entering the same programs were and that immigrants who went to a U.S. high school were more likely than native-born 2-year entrants to transfer to a bachelor's program.

In contrast to the scant literature on outcomes tracked by immigrant origin, vast amounts of research have demonstrated disparities by race/ethnicity. In educational settings, racialization often plays a profound role in immigrant-origin students' experiences and opportunities, which differ among and within racial/ethnic groups. This signals the importance of employing an intersectional lens (Crenshaw, 1991) to contextualize how marginalization occurs at the intersection of multiple social identities (e.g., ethnic groups, races, phenotypes, nationalities) (Suárez-Orozco, Yoshikawa, & Tseng, 2015). Within the United States, educational outcomes vary among racial/ethnic groups, with the highest achievement rates observed for Asian and White students while Latinx and Black students' educational outcomes persistently remain lower (Noguera, 2008). However, an intersectional lens contextualizes these disparities by recognizing the great heterogeneity within groups. For example, among Asian American and Pacific Islander students, the degree completion rates for Hmong and Laotian students are far lower than those for students of Korean or Japanese descent (B. M. D. Nguyen, M. H. Nguyen, Teranishi, & Hune, 2015; Wing, 2007).

In this chapter we explore multiple layers of students' social identities by studying combinations across generations (first, second, third-plus) and racial/ethnic backgrounds. Although imperfect, this examination is an important step in disentangling how social identity intersects with opportunity when students begin their journeys of higher education by enrolling at community colleges.

CHAPTER AIMS

Existing research indicates that there is a vast chasm between students' expectations and their actual educational outcomes. Due to the lack of data on immigrant-origin students, we do not yet have a clear picture of how immigrant-origin community college students' expectations compare with those of their native peers and how their expectations align with their actual outcomes. In this chapter we juxtapose educational expectations with actual graduation rates to highlight the discrepancy between students' expectations and their outcomes, and we explore differences by immigrant generation and race/ethnicity. We address the following research questions:

1. What expectations do CUNY community college students hold regarding their educational trajectories? And how do these expectations differ by immigrant generation, race, and campus attended?
2. What are the actual 6-year graduation rates for bachelor's degrees for students from all CUNY community colleges? And how do these graduation rates differ by race/ethnicity, immigrant generation, and campus attended?
3. When expected graduation rates for students from the Domino and Taino campuses are juxtaposed with their actual graduation rates, how do the rates compare?

In order to address these questions, we drew on two separate but related data sets from the RICC study (see Figure 13.1 for details and Table 13.1 for demographics). Using data collected from the RICC survey (see online appendix for details), we examined the educational expectations of students who were currently enrolled during the 2012–2013 school year. We then used CUNY administrative data (see online appendix for details) to examine the actual 6-year bachelor's degree completion rates for students who had initially enrolled during the 2006–2007 school year (i.e., we reviewed their actual outcomes by the 2012–2013 school year). For RQ1 and RQ2, we tested for group differences by immigrant generation, race/ethnicity, and campus attended. We used *chi*-square tests to study differences between paired variables and one-way ANOVAs to examine group differences for

Figure 13.1. Summary of Data Availability and Sources Utilized per Research Question

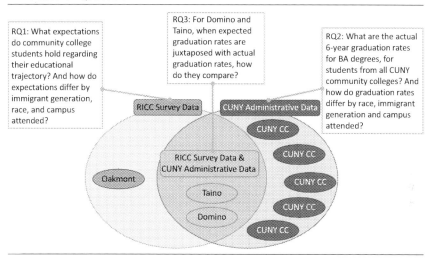

RQ1: What expectations do community college students hold regarding their educational trajectory? And how do expectations differ by immigrant generation, race, and campus attended?

RQ3: For Domino and Taino, when expected graduation rates are juxtaposed with actual graduation rates, how do they compare?

RQ2: What are the actual 6-year graduation rates for BA degrees, for students from all CUNY community colleges? And how do graduation rates differ by race, immigrant generation and campus attended?

Table 13.1. Descriptives

		RICC		CUNY admin	
		n	%	*n*	%
Race/ Ethnicity	Asian	58	9%	3,322	13%
	Black	172	27%	9,184	35%
	Latinx	250	39%	8,760	33%
	White	81	13%	5,204	20%
	Other (other, mixed, Native American)	77	12%	54	0%
	Missing	6	1%	01	0%
	Total	644	100%	26,524	100%
Immigrant Generation	First	213	33%	8,845	33%
	Second	275	43%	5,703	22%
	Third or higher	150	23%	3,582	14%
	Missing	6	1%	8,394	32%
	Total	644	100%	26,524	100%

Note: CUNY administrative race/ethnicity data reported here were imputed, so there is no missing race/ethnicity. The imputed race/ethnicity variable we rely on is very similar to the self-reported race variable, but contains no missing data.

variables with three or more categories. For RQ3, we juxtaposed expectations and graduation rates from the two data sets, comparing expectations and outcomes for students at the same colleges.

We focus on bachelor's degree completion rates in this chapter, although associate's degree completion rates are also important measures of institutional success for community colleges and deliver tangible rewards for the students who attain them (Bailey et al., 2015). We focus on bachelor's degree completion since this certification is the self-reported expectation of most students entering community colleges (Horn & Skomvold, 2011) and since bachelor's degree completion is associated with many long-term benefits that outpace benefits connected with associate's degrees (Toutkoushian & Paulsen, 2016). It is important to note that the CUNY administrative data only provide information on graduation within the CUNY system. However, Conger and Turner (2017) have used National Clearinghouse data to demonstrate that it is exceedingly rare for students who begin their education at CUNY community colleges to graduate from non-CUNY institutions. Thus, students who did not complete their studies within the CUNY system probably did not complete their degrees at all.

RICC PARTICIPANT EXPECTATIONS

According to data from our RICC survey ($N = 625$), 74% of students entering community colleges expected that they would earn a bachelor's degree or higher (see Figure 13.2). Another 16% anticipated that they would earn an associate's degree, and the remaining 10% indicated having some measure of uncertainty about their educational trajectory—that is, 4% anticipated transferring to a 4-year college but not graduating, 4% did not know, and 2% expected to leave community colleges before they graduated.

Demographic Variations in Expectations

Table 13.2 provides a breakdown of students' postsecondary expectations by race/ethnicity and generation ($N = 625$; source: RICC survey). No differences were found among racial/ethnic groups' expectations; however, there were significant differences between immigrant-origin (first and second generation) and third-plus–generation students: $\chi2$ $(2, N = 625) = 4.26, p < .05$. Specifically, immigrant-origin students' expectations of completing a bachelor's degree or higher were greater than those of the third-plus–generation students. A one-way ANOVA by campus indicated that the expectations of students differed significantly by campus: $F(2, 624) = 3.03, p = .049$. Follow-up Bonferroni tests indicated that students' expectations at the Domino campus ($M = .79, SD = .41$) were significantly higher than those at Oakmont ($M = .74, SD = .44$) or Taino ($M = .68, SD = .47$).

Figure 13.2. Postsecondary Education Expectations (*n* = 625)

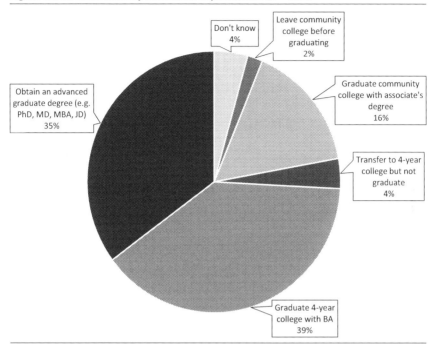

Note: Survey data from the RICC study regarding students' expectations for educational attainment. Approximately three quarters of students entering community colleges expect to graduate with a bachelor's degree or higher.

Six-Year Graduation Rates at CUNY

The figures in Table 13.3 show the 6-year graduation rates (150% of the standard time requirement). The actual outcome rates indicated by the CUNY administrative records of how many students had completed their bachelor's degrees within 6 years of matriculating across all CUNY community colleges (*N* = 18,130; see Table 13.3) are generally very low. Overall, only 9% of all students had completed their bachelor's degrees within 6 years of enrollment. It may be that the 8- or 10-year graduation rates are somewhat higher; however, we did not have access to that information.

Demographic Variations in Six-Year Graduation Rates

The breakdown of bachelor's degree completion rates within 6 years of enrollment by race/ethnicity and immigrant generation is provided in Table 13.3. We found substantial differences by race and immigrant generation. In terms of race, White

Table 13.2. Expectation to Complete BA or Higher by Generation and Ethnic/Racial Group

| | Generation Level | | | |
Race/Ethnicity	1st	2nd	3rd+	Overall
Asian	66%	71%	67%	67%
	($n = 35$)	($n = 17$)	($n = 3$)	($n = 55$)
Black	76%	78%	66%	74%
	($n = 45$)	($n = 78$)	($n = 44$)	($n = 167$)
Latinx	73%	79%	63%	74%
	($n = 92$)	($n = 117$)	($n = 38$)	($n = 247$)
White	87%	80%	73%	78%
	($n = 15$)	($n = 20$)	($n = 45$)	($n = 80$)
Mixed/other	86%	75%	68%	76%
	($n - 21$)	($n - 36$)	($n = 19$)	($n = 76$)
Overall	75%	78%	68%	74%
	($n = 208$)	($n = 268$)	($n = 149$)	($n = 625$)

Note: Source is RICC survey data.

Table 13.3. Actual Rates of Completion of a Bachelor's Degree Within Six Years of Enrollment at All Community Colleges by Generation and Ethnic/Racial Group

| Race/ | Generation Level | | | | |
Ethnicity	1st	2nd	3rd+	Missing	Overall
Asian	16%	13%	11%	14%	15%
	($n = 2,007$)	($n = 527$)	($n = 28$)	($n = 760$)	($n = 3,322$)
Black	8%	5%	3%	5%	6%
	($n = 2,658$)	($n = 1,548$)	($n = 1,630$)	($n = 3,348$)	($n = 9,184$)
Latinx	6%	5%	5%	6%	6%
	($n = 2,821$)	($n = 2,936$)	($n = 726$)	($n = 2,277$)	($n = 8,760$)
White	16%	15%	17%	16%	16%
	($n = 1,336$)	($n = 679$)	($n = 1,188$)	($n = 2,001$)	($n = 5,204$)
Indigenous	4%	8%	0%	0%	4%
	($n = 23$)	($n = 13$)	($n = 10$)	($n = 8$)	($n = 54$)
Overall	10%	7%	8%	9%	9%
	($n = 8,845$)	($n = 5,703$)	($n = 3,582$)	($n = 8,394$)	($n = 26,524$)

Note: Source is CUNY administrative data for all students enrolling in community colleges in school year 2006–2007.

and Asian students had graduation rates of 16% and 15%, respectively, whereas Black and Latinx students each had graduation rates of 6%, and Indigenous students had a graduation rate of 4%: $F(4, 26519) = 181.67$, $p = .000$. There were no differences by immigrant generation within White, Latinx, and Asian American/Pacific Islander (AAPI) student groups. However, within the Black student group, there were significant differences, with the graduation rate of first-generation Black immigrants (8%) being statistically significantly higher than the rate of third-plus–generation Black students (3%) and marginally significantly higher than the rate of second-generation Black immigrants (5%): $F(14, 18115) = 38.78$, $p = .000$. (Within race/ethnicity, differences were tested using Bonferroni post hoc tests.) Combining all racial/ethnic groups, first-generation immigrant students had higher graduation rates (10%) than second-generation (7%) or third-plus—generation (8%) students did: $F(2, 18127) = 24.01$, $p = .000$. In part, this result was driven by the facts that almost four-fifths of Asian students in the sample were first-generation immigrants and that Asian students tended to display higher graduation rates than other racial groups did.

Oakmont is not part of the CUNY system; therefore, only differences in completion rates between students at the Domino and Taino campuses were compared with a *chi*-square difference test. Completion rates of students at the Domino campus were significantly higher than those at Taino: $\chi2$ $(2, N = 4,879) = 50.45$, $p <.000$. This difference is not surprising because, unlike Taino, Domino provides some 4-year degree completion options. However, it is important to note that the overall completion rates remained quite low (see Table 13.4).

Although these differences by race, immigrant generation, and campus are significant, it should be noted that the highest graduation rate—of third-plus–generation White students—was still just 16%. That result means that of 100 White nonimmigrant students who had enrolled at a CUNY community college during the 2006–2007 school year, 84 had not earned a bachelor's degree after 6 years of study. For the sample as a whole, 91 of 100 students who started out at a CUNY community college had not been awarded a bachelor's degree after 6 years. Furthermore, only 19 of these 91 students had attained an associate's degree after 6 years.

Expectations Versus Actual Graduation Rates

When we juxtaposed the expectations of students at the Domino and Taino campuses with their actual bachelor's degree completion rates, the discrepancies were profound (see Figure 13.3). The actual outcome rates showing how many students had completed their bachelor's degrees within 6 years of matriculating at these campuses as indicated by the CUNY administrative records did not remotely align with the expectations expressed by students in the RICC survey, indicating a gap between students' dreams and realities regardless of their backgrounds. Across the racial/ethnic and immigrant-generation groups, the smallest gap between the percentage of students expecting to attain a bachelor's degree

Table 13.4. Expectation of Completing BA or Higher and Actual Degree Completion
Rates by School

	Yes		No	
	n	%	*n*	%
Expect to complete BA degree or higher[a], n = 625				
Taino, *n* = 177	121	68%	56	32%
Domino, *n* = 238	188	79%	50	21%
Oakmont, *n* = 210	155	74%	55	26%
Actual degree completion rates[b], n = 4,879				
Graduated with AA in 3 years				
Taino, *n* = 1,252	110	9%	1,142	91%
Domino, *n* = 3,627	210	6%	3,417	94%
All schools, *n* = 26,254	2,478	9%	24,046	91%
Graduated with AA in 4 years				
Taino, *n* = 1,252	264	21%	988	79%
Domino, *n* = 3,627	554	15%	3,073	85%
All schools, *n* = 26,254	3,945	15%	22,579	85%
Graduated with BA in 6 years				
Taino, *n* = 1,252	52	4%	1,200	96%
Domino, *n* = 3,627	394	11%	3,233	89%
All schools, *n* = 26,254	2,335	9%	24,189	91%

Note: [a]Source is RICC survey data; [b]Source is CUNY administrative data.

and the percentage who actually attained one after 6 years was 52.2% (for first-generation Asian students), and the largest gap was 78.6% (for White third-plus–generation students). Overall, the gap between expected completion and actual completion was 65.3%.

IN SUM

Several notable differences emerged by generational status and campus in terms of students' expectations and by generational status, campus and race/ethnicity for students' degree completion rates. Expectations among students for degree completion were very high, with about three quarters of students anticipating earning a bachelor's degree or higher. Furthermore, immigrant-origin students' expectations were significantly higher than those of third-plus–generation students, and the expectations of students at the Domino campus were significantly higher than those of students at Oakmont or Taino.

Figure 13.3. Taino and Domino: Expected BA Graduation and Actual BA Graduation

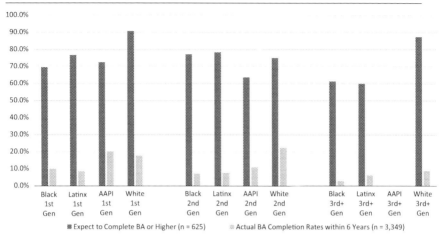

Note: This does not contain information for Indigenous students since the Indigenous category from the administrative data was not comparable to the Native American/Mixed/Other Race category from the survey data. Survey data from the RICC study include students' expectations for completing a BA or higher, and administrative data from the same two CUNY institutions show comparative rates of BA completion within 6 years of enrollment.

Actual degree completion rates were very low overall, with only 9% of students completing their bachelor's degrees within 6 years of enrollment. By race/ethnicity, White and Asian students' completion rates were significantly higher than those of Black, Latinx, and Indigenous students. In terms of racial/ethnic group and generation, first-generation Black students' completion rates were significantly higher than those of second- or third-plus–generation Black students. Among all racial/ethnic groups, first-generation students had the highest completion rates. By campus, degree completion rates at Domino (which provides some 4-year degree completion options) were higher than those at Taino. Despite the variations we found within and among groups as highlighted in our findings, the overarching narrative that emerges from this particular story is one of educational dreams that too often failed to materialize.

This result raises an important question: How can students' expectations be so poorly aligned with their actual attainment? Jacob and Wilder (2010) suggest that the expectations-attainment gap is due to misinformation—that is, "students have misinformation about the cost of college, the preparation they will need, and the difficulty of completing college" (p. 18). We argue that students quite naturally believe that if they put in the effort, they will be rewarded at the end with a credential. There is little reason for them to expect that they will work hard and nonetheless leave empty-handed (Goldrick-Rab, 2016). Young Americans growing up with a "college for all" mentality (Goyette, 2008) may simply be unaware of the dire state of the nation's college graduation rates. Students who are members of the first generation of their family to attend college may be especially naïve about U.S. educational systems. Furthermore, immigrant parents, being new to the United States, may have limited abilities for counseling their children about navigating the perilous community college waters.

It was not until the year 2000 that community colleges began to publish graduation rates in response to the Student Right-to-Know and Campus Security Act of 1990 (Bailey et al., 2015). Graduation rates of first-time, full-time students (a measure that has been highly criticized but that nevertheless provides some guidance) are now reported on the Department of Education College Navigator website (nces.ed.gov/collegenavigator). In principle, students have access to the associate's degree attainment rates (and often also to the student transfer rates) of the community colleges that they are considering attending. However, the fact that the majority of community college students continue to expect to attain a bachelor's degree despite their prospective colleges' reporting of low attainment and transfer rates implies either that they are unaware of this information or that they are aware of it but believe they will be among the small proportion of students who do get through. For immigrant-origin students, this optimism may be further compounded by a greater unfamiliarity with the realities as well as by the power of the "land of opportunity" narrative (Kao & Tienda, 1995; Raleigh & Kao, 2010).

Clearly, the real problem is not the high expectations but the low graduation rates. Unfortunately, the issue of low graduation rates from community colleges is by no means confined to the educational system examined in this chapter. Figure 13.4 shows the national 6-year graduation rates for certificates, associate's degrees, and bachelor's degrees by immigrant generation, split by the level of first institution. It reveals that for the nation as a whole, students from all generations who start out at community colleges are far less likely to attain a bachelor's degree than are those who start at 4-year schools. Of course, a large part of this outcome has to do with the reasons that students choose to attend community colleges in the first place, which are often related to their poor academic preparation during high school and to financial pressures. Nonetheless, such low degree attainment rates strongly call into question the role of community colleges in providing social mobility (Schudde & Goldrick-Rab, 2015). This matter is particularly problematic since education is often seen as the most effective mobility ladder (Greenstone, Looney, Patashnik, & Yu, 2013). Students who are not well served by the nation's public educational system have few alternatives for achieving the American Dream.

Furthermore, such low graduation rates are not only a problem for the individuals whose prospects for social mobility have been constrained. Many companies and health facilities are facing shortages of workers to fill middle-skill jobs such as paralegals, chefs, and health technicians (Holzer, 2015). These are occupations for which community colleges are well situated to provide necessary training. Holzer (2015) attributes the shortages faced in these areas at least partially to the "extremely high" dropout rates at U.S. higher education institutions (p. 6).

As Bailey and colleagues (2015) have argued, "a well-functioning community college system is instrumental in improving educational equity and in efficiently

Figure 13.4. Breakdown of National Graduation Rates by Immigrant Status and Level of First Institution

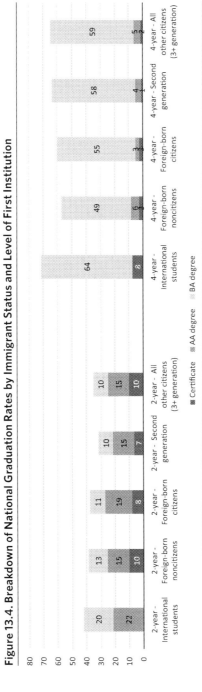

Source: U.S. Department of Education, National Center for Education Statistics, 2011–2012 Beginning Postsecondary Students Longitudinal Study, First Follow-Up [BPS: 12/14]. Computation by NCES QuickStats on 4/25/2017).

developing skills and talents essential for a thriving economy and society" (p. vii). A situation in which more than 80% of entering community college students expect to attain a bachelor's degree and only 12% have actually earned one after 6 years (Horn & Skomvold, 2011) is clearly not a model of a well-functioning community college system.

There is extensive literature on potential reforms for community colleges, much of it highlighting how far-reaching such reforms need to be. For example, Goldrick-Rab (2010) discusses the need for changes on multiple levels such as the macro-level opportunity structure and the institutions themselves as well as changes to address the challenges raised by students' social, economic, and academic attributes. Bailey and colleagues (2015) suggest a major reform to community college design, shifting toward a guided pathways model. Brint (2003) has even gone so far as to suggest dividing the community college into three separate institutions, focusing respectively on job training, academic transfer to 4-year institutions, and community recreational courses (though he also says this change is not likely to occur). Other authors have highlighted issues with the transfer process (e.g., see Monaghan & Attewell, 2015), another area for potential reforms.

The CUNY system studied in this chapter has introduced various innovations intended to increase graduation rates; one in particular has thus far been very effective. Accelerated Study in Associates Programs (ASAP) is a comprehensive program that requires students to enroll full-time and provides them with well-integrated, wide-ranging supports, including benefits such as tuition waivers for students receiving financial aid who have a gap need, New York City Transit MetroCards, block-scheduled first-year courses, and comprehensive and personalized advisement. To date, results have been impressive: Scrivener and colleagues (2015) report that the program has doubled associate's degree attainment rates. Furthermore, Strumbos and Kolenovic (2017) show that this program has also substantially increased students' transfer rates to bachelor's degree programs as well as students' attainment of bachelor's degrees. Levin and Garcia (2018) demonstrate that ASAP requires substantially more funding per student than other programs do but that it is so effective at increasing graduation rates that the cost *per graduate* is much lower than the cost for students not participating in the program. The researchers maintain that ASAP represents a highly productive public investment with high returns to the taxpayer.

ASAP was launched on a small scale at six CUNY schools in 2007. It has subsequently been expanded within CUNY and was introduced at an additional three schools in 2014 and 2015. The analyses of graduation rates in this chapter focus on students who had enrolled prior to the introduction of ASAP. Furthermore, to be eligible for ASAP, students must be New York City residents and be eligible for in-state tuition. Consequently, some first-generation immigrants (such as undocumented students—see Chapter 4) are not likely to be eligible for the program. However, second-generation immigrants as well as foreign-born students who arrive in the United States during their high school years or earlier are likely to be eligible. It is hoped that the positive outcomes of the program, in conjunction with other reforms the CUNY system has been implementing, continue so that students' high expectations can be matched with a more positive reality.

Immigrant-origin community college students face unique challenges (see Chapters 1 through 4), but they demonstrate strong optimism and are even slightly surpassing the graduation rates of their native peers, as the previously discussed analyses confirm. Nevertheless, immigrant-origin community college students, together with all other students attending these institutions, find themselves on the lowest rung of a highly stratified system of higher education. Arguably, community college students' poor rates of degree attainment are even more relevant to the prospects of immigrant-origin youth since they are more likely to enroll in community colleges than their third-plus–generation peers are (see Chapter 1). There is a need for major reforms and innovative programs such as CUNY's ASAP so that the as-yet unrealized promise and potential of community colleges to deliver educational equity and social mobility can be achieved for immigrant and native students alike.

REFERENCES

Bailey, T., & Weininger, E. B. (2002). Performance, graduation, and transfer of immigrants and natives in City University of New York community colleges. *Educational Evaluation and Policy Analysis, 24*(4), 359–377.

Bailey, T. R., Jaggars, S. S., & Jenkins, D. (2015). *Redesigning America's community colleges.* Cambridge, MA: Harvard University Press.

Brint, S. (2003). Few remaining dreams: Community colleges since 1985. *The Annals of the American Academy of Political and Social Science, 586*(1), 16–37.

Conger, D., & Turner, L. J. (2017). The effect of price shocks on undocumented students' college attainment and completion. *Journal of Public Economics, 148*, 92–114.

Connell, C. (2008). The vital role of community colleges in the education and integration of immigrants. *Grantmakers concerned with immigrants and refugees.* Retrieved from www.gcir.org/publications/gcirpubs/college

Conway, K. M. (2010). Educational aspirations in an urban community college: Differences between immigrant and native student groups. *Community College Review, 37*(3), 209–242.

Crenshaw, K. W. (1991). Mapping the margins: Intersectionality, identity politics, and violence against women of color. *Stanford Law Review, 43*(6), 1241–1299. Retrieved from dx.doi.org/10.2307/1229039

CUNY Office of Institutional Research and Assessment (2018, March 30). *Student profile/ demographic information.* Retrieved from www.cuny.edu/about/administration/offices /ira/ir/data-book/current/student.html

Erisman, W., & Looney, S. (2007). *Opening the door to the American dream: Increasing higher education and success for immigrants.* Washington, DC: Institute for Higher Education Policy.

Fuligni, A. J. (2001). Family obligation and the academic motivation of adolescents from Asian, Latin American, and European backgrounds. *New Directions for Child and Adolescent Development, 2001*(94), 61–76.

Fuligni, A. J., & Witkow, M. (2004). The postsecondary educational progress of youth from immigrant families. *Journal of Research on Adolescence, 14*(2), 159–183.

Glick, J. E., & White, M. J. (2004). Post-secondary school participation of immigrant and native youth: The role of familial resources and educational expectations. *Social Science Research, 33*(2), 272–299.

Goldrick-Rab, S. (2010). Challenges and opportunities for improving community college student success. *Review of Educational Research, 80*(3), 437–469.

Goldrick-Rab, S. (2016). *Paying the price: College costs, financial aid, and the betrayal of the American dream.* Chicago, IL: University of Chicago Press.

Goyette, K. A. (2008). College for some to college for all: Social background, occupational expectations, and educational expectations over time. *Social Science Research, 37*(2), 461–484.

Greenstone, M., Looney, A., Patashnik, J., & Yu, M. (2013). *Thirteen economic facts about social mobility and the role of education.* Washington, DC: Hamilton Project.

Hoachlander, G., Sikora, A. C., & Horn, L. (2003). *Community college students: Goals, academic preparation and outcomes.* NCES 2003-164. Washington, DC: U.S. Department of Education, Institute of Education Sciences, National Center for Education Statistics.

Holzer, H. (2015, April). *Job market polarization and U.S. worker skills: A tale of two middles.* Economic Studies, The Brookings Institution. Retrieved from www.brookings.edu/wp-content/uploads/2016/06/polarization_jobs_policy_holzer.pdf

Horn, L., & Skomsvold, P. (2011) *Web tables: Community college student outcomes, 1994–2009.* NCES Publication 2012-253. Washington, DC: U.S. Department of Education, Institute of Education Sciences, National Center for Education Statistics.

Jacob, B. A., & Wilder, T. (2010). *Educational expectations and attainment* (No. w15683). Cambridge, MA: National Bureau of Economic Research.

Jepsen, C., Troske, K., & Coomes, P. (2014). The labor-market returns to community college degrees, diplomas, and certificates. *Journal of Labor Economics, 32*(1), 95–121.

Kao, G., & Tienda, M. (1995). Optimism and achievement: The educational performance of immigrant youth. *Social Science Quarterly, 76*(1), 1–19.

Kirui, D. K., & Kao, G. (2018). Does generational status matter in college? Expectations and academic performance among second-generation college students in the US. *Ethnicities, 18*(4), 571–602.

Levin, H. M., & García, E. (2018). Accelerating community college graduation rates: A benefit–cost analysis. *The Journal of Higher Education, 89*(1), 1–27.

Monaghan, D. B., & Attewell, P. (2015). The community college route to the bachelor's degree. *Educational Evaluation and Policy Analysis, 37*(1), 70–91.

Nguyen, B. M. D., Nguyen, M. H., Teranishi, R. T., & Hune, S. (2015). The hidden academic opportunity gaps among Asian Americans and Pacific Islanders: What disaggregated data reveals in Washington State. *National Commission on Asian American and Pacific Islander Research in Education (CARE).* Retrieved from care.igeucla.org/wp-content/uploads/2015/09/iCount-Report_The-Hidden-Academic-Opportunity-Gaps_2015.pdf

Noguera, P. A. (2008). Creating schools where race does not predict achievement: The role and significance of race in the racial achievement gap. *The Journal of Negro Education, 77*(2), 90–103.

Perreira, K. M., Harris, K. M., & Lee, D. (2006). Making it in America: High school completion by immigrant and native youth. *Demography, 43*(3), 511–536.

Raleigh, E., & Kao, G. (2010). Do immigrant minority parents have more consistent college aspirations for their children? *Social Science Quarterly, 91*(4), 1083–1102.

Rosenbaum, J. E., Deil-Amen, R., & Person, A. E. (2007). *After admission: From college access to college success.* New York, NY: Russell Sage Foundation.

Schudde, L., & Goldrick-Rab, S. (2015). On second chances and stratification: How sociologists think about community colleges. *Community College Review, 43*(1), 27–45.

Scrivener, S., Weiss, M., Ratledge, A., Rudd, T., Sommo, C., & Fresques, H. (2015). *Doubling graduation rates: Three-year effects of CUNY's Accelerated Study in Associate Programs (ASAP) for developmental education students.* MDRC Publications. Retrieved from www.mdrc.org/publication/doubling-graduation-rates

Strumbos, D., & Kolenovic, Z. (2017). Six-year outcomes of ASAP students: Transfer and degree attainment. *ASAP evaluation brief.* New York, NY: City University of New York.

Suárez-Orozco, C., Yoshikawa, H., & Tseng, V. (2015). *Intersecting inequalities: Research to reduce inequality for immigrant-origin children and youth.* New York, NY: William T. Grant Foundation.

Szelényi, K., & Chang, J. C. (2002). ERIC review: Educating immigrants: The community college role. *Community College Review, 30*(2), 55–73.

Toutkoushian, R. K., & Paulsen, M. B. (2016). Private and social returns to higher education. In *Economics of higher education: Background, Concepts and Applications* (pp. 93–147). Dordrecht, Germany: Springer.

Vernez, G., & Abrahamse, A. (1996). *How immigrants fare in US education.* RAND Monograph Report. Retrieved from www.rand.org/pubs/monograph_reports/MR718.html

Wing, J. Y. (2007). Beyond black and white: The model minority myth and the invisibility of Asian American students. *The Urban Review, 39*(4), 455–487.

CHAPTER 14

(Re)Designing Institutional Practices and Policies to Serve Immigrant-Origin Students in Community Colleges

Robert T. Teranishi, Cecilia Rios-Aguilar, & Cynthia M. Alcantar

Students with an immigrant-origin background— foreign-born or children of foreign-born parents—comprise nearly one quarter of the undergraduate population and represent one of the fastest-growing student populations in American higher education. This demographic reality is reason for a deeper understanding of and response to the unique needs and challenges of this student population. Although immigrant-origin students can be found in all sectors of higher education (private/public, 2-year/4-year, and selective/nonselective), their pathway into higher education is disproportionately high in community colleges (Teranishi, C. Suárez-Orozco, & M. Suárez-Orozco, 2011).

In this chapter, we discuss the findings from this book and implications for and connections to effective strategies of practice and policy in the broader field of higher education. Our focus on community colleges is not narrowly tailored to community colleges as a point of access to higher education (i.e., enrollment); rather, we seek to identify key practices and policies related to the findings in this book that promote opportunities for immigrant-origin students to earn a degree or certificate, prepare them for transferring and succeeding in a 4-year institution, and to be gainfully employed. Greater attention to and a deeper understanding of this population is a national imperative; immigrants and children of immigrants are a formidable part of the U.S. labor force, and their impact on the economy and society is even more pronounced as they become a large and growing sector of the U.S. demography (Passel, 2011).

A NEW CONTEXT FOR COMMUNITY COLLEGES

Community colleges have been a fundamental point of access to higher education for a significant proportion of the U.S. population for more than half a century (Rios-Aguilar & Deil-Amen, 2019), and they are a fundamentally important pathway for educating and training America's growing and increasingly diverse immigrant population. Including race, ethnicity, gender, age, sexual orientation, and socioeconomic status, community college students have intersecting and multidimensional identities when it comes to immigration status, full-time/part-time student status, veteran status, language-learner status, and (dis)ability status among others (Bailey, Jaggars, & Jenkins, 2015; Deil-Amen, 2011). But despite high enrollment especially among several groups of underrepresented and marginalized groups of students, community colleges have failed to provide the conditions necessary for students to succeed (The Century Foundation, 2013). Specifically, fewer than 40 percent of community college students earn any kind of certificate or degree within 6 years of enrollment (Bailey et al., 2015). These low completion rates may be even lower for marginalized groups of students, including immigrants. What is evident is that completion rates are noticeably challenging, particularly in light of evidence that completing certificates and degrees are undeniably valuable in terms of earning potential (see Chapter 13).

From existing research, we know that many students who enter the community college system, and immigrant students in particular, are most often placed in a vulnerable position. They are more likely to enter the system academically unprepared (due to attending underfunded and underresourced schools), have less access to financial aid, get trapped in remedial classes, and eventually drop out without transferring or completing a degree or certificate (Deil-Amen & Deluca, 2010; The Century Foundation, 2013). Immigrant students also face unique challenges, such as navigating multiple systems, processes, and services, adapting to new contexts, and becoming proficient in English in addition to being proficient in their native language(s) all at the same time (Connell, 2008). If not served adequately, these students may end up becoming the *new forgotten half*—the half of college students who accumulate credits, but end up with no degree or credential, and few marketable skills (Rosenbaum, Ahearn, Becker, & Rosenbaum, 2015). Especially in the current social, political, and economic climate, it is remarkably important that our nation's community colleges develop the diverse talent needed to fuel democratic engagement, social mobility, and economic opportunity and growth.

To address the persistently poor completion rates, community colleges across the country have undergone significant transformation in the past decade and will continue to do so in the years to come. This sector is characterized by one unique feature: *change*. Recent efforts to boost persistence and completion rates include the simplification and streamlining of course offerings and majors offered, changing the way colleges place students into remedial education (i.e., using multiple measures like high school GPA and course-taking patterns in high school instead of exclusively relying on standardized tests), and changing funding mechanisms/formulas to incentivize colleges to close equity gaps (i.e., performance-based funding).

One of the most significant reform efforts across community colleges in the nation is known as guided pathways (Bailey et al., 2015). The premise behind guided pathways is as follows: College students are more likely to complete a degree in a reasonable time if they choose a program and develop an academic plan early on, have a clear road map of the courses they need to take to complete a credential, and receive guidance and support to help them stay on plan (Bailey et al., 2015). The hope is that this approach helps students to make more efficient decisions and also helps colleges to more effectively serve their students. Some researchers have noted that this model may especially be instrumental for first-generation students as they navigate various "administrative 'silos' on college campuses" (Luna-Torres, Leafgreen, & McKinney, 2017, p. 103). It is assumed that by providing students with a clearer and simpler plan for completion, institutions can be more intentional in targeting resources to make sure students complete their programs faster.

Although these efforts are commendable, they still lack an emphasis on what specifically underrepresented and diverse community college students need the most: help with navigating a highly complex financial aid process, inclusive learning environments, and building and sustaining relationships with key actors to help them succeed academically and in pursuing their occupational goals. This book is a reminder to everyone, including the public, policymakers, college administrators, faculty, and staff, that any effort to restructure and to help improve community colleges must be grounded in an understanding of students' lives, particularly when we talk about immigrant students (and their families and communities; Rios-Aguilar et al., 2019; Rose, 2016).

Findings from this book confirm the fact that policies and practices in this sector must do a better job in taking into consideration students' realities. For instance, findings contained in Chapter 2 remind us that most immigrant students deal with multiple responsibilities including working outside of school, helping parents or relatives, and having community responsibilities, including mentoring and volunteering. Findings in Chapter 3 detail the great linguistic diversity and how immigrant students cope with their linguistic insecurities. Chapter 4, on undocumented students, illustrates the fact that students in community colleges have significantly less access to financial aid and consequently worry more about existing immigration policies, finding safe spaces, and food security and health care. These unique experiences pose several challenges for immigrant students and necessitate specific supports from individual colleges.

CLASSROOMS MATTER

One significant contribution of this book is the attention to and reminder about the importance of the college classroom. In 1999, Norton Grubb wrote a fascinating book, *Honored but Invisible*, describing community college instructors and their classrooms. Since Grubb's contribution, with a few exceptions, there has been virtually no research examining teaching and learning in community college classrooms. This book is a groundbreaking effort to document what actually happens in community college classrooms. We cannot forget that what happens in the classroom matters, as Grubb (1999) suggests, and even Tinto (1993), whose model of college student departure highlights various on-campus modes of social and academic integration necessary for connection and persistence, admits that, for commuting students, "the classroom is the crossroads where the social and the academic meet" (Tinto, 1997, p. 599), and the nature and quality of the community of learning structured by institutions and faculty can greatly enhance both learning and persistence. More recently, Deil-Amen (2011) finds 2-year college students' decisions to persist are shaped by socio-academic integrative moments—interactions within and just outside the classroom with instructors and peers who enhance belonging and encourage/reinforce students' academic identity. This book confirms that, for immigrant students, classrooms are pivotal to their academic experiences and trajectories. However, we learned from chapters in this book that community college classrooms are complex and contradictory spaces. They function both as a place to connect and to facilitate learning, and often they are plagued with deficit thinking and deficit-oriented practices, as well as microaggressions that alienate immigrant students and crush their aspirations to persist and complete their academic goals.

In community college classrooms in particular, students' diverse cultural, work, and family backgrounds, and prior experiences including their immigration and labor histories should inform how educators think about how students approach learning and the educational process generally. Unfortunately, as evidenced in this book, prevailing assumptions commonly frame such student backgrounds and prior experiences as "deficient" or "lacking" rather than as a potential benefit to their learning, especially when those students are immigrant, low-income, lower achieving, and/or from underrepresented racial/ethnic groups. Not surprisingly, teaching pedagogies, services, and interventions that align with dominant deficit models contribute to reinforce deficit thinking that further promotes the framing of immigrant students, students' families, and communities as problems to be fixed in order for students to succeed.

As clearly articulated in this book, classrooms and pedagogies in community colleges are underinvestigated and undertheorized in research on educational opportunity. Existing conceptions of the typical college student are idealized and based on a traditional, imagined norm of someone who begins college immediately after high school, enrolls full-time, lives on campus, has legal status, is financially supported by their family, and is prepared to begin college-level classes (Deil-Amen, 2015). This in no way reflects the reality of today's diverse students, most of whom begin their postsecondary academic trajectories at a community college (Deil-Amen, 2015). Faculty make assumptions about what students know and how they expect them to perform in the classroom (Cox, 2009; Kiyama, Rios-Aguilar, & Deil-Amen, 2018; Mora & Rios-Aguilar, 2018). Frequently, faculty design curriculum by adopting "remedial pedagogy[ies]" (Grubb, 2013) that reinforce dominant narratives of community college students as incapable of learning complex material. Consequently, instructors tend to focus their teaching efforts on providing "discrete and de-contextualized sub-skills through drill and practice procedures" (Cox, 2015, p. 266). As argued by Bensimon (2007), the scholarship in higher education has deliberately "imagined" what students need to have and do to be successful based on what predominant models of student persistence and success have found (Kiyama & Rios-Aguilar, 2018). However, these models have sidestepped our greatest challenge—how to reimagine success for underrepresented and marginalized groups of students, including immigrants who tend to reflect so many traditional predictors of failure. This is particularly challenging in community college contexts, which also face the absence of the conditions that have been shown to promote success generally. Incremental changes will be inadequate. Rather, transformative innovations need our attention. Sadly, approaching immigrant students in community colleges from a deficit orientation has not markedly improved their low levels of academic achievement and high rates of dropping/stopping out. If this open-access, low-cost tier of American higher education is the path to social mobility for the majority of immigrant students, then it is imperative to understand all its complexities, especially those that occur within the community college classroom (Mora & Rios-Aguilar, 2018). This book is a fabulous effort in that direction, but more remains to be done.

We propose that community colleges use asset-based and culturally responsive strategies to create inclusive classroom environments. One possibility is to utilize immigrant students' funds of knowledge (i.e., the varied bodies of knowledge embedded in students' and their families' daily practices, including labor and immigration histories, language diversity, etc.) in the teaching and learning process. Kiyama et al. (2018) provide concrete examples to move beyond just learning about students' lived experiences to concretely exploring how cultural knowledges, lived experiences, and home practices can be validated, incorporated, and developed into culturally responsive pedagogy in higher education curriculum and programming. The first example that Kiyama et al. (2018) offer presents a college outreach program that operates from a funds of knowledge framework and incorporates weekly workshops delivered through the same asset-based approach. The second example details a process for collecting and integrating funds of knowledge into community college classrooms using surveys and community observations to document the wide array of resources and knowledge that students bring to classrooms. And the third example utilizes existing pedagogical tools found in participatory action research methods to integrate funds of knowledge into higher education classrooms. Understanding and integrating students' cultural and social contexts is not an easy task; however, given the current social, economic, and political context it becomes even more imperative to do so. Community college classrooms can become spaces where power dynamics are minimized, teaching and learning are equitably shared among the community, and students' home knowledge becomes the base from which course content is developed (Kiyama et al., 2018). The use of these nondeficit approaches can enhance academic success (Ladson-Billings, 1995) and also be a powerful development and demonstration of student agency and active participation in the pedagogical process (Kiyama et al., 2018).

FINANCIAL AID MATTERS

Although college affordability has been at the forefront of national conversations surrounding higher education for the past decade (Dowd, 2003), the focus has primarily been on the rise in tuition in 4-year institutions (Goldrick-Rab, Harris, & Trostel, 2009). However, while tuition in community colleges is generally less than 4-year colleges, it has also increased and has been found to be a barrier for access to and success for community college students (Goldrick-Rab & Kendall, 2016). In addition to tuition costs, the cost of living for students has increased as well; students no longer just worry about paying for tuition—concerns about paying for housing and basic necessities such as transportation, food, and health care exist as well (Broton & Goldrick-Rab, 2016). Moreover, prominent scholars (Dougherty, 1994; Dowd, 2003) have noted that there is a misconception that community colleges are "affordable," yet, there is confusion as to how much it actually costs to attend community colleges, even with the proliferation of "College Promise" programs around the country. The fact is that not all college costs are covered by available grants and aid at federal, state, and institutional levels. Therefore, students and their families must learn how to effectively navigate this process.

The financial aid process is cumbersome for students and families (Campbell, Deil-Amen, & Rios-Aguilar, 2015; Deil-Amen & Rios Aguilar, 2014). Financial aid is not only related to Federal Application for Student Aid (FAFSA) completion (for those who can file one); it is actually a highly complex process with key dates that must be navigated and met strategically if students want to receive their aid on time. The first step in this process is when students apply for financial aid, whether through the FAFSA application or other applications depending on their immigration status and individual circumstances. Second, after submitting forms and officially applying for aid, they learn about their eligibility for the aid and can be asked to verify the information that they submitted on the FAFSA or any other form. Next, students must maneuver several websites and processes in their own colleges and/or state websites to be able to actually receive the aid on time. After students receive their aid for school, they have to maintain their aid by adhering to federal and state guidelines to remain eligible to receive financial aid. These guidelines establish minimum GPA requirements, courses enrolled and completed, and time to degree. These are also known as satisfactory academic progress requirements. It is important to state that maintaining financial aid has been found to be unclear and confusing for students (Campbell et al., 2015; Deil-Amen & Rios Aguilar, 2014).

Moreover, immigrant students often encounter additional challenges when it comes to completing the already complex hodgepodge of financial aid documents. One of the first and biggest barriers that many students face is explaining to their families the importance of providing the necessary and timely financial information to complete the financial aid forms. When money is scarce, discussing college costs and financial aid can become an even more difficult topic than it is otherwise. In some cases, it may be particularly difficult to get parents to file taxes early or even on time. This puts a lot of stress on family relationships. In addition, many parents do not have a traditional single job—they will work several jobs with the accompanying multiple W-2s, 1099s, and the like. Some parents have jobs that sometimes do not provide income verification. Another huge challenge, of course, is when a parent files taxes, but does not have a Social Security number because they are undocumented. And, students must be able to decipher websites and other forms in English in order to apply for nonfederal financial aid. Finally, it is important to note that many immigrant students are "independent," and others have parents who are not geographically close to provide the information needed to apply for financial aid.

For undocumented immigrant students and mixed-status immigrant families, their immigration status poses yet another challenge to applying for financial aid. Although undocumented immigrant students are *ineligible* for federal student aid, and thus ineligible to complete the FAFSA, U.S.-born and legal permanent resident (LPR) children born to undocumented parents *are eligible* for federal student aid. However, often lack of information and fear of deportation by students and undocumented parents and limited knowledge by institutional agents make it harder for these students to apply for financial aid. Additionally, while *some* states bar undocumented students from receiving state-level financial aid, *other* states have no stipulated financial aid policies for undocumented students or provide access to financial aid but have varying eligibility and application requirements, making it hard to decipher this information (Teranishi, C. Suárez-Orozco, & M. Suárez-Orozco, 2015). The varying and constantly fluctuating state-, institutional-, and system-level student aid policies for undocumented students make it challenging to find information about financial aid for undocumented students and mixed-status families.

Lastly, although financial aid was designed to help students, the implementation of federal and state policy stipulations is often experienced as punitive by the diverse population of students receiving the aid, including immigrant students. Policy regulation and the related policing of aid and climate of penalty experienced by students (see Campbell et al., 2015) may be (re)producing inequities for community college students. This raises social justice concerns in an era in which college attainment is so crucial, particularly for students in poverty (Campbell et al., 2015). For this reason, it is imperative that financial aid reform efforts consider the diversity of experiences of immigrant students and their families.

RELATIONSHIPS AND STUDENT ENGAGEMENT MATTERS

In order for immigrant students to succeed, they must be able to be part of networks that will provide them with the resources that they can utilize to secure the profits to their investment in postsecondary education. However, being part of these networks is not easy. Access to social capital and utilization of it depends on several factors. First, trust and reciprocity must be present. For student SEs to be able to ask for help and to feel they belong to a network, they need to feel safe and that they also have something to offer. Then there is the trust-building process that needs to occur so that students can take advantage of opportunities and resources that networks offer.

In order to help students build meaningful social networks of support, institutions must intentionally engage students academically and socially, especially at community colleges. Students who are more academically and socially engaged in college are more likely to have higher academic achievement, persist in college, and earn a college degree (Kuh, 2008). As this book demonstrates, the relationship between academic and social engagement and student success is due to its likelihood of increasing students' sense of belonging on campus, academic self-concept, and their access to resources and opportunities (Barbatis, 2010; Deil-Amen, 2011; Hurtado & Carter, 1997). However, while 4-year colleges often have the structural (e.g., on-campus housing, student centers) and financial means to create opportunities to engage students, community colleges are dealing with a largely commuter student population comprised of students who are often working full-time off-campus and are enrolled part-time. In addition, community colleges often have limited institutional resources for student engagement. Because of these challenges, the classroom, and more specifically the faculty, have been found to play a critical role in engaging students through impactful pedagogical approaches and curriculum, but also by developing relationships with students and connecting students to one another (Alcantar & Hernandez, 2018; Barnett, 2011; Cejda & Hoover, 2010–2011; Cox, 2009; Umbach & Wawrzynski, 2005).

However, the classroom is not the only place to engage students; community colleges must consider ways to engage students outside of the classroom. For instance, Long Beach City College provides late academic counseling appointments for working students, and South Seattle College offers financial incentives for students to invite faculty to have coffee. Another example is City College of San Francisco's (CCSF) Chinatown campus, which provides citizenship classes, ESL classes, and a space to congregate for the community. Additionally, the main campus offers culturally responsive academic counseling and multilingual tutoring targeted to Latinx, Asian American and Pacific Islander (AAPI), and Black students. These are only a few examples of how community colleges can intentionally create opportunities for students to engage academically and socially and in turn support their success in college.

WHOLISTIC SUPPORT MATTERS

Another important component to the success of immigrant college students is the availability and use of student support services—such as tutoring, academic and career counseling, and mental health services—aimed at student academic and personal development in higher education. Student support services are important for the successful transition into college life and academic outcomes for all students, but especially for immigrant-origin students, many of whom are first-generation college students. Higher education literature has highlighted the importance of strategically delivering comprehensive student support services such as through wraparound services. An example of one the most comprehensive delivery of student support services is the "One-Stop" centers of the City University of New York (CUNY) higher education system in New York City. CUNY "One-Stop" centers were built on the concept of providing wraparound support services—academic advising, career counseling, and financial aid services, and so on—in one location to make it easier to access and connect students to these services (Baksh-Jarrett, 2015). In this "One-Stop" shop model, students are able to talk to an institutional agent who represents the different student support services offices and can answer any question or direct students to the right office.

However, services focused solely on academics, financial aid, and enrollment in higher education can only go so far in supporting community college students. Community college students often face interrelated challenges outside of school, such as poverty, mental health, legal, housing and food security, transportation, and for immigrant and mixed-status students, immigration issues that impact their academic success and persistence in school (Tsui et al., 2011). Thus, it is important for institutions to provide support services that go beyond academic and enrollment support and focus on poverty issues that affect community college students (Broton & Goldrick-Rab, 2016). For instance, one of the important contributions of this book to the higher education literature is the discussion on mental health services—one of the critical, yet little understood support services in community colleges.

CUNY is a leading model for delivering comprehensive support services to students in higher education that go beyond academic support services, particularly the CUNY "Single-Stop" centers. CUNY's "Single-Stop" centers provide "free comprehensive social, legal and financial services to students" by helping students determine their eligibility and applications for federal, state, and local public benefits related to health, food, housing, child care, and utilities and taxes (CUNY, 2018). "Single-Stop" also provides financial counseling and legal services to students (CUNY, 2018). CUNY's "Single-Stop" centers began in 2009 at Kingsborough Community College and later expanded to more CUNY community colleges, and now operate in states across the country (Goldrick-Rab, Broton, & Gates, 2013). In fact, "from 2009 through 2015, Single Stop and its partners served over 77,256 students and families at CUNY, connecting them to more than $183 million in resources, tax refunds, and supportive services" (CUNY, 2016). A study examining the "Single Stop U.S.A. Community College Initiative" at four community college systems found that students participating in the programs were more likely to persist and attempt more college credits compared to students who did not use the services (Daugherty, Johnston, & Tsai, 2016). Given the language, financial, and academic challenges faced by many immigrant-origin students, there is a need for more "one-stop" comprehensive support services in community colleges. This includes tutoring in more than one language, having caring counselors who speak more than one language and can provide culturally responsive academic counseling, and providing culturally responsive mental health services and support centers that can connect students to public social support services.

WHAT CAN WE DO BETTER?

In order for practitioners, scholars, administrators, and policymakers to change the current structures and systems to better serve all students in the community college sector—including immigrants—we need to understand the current conditions in which this sector operates. It is often the case that community colleges are thought of as "not real" colleges and are also conceived as second-class institutions due in part to the varied groups of students they serve and to the multiple missions that they pursue. We must change this deficit mentality and understand that community colleges are now the primary point of entry to postsecondary education for most vulnerable and marginalized groups of students, as well as for more traditional students.

Community colleges are also currently being asked to do everything: offer certificates and associate degrees, help prepare students to transfer, give second chances to many underprepared students, as well as offer a wide range of noncredit classes, training activities, and community services (Rosenbaum, Deil-Amen, & Person, 2006). At the same time, academics and policymakers often use frameworks and benchmarks from the study of 4-year institutions to assess their performance and outcomes. We must interrupt existing conceptions about what these institutions are, who they serve, and their role and function in American higher education. This can and will lead to new ways of defining success for these institutions and the students they serve.

Additionally, this book reveals that community colleges are not only opening doors to higher education, but they are providing hope for immigrants and for many groups of vulnerable and marginalized students who aspire to obtain a postsecondary degree or credential. Thus, we must find ways to expand opportunities and reduce barriers, which are too often driven by deficit perspectives of community college students. An asset frame will build trust between students and the institution, while deconstructing important processes for navigating American higher education. Finally, we must work with community college faculty to better understand and utilize their students' funds of knowledge in classrooms. Immigrant students, in particular, have unique immigration histories and often a strong and unique relationship within their families and communities. Thus, inclusiveness is critical for approaching immigrant-origin students as they develop and work toward their aspirations.

REFERENCES

Alcantar, C. M., & Hernandez, E. (2018, April 4). "Here the professors are your guide, tus guías": Latina/o student validating experiences with faculty at a Hispanic-serving community college. *Journal of Hispanic Higher Education.* doi:https://doi.org/10.1177/1538192718766234

Bailey, T. R., Jaggars, S. S., & Jenkins, D. (2015). *Redesigning American's community colleges: A clearer path to student success.* Cambridge, MA: Harvard University Press.

Baksh-Jarrett, G. (2015, June 5). *One stop enrollment services: An innovative student success partnership.* Presented at CUNY Enrollment Management Conference. Retrieved from www2.cuny.edu/wp-content/uploads/sites/4/page-assets/about/administration/offices/presentations/One-Stop-Enrollment-Services.pdf

Barbatis, P. (2010). Underprepared, ethnically diverse community college students: Factors contributing to persistence. *Journal of Developmental Education, 33*(3), 14.

Barnett, E. A. (2011). Validation experiences and persistence among community college students. *The Review of Higher Education, 34*(2), 193–230.

Bensimon, E. M. (2007). The underestimated significance of practitioner knowledge in the scholarship on student success. *The Review of Higher Education, 30*(4), 441–469.

Broton, K., & Goldrick-Rab, S. (2016). The dark side of college (un)affordability: Food and housing insecurity in higher education. *Change: The Magazine of Higher Learning, 48*(1), 16–25.

Campbell, C. A., Deil-Amen, R., & Rios-Aguilar, C. (2015). Do financial aid policies unintentionally punish the poor, and what can we do about it? *New Directions for Community Colleges. Special Issue: Understanding Equity in Community College Practice, 2015*(172), 67–76.

Cejda, B. D., & Hoover, R. E. (2010–2011). Strategies for faculty-student engagement: How community college faculty engage Latino students. *Journal of College Student Retention, 12*(2), 135–153.

The Century Foundation (2013). *Bridging the higher education divide: Strengthening community colleges and restoring the American dream.* Retrieved from tcf.org/assets/downloads/20130523-Bridging_the_Higher_Education_Divide-REPORT-ONLY.pdf

Connell, C. (2008). *The vital role of community colleges in the education and integration of immigrants. Grantmakers concerned with immigrants and refugees.* Retrieved from www.gcir.org/publications/gcirpubs/college

Cox, R. D. (2009). *The college fear factor: How students and professors misunderstand one another.* Cambridge, MA: Harvard University Press.

Cox, R. D. (2015). "You've got to learn the rules": A classroom-level look at low pass rates in developmental math. *Community College Review, 43*(3), 264–286.

CUNY (2016). *Data report: Single stop.* Retrieved from www2.cuny.edu/wp-content/uploads/sites/4/page-assets/current-students/student-affairs/special-programs/single-stop/Data-Report-CUNY-2009-2016-Q1.pdf

CUNY (2018, November 4). *Single stop.* Retrieved from www2.cuny.edu/current-students/student-affairs/special-programs/single-stop

Daugherty, L., Johnston, W. R., & Tsai, T. (2016). *Connecting college students to alternative sources of support: The Single Stop Community College Initiative and postsecondary outcomes.* Santa Monica, CA: The RAND Corporation. Retrieved from www.rand.org/content/dam/rand/pubs/research_reports/RR1700/RR1740/RAND_RR1740.pdf

Deil-Amen, R. (2011). Socio-academic integrative moments: Rethinking academic and social integration among two-year college students in career-related programs. *The Journal of Higher Education, 82*(1), 54–91. Retrieved from dx.doi.org/10.1080/00221546.2011.11779085

Deil-Amen, R. (2015). The "traditional" college student: A smaller and smaller minority and its implications for diversity and access institutions. In M. Stevens & M. Kirst (Eds.), *Remaking college* (pp. 134–165). Redwood City, CA: Stanford University Press.

Deil-Amen, R., & Deluca, S. (2010). The underserved third: How our educational structures populate an educational underclass. *Journal of Students Placed at Risk, 15,* 27–50.

Deil-Amen, R., & Rios-Aguilar, C. (2014). From FAFSA to Facebook: The role of technology in navigating the financial aid process. In A. Kelly & S. Goldrick-Rab (Eds.), *Reinventing financial aid: Charting a new course to college affordability,* (pp. 75–100). Cambridge, MA: Harvard Education Press.

Dougherty, K. J. (1994). The contradictory college: The conflicting origins, impacts and futures of the community college. Albany, NY: State University of New York Press.

Dowd, A. C. (2003). From access to outcome equity: Revitalizing the democratic mission of the community college. *The ANNALS of the American Academy of Political and Social Science, 586*(1), 92–119.

Goldrick-Rab, S., Broton, K., & Gates, C. (2013). *Clearing the path to a brighter future: Addressing barriers to community college access and success.* Washington, DC: Association of Community College Trustees.

Goldrick-Rab, S., Harris, D. N., & Trostel, P. A. (2009). Why financial aid matters (or does not) for college success: Toward a new interdisciplinary perspective. In J. Smart (Ed.), *Higher education: Handbook of theory and research* (Vol. 24, pp. 1–45). New York, NY: Springer Science & Business.

Goldrick-Rab, S., & Kendall, N. (2016). *The real price of college.* The Century Foundation. Retrieved from s3-us-west-2.amazonaws.com/production.tcf.org/app/uploads/2016/02/18123108/TheRealPriceofCollege_RabKendall.pdf

Grubb, N. W. (1999). *Honored but invisible: An inside look at teaching in community colleges.* New York, NY: Routledge.

Grubb, N. W. (2013). *Basic skills education in community college: Inside and outside classrooms.* New York, NY: Routledge.

Hurtado, S., & Carter, D. F. (1997). Effects of college transition and perceptions of the campus racial climate on Latino college students' sense of belonging. *Sociology of Education, 70*(4), 324–345.

Kiyama, J., & Rios-Aguilar, C. (Eds.). (2018). *Funds of knowledge in higher education: Honoring students' cultural experiences and resources as strengths.* New York, NY: Routledge.

Kiyama, J., Rios-Aguilar, C., & Deil-Amen, R. (2018). Funds of knowledge as a culturally responsive pedagogy in higher education. In J. Kiyama & C. Rios-Aguilar (Eds.), *Funds of knowledge in higher education: Honoring students' cultural experiences and resources as strengths* (pp. 175–188). New York, NY: Routledge.

Kuh, G. D. (2008). *High-impact educational practices: What they are, who has access to them, and why they matter.* Washington, DC: Association of American Colleges and Universities.

Ladson-Billings, G. (1995). Toward a theory of culturally relevant pedagogy. *American Educational Research Journal, 32*(3), 465–491.

Luna-Torres, M., Leafgreen, M., & McKinney, L. (2017). Leveraging guided pathways to improve financial aid design and delivery. *Journal of Student Financial Aid, 47*(2), 101–110.

Mora, J., & Rios-Aguilar, C. (2018). Aligning practice with pedagogy: Funds of knowledge for community college teaching. In J. Kiyama & C. Rios-Aguilar (Eds.), *Funds of knowledge in higher education: Honoring students' cultural experiences and resources as strengths* (pp. 145–159). New York, NY: Routledge.

Passel, J. S. (2011). Demography of immigrant youth: Past, present, and future. *The Future of Children, 21*(1), 19–41.

Rios-Aguilar, C., & Deil-Amen, R. (2019). *Taking history, funding, and current challenges into account when discussing race, ethnicity, and completion in community colleges.* Washington, DC: American Council on Education. Retrieved from www.equityinhighered.org

Rose, M. (2016, June 23). Reassessing a redesign of community colleges. *Inside Higher Ed.* Retrieved from www.insidehighered.com/views/2016/06/23/essay-challenges-facing-guided-pathways-model-restructuring-two-year-colleges

Rosenbaum, J., Ahearn, C., Becker, K., & Rosenbaum, J. (2015). *The new forgotten half and research directions to support them.* New York, NY: William T. Grant Foundation. Retrieved from files.eric.ed.gov/fulltext/ED565750.pdf

Rosenbaum, J., Deil-Amen, R., & Person, A. (2006). *After admission: From college access to college success.* New York, NY: Russell Sage Foundation Press.

Teranishi, R. T., Suárez-Orozco, C., & Suárez-Orozco, M. (2011). Immigrants in community colleges. *The Future of Children, 21*(1), 153–169.

Teranishi, R. T., Suárez-Orozco, C., & Suárez-Orozco, M. (2015). *In the shadows of the ivory tower: Undocumented undergraduates in the uncertain era of immigration reform.* Los Angeles, CA: Institute for Immigration, Globalization, & Education, UCLA.

Tinto, V. (1993). *Leaving college: Rethinking the causes and cures of student attrition* (2nd ed.). Chicago, IL: University of Chicago Press.

Tinto, V. (1997). Classrooms as communities: Exploring the educational character of student persistence. *Journal of Higher Education, 68*(6), 599–623.

Tsui, E., Freudenberg, N., Manzo, L., Jones, H., Kwan, A., & Gagnon, M. (2011). *Housing instability at CUNY: Results from a survey on CUNY undergraduate students.* New York, NY: Healthy CUNY Initiative, City University of New York. Retrieved from web.gc.cuny.edu/che/cunyhousinginstability.pdf

Umbach, P. D., & Wawrzynski, M. R. (2005). Faculty do matter: The role of college faculty in student learning and engagement. *Research in Higher Education, 46*(2), 153–184. Retrieved from dx.doi.org/10.1007/s11162-004-1598-1

RICC Project Description

Research on Immigrants in Community College (RICC) was a multiphase embedded mixed-methods study (Creswell & Plano Clark, 2011) of three urban community college settings, which vary in contexts designed to address this issue. We systematically examined *classrooms* as well as *settings outside of the classroom* that have implications for (1) fostering relational engagement, (2) accessing relevant information/social capital, and (3) fostering academic engagement.

Our data sources included:

Qualitative Phase 1: Ethnographies; 60 structured classroom observations; and 9 focus groups (9/2010 to 6/2012)

Quantitative Phase 2: 644 student surveys (matched to student records) (2/2011 through 10/2012)

Qualitative Phase 3: 60 semistructured student interviews and 45 semistructured instructor and administrator interviews (2/2011 through 10/2012)

Each phase informed the previous phase. The initial phase of the study grounded the research, pointed to important domains of inquiry, and served to inform the design of the survey collected in Phase 2. The last phase drew upon a subsample of the survey participants and served to shed light and explain the survey evidence.

This study was funded by the W. T. Grant Foundation and the Ford Foundation.

CAMPUS SETTINGS

Three distinct community colleges in the New York City metropolitan area were selected to participate in the RICC study with the explicit intention of including institutions with varying campus-level characteristics and contexts. All participating community colleges offer 2-year public associate's degree programs and serve low-income, ethnic minority, and immigrant-origin commuter populations. Brief descriptions of each community college are detailed below (all campus names are pseudonyms).

Located in the poorest congressional district in the nation, Taino is the first 2-year, public, open admissions, and bilingual college in New York, created in response to large-scale protest calling for an institution of higher learning to serve the needs of a local Latino community. Three major buildings connected by a pedestrian bridge that spans a central street comprise this urban campus. The number of applicants has more than doubled from 3,000 in 2000 to 6,500 in 2010, resulting in wait listing of prospective students due to lack both material (e.g., printing services, classroom supplies) and physical resources (e.g., campus, classroom, and computer lab space). Taino serves predominately Latino (64%) and Black (31%) students. In 2012, only 2% of the students were White, and 3% were Asian/Pacific Islander. More than 90% of the student body report speaking a language other than English at home. Taino has the highest rates of remediation in the 2-year public college system. In 2012, only 10.3% of entering freshmen passed all "college readiness" skills (i.e., reading, writing, and math tests). Nearly one-third of entering freshmen are "triple remedial," failing all three readiness exams—a disproportionate number in comparison to other colleges in the system.

Located in the burgeoning downtown section of a large urban center, Domino began as a trade school in a former industrial neighborhood and now focuses heavily on technological education. The campus consists of multiple disconnected specialized buildings spanning over a half mile of city blocks. Buildings on campus have been under renovation for years, and the school has an alarming number of health code violations. In 2012, Domino reported serving 11,000 associate degree program students. Forty percent of the students were born outside of the United States representing 134 countries, and 62% report speaking a language other than English at home. The racial/ethnic background is highly diverse, and the majority of students report being non-White: 32.5% Black (non-Latino), 33.2% Latino, 19.2% Asian/Pacific Islander, 11.2% White (non-Latino), 0.5% Native American, and 3.4% other.

Although a commuter school, Oakmont physically resembles more of a traditional 4-year university campus, located in an affluent suburban county roughly 1.5 hours away from a major urban city center known for long-standing class-based (i.e., socioeconomic) segregation. It is the county's largest educational institution with a campus enrollment of over 12,000 part- and full-time students. Oakmont is abundant in material and physical resources, including parking for commuter students, a large student center with cafeteria and café, state-of-the-art technology centers, and more than 60 associate and certificate programs. Reflecting our country's rapidly shifting demographics, the college has recently dipped to just under half its students representing a majority population (49% White); it currently has the highest percentage of minority students in the *state* system with the largest growth occurring in the low-income Latino (28%) and Black (21%) student population. Foreign-born students make-up a particularly large segment of this demographic transformation, currently representing 42% of the students attending the campus.

OVERVIEW OF RICC DATA

The different data types collected during the study are introduced very briefly below. Figure A.1 provides an overview. *For further details, please see the online appendix.*

Figure A.1. Overview of RICC data

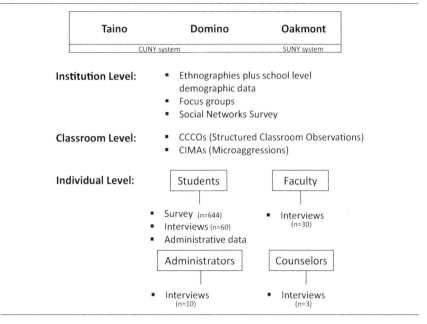

ETHNOGRAPHIES

Graduate research assistants were provided training in conducting ethnographic evidence and were tasked with observing public spaces (common hall, buildings, campus grounds, bathrooms, and classrooms), taking extensive field notes. Two to three researchers spent 10 hours a week per campus for a semester. The notes were entered into Dedoose and coded in analytic teams using grounded theory.

FOCUS GROUPS

Twenty-one participants took part in three consecutive weekly focus groups that explored the experiences and perceptions of immigrant community college students at three different sites. The first session explored the individual experiences of students by probing for the competing responsibilities students faced and the challenges they experienced both on and off campus. The second session explored the interaction of students and the community college setting, specifically probing for students' use of campus space when not in classes, and students' experiences in various administrative, support, and virtual spaces on campus. The last session focused on student experiences in classroom spaces and explored their experiences as "emerging adults." Each focus group session lasted

for approximately 2 hours and took place on campus. All participants were between the ages of 18 and 25, attended classes full-time at the campus from which
they were recruited, and were from diverse ethnic backgrounds and generational
statuses.

THE COMMUNITY COLLEGE CLASSROOM OBSERVATION PROTOCOL (CCCO)

Classroom-level engagement was assessed in Phase 1 of the study using the
Community College Classroom Observation (CCCO) Protocol. The CCCO is a
qualitatively grounded quantitative measure, which taps specific *observable* behavioral and interactional indicators of three dimensions of classroom engagement—
behavioral, relational, and cognitive. Measurement development was an iterative
process informed by the CLASS-S, an observational instrument developed to
assess the quality of interactions in high school classrooms (Pianta, La Paro, &
Hamre, 2008), and the Center for Community College Student Engagement
Classroom Form (CCSEC; www.ccsse.org), which assesses community college
students' perceptions of their school environment. These measures, along with
focus groups conducted by the RICC research team, informed CCCO content and
method procedures.

Our measure specifically assessed three primary dimensions of classroom engagement: behavioral engagement, relational engagement, and cognitive engagement. Each engagement dimension is comprised of items that reflect interactions
theoretically and empirically related to these respective dimensions. Items were
placed along a scale with behaviorally anchored descriptors of types of interactions between all members in the class (i.e., student–student, student–teacher) on
a continuum from (1 = low engagement) to (5 = high engagement). Classroom
observers completed item ratings on all dimensions for each observational segment. A composite score was created for each item based on an average of the
item's ratings across all observation segments. Sixty classrooms were assessed using the CCCO.

CLASSROOM INTERPERSONAL MICROAGGRESSIONS (CIMAS)

Lau and Williams (2010) recommend enhancing current microaggression research by conducting "real-life setting" observations directly capturing microaggressions. To that end, we developed an instrument to capture "in-vivo"
microaggressions while observing 60 classrooms across three community college
campuses. The Classroom Interpersonal Microaggressions (CIMAs) form was
developed to document microaggressions in context as they occurred during the
course of classroom observations. Observers were trained to make note of occurrences that might have shifted the tone of the class, and insulted, invalidated,

or demeaned any person in the class while conducting a structured classroom observation and ethnography. The form required the observer to note the CIMA statement (or episode); the event(s) immediately leading up to and following the CIMA; who initiated the event (student or instructor); to whom the CIMA was directed (student, instructor, or unclear); student(s)' responses (ignored/oblivious; intervened; escalated; visibly upset, withdrawn, other); and instructor responses (ignored/oblivious; intervened; escalated; visibly upset, withdrawn, other).

STUDENT SURVEY

In Phase 2, the research team developed a survey addressing the constructs of interest for the study. Scale development was informed through ethnographic fieldwork, focus groups, and grounded emerging findings, building on the mixed-methods synergetic foundations of this study (Crewswell & Plano Clark, 2011). Our protocol development teams included a cultural developmental psychologist, an educational sociologist, an anthropologist, a community college instructor, and bicultural immigrant college students from a variety of origins. Each item of every scale included in the protocols was discussed and wording was tweaked until there was agreement that the items were meaningful and appropriate. Interviews were piloted with immigrant-origin college-age participants and then reviewed in the development team and modified to make them as accessible as possible.

The survey was administered through Qualtrics online software. The survey was made available in Spanish, Chinese (Mandarin), and English. Students were qualified to participate if they met the following criteria: (1) they were between the ages of 18 and 25; (2) they attended one of the campuses we are studying; and (3) they were enrolled in a degree-seeking program. Efforts were made to obtain an ethnically and gender-balanced sample representative of the three participating campuses through targeted recruitment as needed, and newly enrolled and continuing students. Six hundred forty-four students completed the survey. Participants received $25 dollars cash or an Amazon gift certificate for completing the survey.

SEMISTRUCTURED INTERVIEWS

In Phase 3, in order to gain insights from participants on our emerging results, semistructured individual interviews were collected from students, faculty, administrators, and counselors. In order to develop interviews that were relevant across groups, questions were informed by the ethnographies, focus groups, and grounded emerging findings, in keeping with its mixed-methods sequential embedded design (Creswell & Plano Clark, 2011). All interviewees received $40 dollars cash or an Amazon gift card for their participation.

Student Interviews

Ten percent (N = 60) of the students surveyed were randomly selected to be interviewed. The student interviews took from 1.5 to 2.5 hours to administer. The semistructured student interviews were developed to systematically gather data on a variety of relevant topics: their motivations for attending college; their classroom experiences; their assessment of their developmental and ESL courses (if applicable); their perceptions of their academic workload; their relationships with their faculty; their relationships with their peers; their experiences on a diverse campus (including microaggressions); how they use their time out of the classroom on campus; their sources and experiences with institutional services; their extracurricular roles, activities, and pressures as emerging adults; their civic engagement; and finally recommendations for improving community college settings.

Faculty Interviews

A total of 30 faculty were interviewed across the three campuses in order to gain insights into their experiences regarding the campus climate as well as their perspectives about teaching students of immigrant origin backgrounds with a particular lens to their strengths and challenges. We made a concerted effort to recruit faculty representing divergent disciplinary backgrounds. Thus, we sought to recruit faculty teaching in math, science, English, and humanities: (1) *general education* as well as (2) *remedial* and (3) *vocational* courses, across all three campuses. The semistructured faculty interviews triangulated a number of topics covered in the student interview including, for example, their perspectives on the strengths and challenges of their immigrant-origin students, perspectives on a diverse campus, the ways in which their students use of institutional supports, and recommendations for improving community college settings. The interview also uniquely covered faculty perspectives on their own roles, activities, and pressures. The interviews were done on campus, and each interview took an average of 1.5 hours to conduct.

Administrator and Counselor Interviews

Ten college high-level administrators and three college counselors were also interviewed across the three campuses in order to gain insights into their experiences regarding the campus climate as well as their perspectives about working with students of immigrant-origin backgrounds with a particular lens to their strengths and challenges. As with the teacher interviews, many of the questions served to triangulate the survey and student data, and a few questions focused on information on which the administrators or counselor might be uniquely positioned to provide perspective. The interviews were done on campus, and each interview took an average of 1.5 hours to complete.

SOCIAL NETWORKS SURVEY

Of the 644 students who participated in the RICC study, 195 students completed the ego network survey. Ego networks are reports from a person about people to whom they are connected, and are theorized as the optimal way to estimate individuals' social capital (Burt, 2000). See Alicea (2015) for a full description of this data.

ADMINISTRATIVE DATA

As part of this project, CUNY provided us with de-identified administrative data for full cohorts of students enrolling as first-time full-time freshmen between 2005/2006 and 2012/2013. This data contained measures of various demographic characteristics, academic outcomes, and other information. We used this data to record the grade point averages for students who took the survey. Furthermore, we analyzed the whole dataset to examine and report on general patterns.

REFERENCES

Alicea, S. (2015). *Social networks in CCs: Influences on social capital, academic achievement, employment skills and psychosocial wellbeing.* Doctoral dissertation. Retrieved from Proquest LLC (UMI No. 3705207).

Burt, R. S. (2000). The network structure of social capital. *Research in Organizational Behavior, 22,* 345–423.

Creswell, J. W., & Plano Clark, V. L. (2011). *Designing and conducting mixed methods research* (2nd ed.). Thousand Oaks, CA: Sage.

Lau, M. Y., & Williams, C. D. (2010). Microaggression research: Methodological review and recommendations. In D. W. Sue (Ed.), *Microaggressions and marginality: Manifestations, dynamics, and impact.* New York, NY: Wiley.

Pianta, R. C., La Paro, K., & Hamre, B. K. (2008). *Classroom Assessment Scoring System (CLASS).* Baltimore, MD: Paul H. Brookes.

About the Contributors

Cynthia M. Alcantar is an assistant professor of Higher Education Leadership at the University of Nevada, Reno. Her research focuses on the factors that impact the social mobility and integration of racial/ethnic minority and immigrant populations in the United States. She is particularly focused on the influence of schools (i.e., K–12 schools, community colleges, and minority-serving institutions) on the educational pathways and civic participation of racial/ethnic minority and immigrant students. She earned her PhD in Social Science and Comparative Education at the University of California, Los Angeles.

Stacey Alicea, PhD, MPH is the associate executive director of Training, Strategic Learning, and Evaluation at Ramapo for Children. Stacey is a community psychologist and practitioner-researcher with a deep commitment to grounding work in meaningful and authentic relationships, and leveraging the resources embedded in and generated by the betweenness of those relationships to drive youth social and human capital accrual in educational settings. She has over 15 years of experience directing applied research intervention, direct service, and capacity building programs supporting youths' health, education, and holistic development across multiple domestic and international contexts.

Saskias Casanova is an assistant professor of Psychology at UC Santa Cruz. She researches individual and contextual factors that relate to the psychological processes and educational outcomes of Latinx and immigrant-origin students. Her work appears in journals such as *Teachers College Record, Journal of Negro Education,* and *Latino Studies.*

Janet Cerda is a doctoral candidate in Human Development and Psychology at UCLA. She is a graduate student researcher at the UCLA Center for Community Schooling and at the National Center for Research on Evaluation, Standards, and Student Testing (CRESST) at UCLA.

Natacha M. Cesar-Davis is a Ph.D. student at the University of California, Los Angeles in the Higher Education and Organizational Change Program. Prior to arriving at UCLA, Natacha worked in higher education for about 6 years in a variety of roles and at different types of institutions. Her most recent position was working at Bunker Hill Community College as a tenure-track faculty in the Behavioral Science department. At UCLA, Natacha has worked at the Higher Education Research Institute and on numerous research projects focusing on community college faculty and students.

Monique Corral is a doctoral candidate in the Human Development and Psychology program in the Department of Education at UCLA. She serves as a research associate for the

Institute for Immigration, Globalization, and Education at UCLA. Her research interests center on the educational trajectories and career development of culturally diverse students, nontraditional pathways to success, and mixed methods research. She has taught in adult education and has served as a program coordinator and case manager for social services and family service programs in partnerships with nonprofit agencies and public services.

Tasha Darbes is currently a professor of TESOL and Bilingual Education at Pace University. Her research examines the intersection of educational access, immigration and language acquisition. She has received grants from the Sociological Initiatives Foundation, the Mayor's Office of Adult Literacy and The International Research Foundation for English Language Education. She also co-produced a documentary on the experiences of undocumented youth in higher education, Admissions, which was awarded Best Amateur Film by AERA.

Sandra I. Dias earned her doctorate in Counseling Psychology from New York University. She is currently a clinical psychologist with experience in health psychology, trauma, PTSD, and evidence-based treatments such as cognitive behavioral therapy, motivational interviewing, cognitive behavioral therapy for chronic pain, and cognitive processing therapy for adults. Dr. Dias is also experienced in psychodynamic, group, couple, and family therapy, and organizational, immigration, and acculturation issues.

Edwin Hernandez is an assistant professor in the Counseling and Guidance Program in the Department of Special Education, Rehabilitation and Counseling at California State University, San Bernardino. His research and teaching interest are focused on issues of equity and access in education, with a focus on institutional culture and how it shapes underrepresented students' experience and opportunity across the educational pipeline. His research has been published in *The High School Journal, Journal of Hispanic Higher Education, Teachers College Record,* and *Qualitative Psychology.*

Heather Herrera is the assistant dean of Assessment and Accreditation for the University of San Diego's School of Leadership and Education Sciences. Her research interests focus on immigrant-origin students in higher education, higher education policies and practices as they pertain to access, retention, and completion, and the role of language and literacy on student academic achievement.

Juliana Karras-Jean Gilles is a postdoctoral scholar at UCLA and is leading the Making the Invisible Visible: Systematically Examining Classroom Bias with MET Data study. She studied Developmental Psychology at the Graduate Center, City University of New York, and received her MA in Human Development and Social Intervention at NYU Steinhardt. Her multimethod work straddles both developmental and social research by focusing on the social development of children and adolescents in context. Using a structural lens, the goal of her work regarding racial inequality in education, children's rights across contexts, and inequality in civic development, is to generate knowledge that can be used to challenge social systems which reproduce inequality in development

Dalal Katsiaficas is an assistant professor of Educational Psychology at the University of Illinois at Chicago. Her research examines the social development of immigrant-origin adolescents and emerging adults, with regards to the development of multiple identities and social and academic engagement. Her recent work has explored the experiences of undocumented youth as they navigate educational settings and bridging theories of intersectionality with developmental science.

Guadalupe López-Hernández is a doctoral student in Human Development and Psychology at UCLA and a research assistant in the Institute for Immigration, Globalization, and Education. Her research focuses on exploring how an undocumented status impacts the mental health and school engagement of children and youth in mixed-status families.

Margary Martin, Ph.D. is an assistant professor of Educational Foundations at the University of Hawai'i at Hilo, and the executive director of UH Hilo's Center for Place-Based Social Emotional Learning. Her current research examines how place-based, culturally sustaining initiatives shape the socioemotional development of children and youth from culturally and economically subordinated communities. She received the 2018 College of Arts and Sciences Faculty Achievement Award at the University of Hawai'i at Hilo. Her most recent publications appear in Theory In Practice, Education Studies, Education Researcher and Teachers College Record, and she is a co-author of the book Schooling for Resilience: Improving the Life Trajectory of Black and Latino Boys.

Alfredo Novoa is a doctoral student in the Human Development and Psychology program at UCLA's Graduate School of Education and Information Studies. He is interested in understanding the ecological factors that shape the sociocultural experiences and academic development of immigrant-origin youth. His other interests include applying translational science within academic contexts. Alfredo received his Bachelors of Science in Applied Psychology from New York University.

Olivia Osei-Twumasi is an assistant adjunct professor of Economics at the University of California, Los Angeles (UCLA) where she teaches labor and development economics. Her research focuses on educational access and outcomes for underprivileged students, including students from low-income families, undocumented students, and racial/ethnic minorities.

McKenna Parnes is a current doctoral student in Clinical Psychology at Suffolk University. She earned a master's degree in counseling and mental health services at the University of Pennsylvania. She has coauthored several papers exploring the impact of social support on outcomes for underrepresented students and for individuals working in the human rights field.

Sarah Schwartz is an assistant professor of Psychology at Suffolk University in Boston. She holds a doctorate in Clinical Psychology from the University of Massachusetts Boston and a master's degree in Education from the Harvard Graduate School of Education. Her research aims to identify, develop, and evaluate effective strategies to foster healthy developmental outcomes during adolescence and the transition to adulthood, with a particular focus on the role of mentoring relationships and networks of support

Sukhmani Singh is a postdoctoral associate with both the Office of Juvenile Justice and Delinquency Prevention (OJJDP) and NoVo Foundation funded Ending Girls' Incarceration Initiative, as well as the NIH-funded SAFE Spaces study at New York University. She is also Co-PI of the ROSEBuds Visionary Scientists Project, a participatory research project funded by the Ford Foundation that centers the expertise and lived experiences of co-researchers who are formerly juvenile justice system involved girls of color.

Cecilia Rios-Aguilar is professor of education at UCLA's Graduate School of Education and Information Studies (GSEIS). She also serves as associate dean of Equity, Diversity, and Inclusion. She is past director of the Higher Education Research Institute at UCLA. Her research is multidisciplinary and uses a variety of asset-based conceptual frameworks (including funds of knowledge, community cultural wealth, and the forms of capital) and statistical approaches (such as econometric models, multilevel models, spatial analyses and GIS, and social network analysis) to study the educational and occupational trajectories of marginalized students. Dr. Rios-Aguilar obtained her PhD in Education Theory and Policy from the University of Rochester, her MS in Educational Administration from the University of Rochester, and her BA in Economics from the Instituto Tecnológico Autónomo de México (ITAM).

Carola Suárez-Orozco is a professor of Human Development and Psychology at UCLA and the co-founder of Re-Imagining Migration. Her prior books include *Children of Immigration* and *Learning a New Land* as well as *Transitions: The Development of the Children of Immigrants.* She has been awarded an American Psychological Association (APA) Presidential Citation for her contributions to the understanding of cultural psychology of immigration, has served as Chair of the APA Presidential Task Force on Immigration, and is a member of the National Academy of Education.

Marcelo Suárez-Orozco is the Wasserman Dean and Distinguished Professor of Education at the Graduate School of Education and Information studies at UCLA. His most recent volume, *Humanitarianism and Mass Migration: Confronting the World Crisis* was published earlier this year by the University of California Press.

Robert T. Teranishi is a professor of Social Science and Comparative Education, the Morgan and Helen Chu Endowed Chair in Asian American Studies, and co-director for the Institute for Immigration, Globalization, and Education at UCLA. His research is broadly focused on race, ethnicity, and the stratification of college opportunity. His work has been influential to federal, state, and institution policy related to college access and affordability. He has provided congressional testimony regarding the Higher Education Reauthorization Act and No Child Left Behind, informed state policy decisions related to selective college admissions, and his research has been solicited to inform U.S. Supreme Court decisions on affirmative action and school desegregation. Prior to his appointment at UCLA, he served as a professor at New York University and the University of Pennsylvania. Dr. Teranishi also served as a member of the Board of Directors of the National Board for Education Services under President Obama.

Index

Note: Page numbers followed by *f* indicate figures and those followed by *t* indicate tables.